THE HISTORY

OF

THE EARLY PURITANS

Tentmaker Publications
121 Hartshill Road
Stoke-on-Trent
Staffordshire, UK
ST4 7LU

www.tentmaker.org.uk

ISBN 1 899003 81 9

Published in 1850
Reprinted 2002
Reprinted 2005

THE HISTORY

OF

THE EARLY PURITANS:

FROM THE REFORMATION

TO THE OPENING OF THE CIVIL WAR

IN 1642.

BY

J. B. MARSDEN. M.A.

VICAR OF GREAT MISSENDEN.

LONDON:

PUBLISHED BY HAMILTON, ADAMS, & CO.

PATERNOSTER ROW.

J. HATCHARD AND SON, PICCADILLY.

SANDERS, TOOTING.

M.DCCCL.

ADVERTISEMENT.

THE following pages are intended to form a work complete within itself. Should life and leisure be afforded to the author, he hopes, at no distant period, to publish a second volume upon the history of the later puritans; from the opening of the civil war to the close of the seventeenth century.

Many events of great interest in the political, and in the religious history of England, are passed over in this volume, with a slight reference or with none. This needs no apology. It was not the author's intention to write a history of England, or even of the church of England. The former task lay far away from his studies, his tastes, and his sacred duties; the latter has been done so lately, and so well, by others, that his chief anxiety has been to avoid the ground from which the harvest has been gathered.

The stream of puritan history runs deep and clear. The facts are well authenticated, and they are recorded by the historians of each party with a singular agreement. With all their faults, religious writers have shewn a regard for truth, in the relation of facts, from which secular historians might yet learn some useful lessons. The author has not felt it necessary to encumber his pages, and to distract the reader's attention, with a reference to every volume he has consulted, or a confirmation of every fact he has mentioned,—a practice which modern writers of history seem to have carried to excess. Still he has endeavoured to indicate the sources of his information upon important, still more upon disputable, points : and the candid reader, whether friend or foe, will be at no loss to track his path, confirm his statements, or convict him (if he has unconsciously erred) of incorrectness.

In conclusion, the author contributes this volume to the cause of christian charity, of moderation, and of peace.

May, 1850.

CONTENTS.

CHAPTER I.

A. D. 1547.

CHAPTER II.

A. D. 1558.

CHAPTER III.

A. D. 1565.

CHAPTER IV.

a. d. 1575.

CHAPTER V.

a. d. 1583.

CHAPTER VI.

A. D. 1583.

CHAPTER VII.

A. D. 1590.

CHAPTER VIII.

A. D. 1592.

CHAPTER IX.

A. D. 1595.

CHAPTER X.

A. D. 1602.

CHAPTER XI.

a. d. 1610.

CHAPTER XII.

A. D. 1618.

CHAPTER XIII.

A. D. 1624.

CHAPTER XIV.

A. D. 1640.

HISTORY OF THE EARLY PURITANS.

CHAPTER I.

1. The reformation was scarcely accomplished in England, when a large party began loudly to express its discontent. Great as the change was, it seemed to many of the reformers still imperfect, and they were anxious to give it a new impulse, and to extend it further. The chains in which the English church had been fettered for a thousand years were broken; and now the task remained to model it anew, yet so as to retain the visible unity which it had worn beneath the papacy. But here the difficulties were great. For the same resolute and dauntless spirit which had carried the nation through its conflict with Rome, re-appeared under another form. It distrusted all interference in spiritual affairs, and seemed ready to abjure all authority, as though to acknowledge a superior had only been to submit to another and a meaner usurpation. More intent upon the end to be attained than cautious in the means employed, it would have hazarded one reformation in order to have brought about another; and

CHAPTER I.

EDW. VI.
A.D. 1547.

risked the vast advantages already secured, for the sake of further changes of inferior moment, if not of questionable utility.

2. To a great extent this was the legitimate consequence of the reformation, and its further and inevitable development. Great changes, especially if sudden, generally leave their authors dissatisfied: for anticipation outruns fulfilment, and more has been expected than can possibly be achieved. And the wisest reforms, since they provide no security against the prejudices and ignorance of the multitude, while at the same time they inflame their passions, are often bitterly decried by those who were most clamorous to effect them. Reformers in all ages complain of this ingratitude. They are blamed for failures which were unavoidable; the imperfections of their toil and labour are magnified; the real worth of their services in the cause of truth is undervalued. Their difficulties meet with no sympathy: it is only their infirmities that are viewed with stern justice and without abatement.

3. And yet, upon the other hand, it seems unreasonable that the ardent love of truth and the spirit of inquiry, once quickened into life, should consent to stay its progress whenever the first leaders of the movement announce a difficulty, or decline a fresh encounter. The leader who blames his followers for rashness may himself have been overtaken with incapacity. In such circumstances wisdom lies no doubt between a servile aquies-

cence and a hot and precipitate daring. These opposite vices are, in their consequences, alike unfavourable to the best interests of man. The one crushes the spirit ; the other blinds the judgment. The former extinguishes the desire of improvement; the latter too often renders all progress impossible. The perfection so eagerly sought may be visionary and unattainable, and the time lost in the pursuit of it may be fatal to other and more important, because more reasonable, projects of advancement.

4. Thus, the reformation was yet in progress when the PURITANS sprang at once into a vigorous existence. Under this name were very soon comprised all those, however differing amongst themselves, who sought for further change in the forms and discipline of the English church. The name itself confers no dishonour, though borne with impatience, and often resented as a grievous wrong. It was applied in scorn : but age and use have made it venerable. No clear account of the origin of this now famous title has been handed down. It seems to imply that if the professions of those to whom it was first given were high, their lives at least were consistent, and their morals *pure*. The name occurs soon after the accession of queen Elizabeth, though it was not much in use for ten years afterwards. It then became the title of a party which, for upwards of a century, exercised in England an influence, whether for good or evil, such as no other party, civil or religious, has obtained at any period of

CHAPTER our history. And this influence, though weakened,
I.   still survives. Of this we have at least one pain-
EDW. VI. ful and conclusive proof. Men still approach the
A.D. 1547. history of the puritans on both sides, with violence and prejudice ; and it is only a living principle that can call up these strong passions. We
do not war in earnest with the dead. The memory
of things which have no existence but in history,
provokes no real animosity. The eager conflict
indicates the presence of a real foe.

5. Except by the writers (a large class unhappily) who treat religion with indifference, scarcely
an attempt has been made to present the history
of the puritans to their countrymen with impartial fairness. Their own partisans have defended
them with warmth, but without discrimination ;
and they have been assailed with all the rancour
of civil and religious hatred : an impartial history
has scarcely been essayed, still less accomplished.
And yet, oppressed as it has been with grievous
slanders on the one hand, and with adulation
scarcely less injurious to a lasting reputation on
the other, the name survives. Wherever the religion, the language, or the free spirit of our
country has forced its way, the puritans of old
have some memorial. They have moulded the
character and shaped the laws of other lands, and
tinged with their devouter shades unnumbered
congregations of Christian worshippers, even
where no allegiance is professed or willing homage done to their peculiarities. It is a party
that has numbered in its ranks many of the best,

and not a few of the greatest, men that England has enrolled upon her history. Amongst the
puritans were found, together with a crowd of our
greatest divines and a multitude of learned men,
many of our most profound lawyers, some of
our most able statesmen, of our most renowned
soldiers, and (strangely out of place as they may
seem) not a few of our greatest orators and poets.
Smith and Owen, Baxter and Howe, were their
ministers, and preached amongst them. Cecil
revered and defended them while he lived; so did
the illustrious Bacon; and the unfortunate Essex
sought his consolations from them when he came
to die. They were the men whom Cromwell
dreaded and deceived, and amongst whom Hampden fought and perished. Milton owned allegiance to their principles, and lent them a pen still
immortal though steeped in gall. Of wealth and
wit and patriotism they had at least their fair
proportion. They boasted, not without reason,
that the first college, in either university, founded
by a protestant, was the magnificent donation of
their own Sir Walter Mildmay at Cambridge;
dedicated, not to legendary saints or superstitious
fears, but to the divine IMMANUEL; and built,
not for the promotion of a stupid superstition,
but in the pious hope that the gospel of the Son
of God might never want an advocate while its
foundation should endure. They were our own
countrymen; and their history is, in its glories or
its darker shades, in truth our own. During
the period of which we shall attempt to write,

they were members of the church of England. They were anxious for improvement, sometimes fretful for change, but they revered the great principle of an established church, and did not entertain a thought of separating from its communion. Some of them would have moulded it anew; but few or none of them desired its overthrow.

6. It shall be our aim in the following pages to do justice both to these men and to their opponents: to write a faithful record of the virtues of the puritans and of their faults; to shew how much we owe to the one, and how much we suffer from the other; to describe their wrongs with respect and sympathy, and yet to display in its turn their own intolerance. It is an enterprise not without its perils: even now the historian has need of caution when he plants his foot amidst the ashes of a departed age. Its fires yet smoulder, and its passions are not extinguished. Yet the pursuit of truth is pleasant, whatever dangers we encounter by the way; and in the study of the virtues and sufferings of our forefathers, nay in the dispassionate review of their weaknesses and faults, we shall meet with our reward. Nor must we forget that by these men, whatever their infirmities, the foundations of our English liberties were fastened and secured. We enjoy the fruits for which they toiled; and warned by their misfortunes, we may escape the rocks on which they perished.

7. The reformation in England originated with the monarch, and was transmitted to the people

through the regular forms of the constitution.
Upon the continent and in Scotland, the order
was reversed. With the exception of a few of the
minor German states, in which the reigning princes
led the movement they were unable to control, the
reformation was begun by the people, and carried
into effect against the will of the higher civil authorities, or without their assistance. The character of this vast revolution, both at home and
abroad, partook of the circumstances of its origin,
and in each case still retains the visible impression of its peculiar parentage. In England, the
reformed religion immediately assumed the outward symbols of a monarchical institution, and
the church, represented by its higher clergy,
again, as before the reformation, took its place in
the constitution, without exciting jealousy in the
crown, or stimulating those passions, which the
possession of a new and formidable power invariably creates, amongst the people. The spirit of
the institution was naturally tinged by the same
circumstances. It was a matter of course, in a
reformation of which a succession of sovereigns
were the first promoters, that episcopacy should
be retained, and not less so that a certain degree
of magnificence and splendour should invest the
national church, and display itself both in the
dignities of its hierarchy and in the ceremonial
of its public worship : and thus the church of
England assumed, and has ever since retained,
a more exact gradation of spiritual dignities, and a

more stately mode of worship, than the reformed churches of other lands. Upon the continent the higher clergy, following the general example of the civil powers, stood aloof, or met the reformation with fierce hostility. Scarcely a churchman of rank joined with it. Princes and prelates viewed it at first with equal scorn, and afterwards, as they learned something of the vast and awful power it wielded, with equal hatred. Thus the reformation in Germany, France, and Switzerland was a popular, and sometimes a plebeian, movement. To a certain extent the case was similar in Scotland; except that the barons and chief estates of the kingdom being already arrayed against the sovereign, the management of the reformation fell into their hands; and the struggle between the new and old opinions became political, and was embittered with another element of civil strife.

8. Thus the reformation in the foreign churches, originating among the common people and the inferior clergy, took a democratic form. They became presbyterian in their government, and simple even to excess in their modes of worship. For the one they pleaded necessity; for the other the sanction of primitive antiquity, and the tenor of the new testament. None of them at first rejected episcopacy as unlawful. Calvin and others have recorded their concurrent sense of its importance; though in effect they considered themselves at liberty, under the circumstances in which they were placed, to reconstruct the reformed churches

upon another model. For the simplicity of their
forms of worship they made no apology ; differing
in this, though without personal animosities or
any feeling of unkindness, from the great reformers of the church of England. In fact, the
closest friendship existed between the leaders of
the reformation throughout the whole of Europe.
Their cause, their dangers and triumphs, and their
great foe the papacy, were every where the same ;
and it would be difficult to say whether the
warmth of their affection for each other or their
hatred of papal superstition, their catholic spirit
or their righteous and unsparing zeal, were the
master passion of their breasts.

9. Amongst the first who introduced into England the controversy which soon afterwards ripen-
ed into puritanism, was a name no less revered
than that of the martyr-bishop Hooper.* He had
lived some time abroad, and was the friend of
Bullinger and Gualter, the two leaders of the
protestant cause in Germany and Switzerland.
Returning home in the days of Edward the Sixth,
his piety and talents were at once appreciated, and
he was nominated, in the spring of 1550, to the
see of Gloucester. But his conscience was em-
barrassed ; and in his person a contest began
which has never since been stilled. He demurred
first to the oath of consecration, and secondly to
the robes in which the episcopal investiture usually

* Burnet, Hist. of the Reformation, part iii. book iv. Strype's Memorials of Cranmer, vol. ii. ch. 17, § 212. Foxe's Martyrs.

took place; and he wrote to the king an earnest request that he might be allowed either to decline the bishoprick, or to be admitted to it without the usual oath and ceremonial. His objection, so far as the oath was involved, seems to have been easily removed. The obnoxious passage, in which he was required to swear " by God, *by the saints,* and by the holy gospels," was at once altered by the king's own hand, in the presence of the council, when Hooper's protest against the impiety of a solemn appeal to the departed saints was placed before him. But the greater difficulty still remained. Hooper would by no means consent to wear the vestments. He refused to be consecrated in the dress which had been worn by the bishops of the church of Rome, and which he regarded as a badge of antichrist. Cranmer was then archbishop of Canterbury, and Ridley bishop of London; and they endeavoured to convince him that his scruples were unfounded. But their persuasions and arguments failed; and the three illustrious men gave a short triumph to the enemies of the reformation by a contention not free from human weakness. The council, in the king's name, requested Cranmer to give way and proceed with Hooper's consecration; but Cranmer refused to do so; not thinking, says his biographer, that even such a mandate was a sufficient authority for the breach of an existing law.* Still he does not appear to have been insensible of Hooper's

---

* Strype's Memorials of Cranmer, book ii. c. 17.

worth, far less influenced by any private dislike or jealousy.* His conduct claims our respect, as that of a man who, in arbitrary times, revered the au- thority of the law, and held it to be superior to the mere commands of the sovereign. The professorships of divinity at Oxford and Cambridge were then filled by two eminent foreigners, Peter Martyr and Bucer, whom the archbishop, by the king's command, had invited to those posts of distinguished honour, and, in those changeful times, of equal danger. He desired each of them to write to Hooper on the subject of the vestments, supposing that the judgment of those who were esteemed in their own churches abroad as leaders of the reformation, would have great weight. Meanwhile Hooper continued to inveigh in his sermons, and often with some asperity, against the vestments. The privy council, in consequence, confined him to his own house : but his ardent spirit disdained to be silent. His zeal was not always tempered with discretion. He could not preach upon the decalogue without

---

* In Stowell's History of English Puritans, p. 65, I find a passage quoted from the early *Latin* Edition of Foxe's Martyrs, but omitted in the English translation, as the author says, *out of too great tenderness towards that* [the bishop's] *party*, to this effect, " There are those who think the bishops would have endeavoured to take away his life : for his servant told me the duke of Suffolk sent such word to Hooper, who was not himself ignorant of what they were doing." It is much to be regretted that Foxe should ever have listened to such an accusation, supported on no better evidence than a mere hearsay, reported at second hand by a servant. But it is a painful evidence of the spirit in which even living authors continue to write on the puritan history, that an act of justice on Foxe's part, in not repeating a rumour unsupported by a shade of evidence, should be construed into " too great tenderness" to the maligned party, at the head of which stand the revered names of Ridley and Cranmer.

including " the Aaronic garments" among the violations of the fourth commandment.* He still preached in London, and did not spare the forbidden topic. He even published a book upon the subject, in answer to his opponents; which seems to have been regarded as an act of great contumacy. By order of the privy council he was now silenced, and imprisoned in the Fleet.

10. The letters of Martyr and Bucer upon the subject are still extant. Each of them, but especially the latter, enters at large into the merits of the question. The conclusion at which Martyr arrives is, that Hooper should consent: " yet," he 4th Nov. 1550. adds, " when I consider the superstition and contention the vestments have occasioned, I could wish they were abandoned." Bucer considers them "as in themselves indifferent;" and implores S D c. him for the sake of the church of Christ to dismiss his scruples and accept an office of such vast importance, and one to which, in his judgment, he was especially called, no less by the voice of the sovereign and the necessities of the church, than by his possession of those gifts which qualify for so important an office.†

11. Whatever our decision may be upon the question at issue, no man who now reads the correspondence will lightly condemn Hooper for fickleness of purpose, if, swayed by such advisers, he consented to use the vestments in the ceremonial of his consecration, and to preach in them, once at least, before the court. It seems uncertain

---

* See Hooper's Sermons on the Decalogue. 4th Commandment.
† Strype's Mem. Cran. ii. 17, § 213.

whether he ever wore them afterwards. Thus he exchanged his prison for a bishoprick. His friends were overjoyed. Peter Martyr waited at Oxford to receive him on his progress to his diocese in the west; and wrote to Bullinger expressing the happiness he felt in common with all good men at so great a triumph.* On the 8th March, 1551, he was consecrated bishop of that cathedral, in sight of which, four years afterwards, he died a martyr. Ridley, in whose diocese he had been so harshly used, was brought, and almost at the same time, to the same fiery ordeal. It was a touching message which the one of these devoted men sent to the other, when death in its most dreadful form was near, though disfigured in the quaint language of their times. "We have been two in white : let us be one in red." The "chimere and rochet" now appeared to both of them in another light. So the greatest contentions of good men dwindle on the approach of death.

12. This affair of bishop Hooper made a deep impression. His elevated position, his popular eloquence, his dauntless courage, and above all his glorious martyrdom, embalmed his memory, and rivetted his opinions in the hearts of the reformers. Other circumstances occurred to keep alive the controversy which had now unhappily

---

* Aliquos episcopos habemus, non pessimos, inter quos est uti signifer Cantuariensis. Deinde co-optatus est in eorum album, Hooperus magnâ porrò bonorum omnium letitiâ. Martyr to Bullinger, 1 June 1550. in Burnet's Collection.

arisen.   Several congregations of German protestants, fleeing from continental persecution, had
found an asylum in England.   One of the principal of these was settled in London under the
pastoral care of John Alasco, a man of great
repute, the friend and patron of Erasmus;
while another was placed by the patriotic
wisdom of the duke of Somerset, the protec-
tor during the king's minority, at Glaston-
bury, upon the lands of the famous monastery
then recently dissolved.   Here they introduced
their peculiar craft.   They were cloth workers;
and from them the kingdom derived one of its
greatest manufactures; and the western counties
of England, after three centuries, acknowledge
with gratitude that the boundless fields of enterprise and wealth they still cultivate were first
pointed out by a persecuted band of Flemish refugees.   But at that period the strangers met with
little sympathy.   The neighbourhood was one of
the last strongholds of popery; and the common
people were taught to insult and thwart the
strange society of men whose language was unknown, whose religion was abhorred, and whose
industry was not appreciated; but who profanely
tenanted the lands so long held sacred, and which
a hoary superstition connected in every mind with
Joseph of Arimathea, the reputed apostle of the
western country.   The effect, however, of these
various colonists upon the religious parties in
England, though at length considerable, was not
immediately apparent.

13. But a change was again at hand. Mary
succeeded to the throne, and the antient superstitions were restored. The influence of the
foreigners in matters of religion, however imper-
ceptible, must have been already such as to excite
suspicion; for they were commanded to leave
the kingdom without delay. Nor did they retire
alone. A furious burst of persecution drove with
them a thousand of our countrymen,—who possessed the means of thus providing for their safety,—
who wanted the iron nerve which God bestows on
those he calls to martyrdom,—or who felt that to remain at home was to incur a needless hazard, since,
for the present, nothing could be done. The Low
Countries, the free cities of the Rhine, and Switzerland, were now filled in turn with the English
wanderers. Frankfort, Basle, Zurich, and Geneva,
were the towns of their chief resort; for there the
doctrines of the reformation had taken the strongest
hold, and there its most eminent professors dwelt.

14. A conference of eminent divines, mingled
with a crowd of learned and pious men of secular
pursuits, was thus assembled, though without
design, to which the annals of the church affords
no precedent, and in some respects no parallel.
They were men of various nations, but intent upon a
common object; the greatest that has ever occupied the energies of man. To vanquish the great
antichrist, and restore the religion of Christ to the
myriads from whom it had been so long withheld;
to make provision for its continued establishment
among the nations of Europe, and for its preser-

CHAPTER
I.

MARY

A. D. 1553.

vation from decay by any future corruptions; to continue the fight with popery, now that the tide of battle was rolling fearfully against them, with that assurance of success which nothing could warrant except (what they largely possessed) faith in the written word of God, and a masculine hold upon its prophetic intimations of the certain fall of antichrist; such was the burden of their thoughts and the subject of their frequent conferences as they met during several successive years in social intercourse. And the men were equal to their task. They were scholars of high attainments; and the differences of race and language were insignificant in an age when Latin was the vernacular tongue of educated men.

15. The Zurich Letters* still remain to testify that, in classical taste as well as in theology, the monkish puerilities had been marvellously dissipated from the minds of men who one and all were tutored in their youth under monkish discipline. Nor was scholarship their only boast. They were men of great and diversified experience; of practical habits; of energy and zeal; and above all of fervent and exalted piety. Here were to be found the firm and gentle Jewel, the future apologist, and bishop, of the church of England; and the resolute Knox, the reformer of the north. Here too were Grindal, Sandys, and Pilkington; besides Parkhurst, and Humphrey, and Wittingham, and others scarcely less renown-

---

* First published in part by Bishop Burnet in his Hist. Reformation, and now at large by the Parker Society, in 2 vols.

ed as the champions of the English reformation.
And with these there was a host of names scarcely,
if at all, inferior:—Coverdale, ever honoured by
those who reverence the bible : Nowel, the future
dean of St. Paul's, whose catechism, approved
in convocation and sanctioned by the church of
England, it would be needless to mention, and
presumptuous to applaud ; and Foxe, whose
plaintive and authentic story of the martyrs will
be read, while time shall last, with indignation or
with tears. In short, besides five bishops and an
equal number of deans, the character of those who
fled may be surmised from the fact, that no less
than fifty were doctors in divinity of English universities. And even of the laity, including noblemen, merchants, and artificers, who had less to
fear, the number was about a thousand. Mingled
with these were the leaders of the continental reformation. The English refugees had constant intercourse with Calvin, (a name as much honoured
then as it has been since depreciated in England),
with Gualter, and with Peter Martyr and Alasco,
whom the refluent surge of persecution had beaten
back upon their native shores ; and above all with
Henry Bullinger. Of the last the historical fate
is singular and affecting. Scarcely known in England in the nineteenth century, he was the spon-
sor of the English reformation. Jewel and Parkhurst, and Cox and Horn and Pilkington, who
became bishops—and Sandys and Grindal, archbishops—of the church of England ; not to men-

tion John Foxe and Wiburne, Richard Hilles (a London merchant) and Humphrey and Sampson, worthies of our church in its first days, were amongst the affectionate, it might be said the reverential, correspondents of this great man. They address him with every title of respect; as their father and their counsellor. The tidings of his death draw forth a burst of tenderness, and they console each other with the assurance that his fame shall be immortal. And those who read in his still extant letters, and in his more elaborate writings, the record of his wisdom, are at no loss to comprehend the secret of their respect and reverence, however they may be perplexed to understand the oblivion of his name—a name that once promised, at least in the reformed churches, honor and immortality. But such men are satisfied to receive their honours in a better world.

16. The results of this great congress of wise and thoughtful men were such as universal experience would teach us to expect: continued diversities on those points on which they previously differed; and greater steadfastness on those on which they were all along agreed. Their detestation of the papacy, and their views of evangelical truth, were confirmed; for on these points few differences, if any, had crept in; and their mutual conferences served to strengthen each other in the common quarrel and in the common faith. On points of church government it was

different. The fusion of parties produced no perfect coalescence. Each adhered to his national
forms of worship in preference to the rest; or if
some occasionally went over to the episcopal
party, their place was filled by deserters to the
presbyterian camp. The relative strength of the
two infant parties, the episcopal and presbyterian,
was not immediately changed. What was gained
was an equal advantage to both sides,—on both
sides an increase of mutual confidence and christian love. On the death of Mary our English
exiles returned home, bringing nothing back with
them, as a quaint and not unfriendly chronicler
has said, but much learning and some experience.* Still it is likely that they were swayed
unconsciously by the manners of the German
churches. On their return to England, the contrast between the splendour of the English ceremonial and the simplicity of that abroad would
be more striking. Their opponents never ceased
to attribute much of the discontent that followed
to the Genevan exile;† though the puritans less
frequently adverted to it ; founding their scruples
more upon what they conceived to be the absence
of scriptural simplicity than upon the practice
of other churches. But the question of the habits,
or as it has since been termed the vestiarian controversy, was unsettled : and it now began to
wear an anxious if not a threatening aspect : and
other difficulties already lowered upon the hori-

* Fuller : Church His. Vol. II. Book viii.
† So Heylin, Hist. Reformation, ann. 1560 to 1565, &c.

zon, even in this the early morning of the English reformation.

17. This dispute with regard to the vestments to be worn by the ministers of Christ when discharging their official duties, lay at the root of many other controversies, and was the source from which they sprung. The controversy was a vital one ; and few questions in the history of the christian church are more deserving of a calm dispassionate consideration. It will appear insignificant to those only who are unable to comprehend that the colours of a regiment are to be surrendered only with the life of the soldier who proudly bears them into battle ; that they are symbols, insignificant in themselves it may be, but in their meaning most important. In the great conflicts in which mankind unhappily engage some visible sign is always found to express and represent the sentiment or principle most cherished or most abhorred. These are often arbitrary. The white and red roses of the houses of York and Lancaster were purely so; though ranged beneath them England poured out for half a century its noblest blood. But the vestments, at the time of the reformation, were not admitted, at least by one of the contending parties, to be merely conventional ; they were supposed to represent principles of which, it was said, they formed an integral and inseparable part.—But it is necessary to pause and consider the arguments on each side as they were stated at first by the respective pleaders. During the reigns of Edward

VI. and Mary, and the first years of Elizabeth, the CHAPTER
controversy was managed with great ability, and _{I.}
generally with temper and forbearance; but as ELIZ.
the first leaders of the reformation disappeared, A.D. 1558.
it fell into the hands of other disputants, and was
conducted on both sides in a very different spirit.

18. It was urged by the dissatisfied party that
the imposition of the vestments was an infringe-
ment of their christian liberty. They were called
under the gospel to worship God in spirit and in
truth : and no outward forms or splendours could
contribute in any measure to assist the devout
mind in a service so spiritual and exalted. On
the contrary, the tendency of these official garments was to distract the worshipper, and to
debase his devotions by an admixture of those
sentiments which are allowed no place in spiritual
things : namely, the awe inspired by official pomp
and the admiration of outward grandeur. The
church had ever maintained or lost its purity just
as it had resisted or allowed the allurements of
external splendour. It was only safe in its simplicity ; and such was its inward glory, that any
attempts to decorate could but in fact degrade
it. Men had been too long the dupes of artifice
and superstition ; and it became a reformation
which professed nothing less than to restore to
the churches of Christendom the liberties of which
they had been so long deprived, as well as the
truths which a vile imposture had perverted or
concealed, boldly to lay aside the stratagems of

superstition, and to rest its influence upon the naked force of truth.

19. Besides, the vestments against which they were now contending had a jewish origin, and belonged not to the christian ministry, but to the priesthood of the house of Aaron. To introduce them into the church of Christ was to pervert their meaning. They were a part of the divinely appointed constitution of the jewish church ; and had passed away together with the rest of its figurative and mystic ceremonial. If they were not retained as symbols, they were merely childish, and unworthy of the dignity of christian worship. If their symbolic character was admitted, then the priesthood of the clergy, one of the many corruptions of the papacy, was involved. A sacrificing priest must wear a linen ephod. If the sacrificial vestments were now retained, the sacrifice of the mass itself would probably but too soon return. As a safeguard against popery, no less than as a guarantee for the continued purity of evangelical doctrine in the reformed church, they protested against the use of garments which were at once so unnecessary and, as it seemed to them, so full of danger.

20. It was a further objection, and one that appealed not only to divines and controversialists, but to the feelings of the common people, that the vestments were identified with all the superstitions of popery. They were looked upon as the badge of antichrist ; and they who wore them were re-

garded with suspicion as men either indifferent to the cause of the reformation, or not yet suffi- ciently enlightened as to the danger, and indeed the sinfulness, of approaching the most distant confines of a system which ought to be avoided with alarm and horror. In similar robes the " massing priests" had performed their idolatrous services. Thus arrayed the papal bishops had de- nounced the reformation from their superstitious altars. Into these hated garments the martyrs had been thrust, in order that being again stripped of them, and thus degraded from the priesthood, they might, as laymen, perish in flames kindled by the secular power. Nor was it forgotten that if Hooper refused to wear them at his consecra- tion, Cranmer and Latimer, and Taylor of Had- leigh, had expressed their contempt of them, in their last moments. Thus the detestation of the habits, as popish relics, became a popular cry and passion: and it broke out from time to time in rudeness and acts of violence.

21. And admitting the vestments to be in themselves indifferent, it was contended by the clergy who opposed their introduction, that under present circumstances they were still unlawful. For having been once consecrated to idolatry, they had received a taint which, like the leprosy of Gehazi, must cleave to them for ever. Some of their hearers still thought their ministrations in- valid, or not acceptable to God, unless performed in popish apparel: some mysterious virtue was still supposed by the superstitious to be connected

with them; and this, said they, being a prevailing opinion, we apprehend that it is highly necessary to disabuse the people. And lastly they urged that one concession would only be the prelude to fresh demands: an argument upon which the weaker party is apt, it is true, to place too much reliance, and one upon which it is always sensitive. " If we are bound to wear popish apparel when commanded, we may be obliged to have shaven crowns, and to use oil, and cream, and spittle, and all the rest of the papistical additions to the ordinances of Christ." Such were their objections, and thus they were expressed.

22. These arguments received, no doubt, additional weight and confirmation from the fact that of all the reformed churches, the church of England was the only one which had retained the vestments. Other churches had abandoned them. Something then was due to the judgment of other churches, especially when their decision was unanimous. Something, too, was due to the great principle of godly union; an agreement in externals ought to prevail amongst all the reformed without exception. Shall the body of Christ, it was inquired, be rent in the garments of his own ministers? Shall the divisions of true christians, upon such a point, afford a triumph to the enemies of the gospel and of the reformation? For the sake of peace let the English church abandon a peculiarity which many of its own members submit to with impatience, and which all other churches have rejected with disdain. Were it nothing else

than a concession to weak consciences and per-verse men, ill-informed, still it ought to be made; except it could be shewn that conces-sion was absolutely sinful. And when every reformed church in Europe had rejected them, it would scarcely be contended that they were essential to the purity of the faith. The apostolic precept ought to decide the question. In things indifferent the weaker party must be allowed the triumph. However painful it might be, still it was a duty in the rulers of the church to "suffer all things for the elects' sake;" to give up the most harmless indulgences if they caused the feet of the lame to stumble, or cast a stone of offence in the way of the meanest of Christ's dis-ciples.

23. Such were the arguments of those who ob-jected to the use of the vestments. They were urged with the utmost sincerity, and, it is not too much to say, they were listened to with profound respect. During the troublous days of queen Mary the controversy was still carried on, around the fires of the martyrs and in the strange homes of the self-banished exiles. But there was at present little or no bitterness displayed. Happily for mankind the reign of Mary was brief. When her sister Elizabeth succeeded to the crown, some concessions were eagerly looked for; but none were made. It was natural that a minority who now began to think themselves oppressed should urge their cause with warmth; and by no means surprising that a popular question should be ad-

CHAPTER vocated sometimes with clamour and impatience.
I. For this the leaders of the church made, during
ELIZ. the first period of the controversy, a generous
A. D. allowance. They viewed with deep concern a
1558—1560. division in the English church, which might end
in a secession from it. Why then did they not
give way?—why not abandon the vestments, and
quench the growing discord? Why not at once
adopt the fashions of the continental churches?
It is due to some of the greatest men that England has nourished to listen dispassionately to
their reply.

24. Every christian church contains within
itself the principles of self-government. If it be
not only an independent but a national church,
the right of self-control is one that it cannot part
with without disloyalty. It may receive advice,
but it may not submit to foreign interference.
The church of England has retained the vestments
in the exercise of its undoubted right to decree
rights and ceremonies for its own use, guarding
itself only against the introduction of any thing
contrary to God's word. The vestments are
decent and becoming, and in themselves indifferent. And in matters of order and church discipline, it is surely a maxim of caution to introduce no unnecessary changes: for these unsettle
the minds of the multitude; turn them aside
from what is really edifying; and excite them to
the desire of still fresh experiments. Besides, the
example of the primitive church, long before the
rise of popery, favours some distinctive habits in

those who discharge a public function. Saint
John himself, as the historian Eusebius relates,
wore a *petalon*, which some translate a mitre,
some a plate, or coronal of gold; but all acknowledge that it was a badge of dignity which belonged to him as bishop of Ephesus. The cate-
chumens in the earliest ages were clothed in white
when they presented themselves for baptism, a
modest sign of the purity they now professed.
Even their pagan forefathers, the citizens of
Rome, had used a white robe in the same manner
when they were *candidates*, (the word itself being
expressive of the fact) for public offices. The
surplice was used in the church of Christ long
before the introduction of popery : and is retained
by us, they said, together with some other forms,
not for superstition but only for distinction; that
order and decency may be preserved in the ministry of the word and sacraments. " And neither
good pastors nor pious laymen," they affirmed,
" are offended at these things."*

25. With regard to the charge of returning to
the usage of the jewish church and restoring the
garments proper to its priesthood, it was surely
enough, they thought, to remind their opponents
that every document they had uttered was at
variance with the supposition that they regarded
the ministry of Jesus Christ as a succession of the
jewish priesthood, or desired to see it invested, or
degraded rather, with sacrificial robes. They now

---

* So Grindal, Parkhurst, Sandys, and even Pilkington and Jewel,
in the Zurich Correspondence.

CHAPTER protested against such a perversion of their sen-
I.   timents. The christian church acknowledged
ELIZ.   only one priest, in the person of its LORD. From
A. D.   this doctrine they had never swerved. It was for
1558—60. this they fought; for this they had suffered.
Indeed, there was at present no difference amongst
the reformed churches upon this cardinal truth.
With one consent they dismissed the fiction of a
priesthood as inconsistent with the scheme of
redemption perfected in the one offering of the
Lord Jesus Christ. It was rather with a view to
the probable consequences than the present evil
of the vestments, that the dispute under this
head of objection, was carried on by the opposing
party. And the argument on the episcopal side
was briefly this, that the vestments could mislead
none who cared to listen to the doctrinal teaching
of the English church.

26. Still less could they reasonably be charged
with any disposition to popery. What church
had been so much and so long in deadly conflict
with the man of sin ? What church had given
so many, and they such illustrious, pledges of
the depth of its hatred of the great antichrist ?
Nobles and gentry, bishops and archbishops, the
laity and the clergy, men, women, and children,
had yield themselves a ready sacrifice to his
fury in prisons and at the stake : not accepting
deliverance, when deliverance was thrust upon
them on the sole condition of admitting a real
presence in the mass. They felt, and may well
be forgiven if they expressed, some indignation

when, because they retained a surplice, they were charged with a return to popery.

27. If these reasons were not sufficient, another yet remained. The reformation was itself in jeopardy in England from the continued agitation of these unfortunate, and as the episcopal party maintained, these insignificant, disputes. During the short reign of king Edward the controversy arose, and might then perhaps have been set at rest by mutual concessions; but his early death put a stop to the progress of the reformation. During the reign of Mary it was evident that nothing could be done; for the reformed church was broken up and scattered. And now that Elizabeth held the sceptre, fresh difficulties crowded in. The queen, as a sovereign and a woman, was equally tender of her mother's honour and her own legitimacy. The Romish party were powerful and restless; and numbers of the gentry as well as the nobility, and not a few of the clergy, were supposed to yield but a hollow consent to the principles of the reformation. The ascendancy of the Romish party would have been fatal to the queen's happiness, if not to her throne. For the pope had already taken his position and de. nounced her claims. She was deeply attached to the reformation when she began her reign. And when she kissed the bible presented to her at Paul's cross on the day of her magnificent procession through London, and then pressed it to her heart, it is probable that no bosom in that vast enthusiastic crowd beat with more fervent

loyalty to the protestant cause. It was with difficulty she could be prevailed upon to assume the title of head of the church. This, she said, belonged not to a sovereign, still less to a woman, but to Christ. It has been urged, indeed, that a lingering reverence for the papal claim of universal supremacy had some share in this unwillingness. Every thing, however, portended a happy settlement of past differences. Sound doctrine was rapidly diffused. " The true religion of Christ is settled among us : the gospel is not bound, but is freely and faithfully preached. As to other matters there is not much cause for anxiety. There is some little dispute about using or not using the popish habits : but God will put an end to these things also." So wrote bishop Sandys, of Worcester, in January 1566.

28. But the queen was extremely anxious that no needless offence should be given to the Romish party ; and the removal of the surplice would, she feared, afford a pretext for some new outrage. If it were a thing not sinful in itself, as not only her own divines, but those of Germany and Switzerland, informed her, then it became a question of state policy, not simply of religious controversy. The continued use of a thing indifferent in a religious sense, but important in its political bearings, must be determined not by the clergy but by the sovereign. If therefore the reformation were not injured, policy was in favour of the vestments. This seemed a reasonable conclusion, even upon the view of the

question taken by the foreign reformers. Adverse
as they were to the use of the surplice, they
counselled the English clergy by no means to
refuse it, since the progress of the reformation
seemed to depend on their compliance. The
question then, as soon as it ceased to be one of
conscience, became one of convenience and expediency, and of that expediency the queen and
her council must judge. The foreign reformers
themselves acted on this principle : for they admitted episcopacy to be scriptural, and in itself de-
sirable; and yet established presbyterian churches
on the ground of expediency. Just at the same
period other influences produced a painful impression on her mind. The puritans preached
before her with unmeasured vehemence. " She
is in the habit of listening with the greatest
patience," says bishop Cox, " to bitter and sufficiently cutting discourses."* There is unhappily
no reason to think that the bishop in a courtly
mood overdrew the picture. It is a fact constantly
repeated by the leaders of the reformation, " that
the queen was irritated, the minds of the nobility
alienated, the diseased and weak debilitated,"† by
the violent appeals with which the pulpit now
rang. One preacher‡ informed her majesty that
she had begun her reign with the meekness of a
lamb—but she was now an untamed heifer. *Olim
tanquam ovis, nunc autem indomita juvenca.*

29. The vestments in short were now unhappily

---

* Zurich Letters. Cox to Gualter. 1. 234. † Ibid.
‡ Dering. The story is related by all the puritan writers.

CHAPTER
1.

ELIZ.
A. D.
1565—68.

regarded as badges not only of canonical obedience but of loyalty to the queen herself. To abandon them, or to join in the inconsiderate zeal which assailed what was by law established, would be in effect to abandon the ministry: "and then, verily," said the prelates,* "we shall have a papistical, or a Lutherano-papistical, ministry, or none at all." They complain that "an ungovernable zeal for discord" was abroad; and it seemed to threaten danger to both church and state. It was to save England from these calamities; to save the reformation from the indiscretion of its friends, as they had saved it once from the fury of its enemies, that they decided on the course from which they never swerved. But was the danger real, or were their fears groundless? We have perhaps at this distance of time no answer more reasonable than an appeal to their private characters. They were not crafty politicians, but a body of christian ministers of calm wisdom, of tried courage, of dauntless resolution. The fears and apprehensions of such men are never to be treated with disdain: there must have been some grounds for alarm. They submitted from necessity, not from choice. The bishops of London and Winchester "protest and solemnly make oath," in a letter they jointly addressed to Bullinger and Gaulter, "that the dissension was not caused by any fault of theirs, and that it was not owing to them that vestments of this kind had not alto-gether been done away with."† Jewel expresses

* Grindal and Horn to Bullinger, Feb. 6, 1567.   † Ibid.

himself if possible more strongly : " They are the
relics of the Amorites ; *that* cannot be denied."
And yet he speaks of the contest as a trifling
matter that " somewhat disturbs weak minds."*
In short, they brought the matter to this issue :
" We are brought into such straits, that since we
cannot do what we would, shall we not do, in the
Lord, what we can ?"† Calmly viewed, the whole
question hinges upon this : when men cannot
do what they would, shall they do what they
can ; or, rigidly adhering to an abstract notion
of that which in itself is best, shall they abandon
their posts, and risk the consequences ? The
fathers of the church of England were at length
unanimous " to do what they could ;" they received the vestments themselves, and, though
with very different degrees of rigour, enforced
them on their clergy. They hoped the ferment
would soon subside ; but ages have passed, and
the controversy is not yet decided. So little do
the wisest men foresee the consequences of all their
actions. And so difficult is it to appease the
quarrels on which all parties at first enter with
too much alacrity !

* Feb. 8, 1566.
† Zurich Letters, Parker Soc. Edit. Vol. i. p. 175, Grindal and Horne
to Bullinger, &c., Jewel to Bullinger, p. 147. I have used throughout the admirable translation of the Zurich Letters by Dr. Hastings
Robinson.

CHAPTER II.

CHAPTER II.

ELIZ.

A.D. 1558.

1. A great question is not long in agitation without invoking its tributary discords. Consequences not at first suspected are found to hang upon it. What appeared to be a single point of difference, is perceived to be no more than one amongst many others, on which all insist upon their right to swell the general clamour. The contest begins with facts; but it soon spreads itself among the principles of which those facts were only the exponents. Thus a great controversy, like a great battle, is seldom decided upon the ground previously marked out. The conflict widens on all sides, and the confusion at length becomes universal.

2. The question of the vestments was very soon followed up with other questions equally irritating. From dislike to the habits the progress was easy to a dislike of the service book; and that of king Edward was by no means free from superstition. All forms of prayer fell under a suspicion of popery. So that the revisal of the prayer book, on the accession of Elizabeth, gave

little satisfaction to those, already a considerable CHAPTER II. party, who had begun to think all forms unlawful. Others again, ignorant of the difficulties ELIZ. with which the bishops were contending, and A.D. 1558. smarting, it must be owned, from their unreasonable severity, began to associate prelacy with popery. In a short time the former was loaded with the same obloquy which, ten years before, had fallen upon the latter; and bishops were denounced with as much vehemence as the pope himself. Thus fresh wounds were opened from day to day, and at last they became incurable. Thus there were from the first, dissenters from the English church of the reformation. Their story must be briefly told, though in fact they were disowned by the puritans; nor did they seek to be reckoned their associates, regarding both prelatists and puritans as equally inconsistent, or on spiritual matters ignorant and dark.

3. The first actual secession took place abroad. Anno 1554. The English residents at Frankfort* entered into an agreement with a congregation of French protestants, in whose church they were allowed to assemble as their place of worship, binding themselves not only to subscribe to the French confession of faith, which evangelical christians of almost every name might safely do, but further, not to make responses after the minister, nor to use the litany or surplice; and (a condition of no less importance,) not to quarrel about ceremonies.

* Hist. of the Troubles at Frankfort. Neale, Hist. of the Puritans, vol. 1. c. 111. p. 86 et seq.

CHAPTER II.

ELIZ.

A.D. 1558.

Their church discipline seems to have been rather *independent* than *presbyterian*. They looked upon themselves as under God himself, the source and fountain of ecclesiastical power. They proceeded to choose their own minister and deacons, and to invite their brethren dispersed through the neighbouring cities, to join a community where, they said, God's word was faithfully preached, the sacraments rightly administered, and scripture discipline enforced. Their public service was conducted thus : it began with extemporaneous prayer ; a hymn was sung ; the minister then prayed a second time and more at large, concluding with the Lord's prayer. Then followed another psalm, and a sermon, if a preacher were present ; or otherwise the recital of a confession of faith. The congregation was then dismissed with the apostolic benediction.

4. This form of worship has been retained, with a few variations, and is still used, by almost every class of nonconformists in England. The objections to it are obvious. It leaves too much to the piety, and too much to the discretion, of the minister. Such is human nature, even in its best estate, that the fervour of the most devout is often cold, and the zeal of the most ardent is often languid. And whenever this occurs, the whole congregation suffer from their minister's weakness. On the other hand, it must be admitted that such a mode of worship, if conducted by ministers equally eminent for talents and for piety, is not without its advantages. It excites a more ready

sympathy in the hearer : it is capable of a more
frequent and graceful accommodation to passing
events,—and to the ever varying circumstances,
the joys, trials, and temptations of the flock ; and
since it is easier to speak than to read in a manner
at once devout and natural, it often has an air of
more reality. And these are no mean advantages.
Perhaps the perfection of a ritualistic church
would be found between a liturgy rigidly enforced
in some of its greater services, and the free use of
unpremeditated acts of worship in those of a more
social character.

5. The experiment, however, was not successful.
The English divines at Strasburgh, Zurich, and
Basle, declined, in succession, the invitations of
the newly formed congregation. They next applied to Knox, and he with two assistants became
their pastor. But difficulties arose amongst themselves; for many of them were attached to the
English forms, and even the fervour and eloquence of Knox himself, the fiery meteor of the
north, did not convince them of the superior
value of extemporary worship. These it seems
were the majority ; they elected Dr. Cox, who had
been tutor to Edward the Sixth, their minister, and
Knox found himself displaced, and was required
by the government to leave the city. He retired
to Geneva, and immediately gathered another congregation amongst the English exiles. But the
death of Mary, which happened in the following
year, again broke up his flock, and their pastor
was now free to return to his native land, where

CHAPTER a greater work required his presence. Meantime,
II. however, Cox resigned his pastoral care at Frank-
ELIZ. fort, and removed elsewhere ; and the congrega-
A.D. 1559. tion again quarrelled, and divided. The magistrates were obliged to interfere ; for the heat and
scandal occasioned by a handful of strangers became, they said, intolerable. Once more the
minority left the city ; the congregation soon
afterwards dispersed ; and thus the affair ended.
The crowds of foreigners who hastened to England
on the accession of Elizabeth, or who had lived
amongst us since the days of Edward VI., brought
with them similar quarrels, and tempers still more
ungovernable. They were chiefly artizans; persons
of inferior education and lower rank than the
English exiles, and their conduct is to be judged
with more forbearance. Four thousand of them
settled in Norwich, and John Alasco returned
with his flock to London. The latter were sometimes troublesome, but the artificers at Norwich
set no bounds to their contentious violence. There
were several congregations, and each, with its
minister at its head, was in bitter warfare with
the rest. The value of episcopacy, and the reason-
ableness of a secular head in the national church,
might be learned from the unhappy differences of
these foreigners. Each church was a rival republic; and when they had nothing to fear from
without, they turned their arms against each
other. Parkhurst was then bishop of Norwich,
and, in a letter to their countryman Bullinger, he
describes their quarrel as implacable. The whole

congregation, he says, is nearly broken up. The English, I allow, were somewhat troublesome in Germany; but if you compare them with these men, they are quietness itself.*

6. But these troubles passed over, and left no serious consequences. They were, however, the harbingers of greater and more lasting conflicts, in which the interests of the church of England were more immediately concerned.

7. The puritans were the extreme party of the reformation; and they naturally looked forward to the accession of Elizabeth with sanguine hope. During her intolerant sister's reign, she had suffered much in common with themselves. They had fled from England, or remained at home at the peril of their lives; and she too had been a prisoner in fear and constant apprehension. Her attachment to the reformation was not doubted; it was supposed indeed to be in Mary's sight her one great delinquency; and she was regarded as a fellow-sufferer for conscience sake. They expected to find in her a patron and a friend; and deep and bitter was their disappointment. However the conduct of the prelates may be justified, that of the queen admits of less excuse. It committed her to a course of policy which embarrassed her through life, led her into many acts of injustice and not a few of cruelty, and continues to this day to be the greatest blot on her otherwise glorious reign. Contrary to her usual policy, she placed herself in opposition to a large body of her

* Aug. 10, 1571.

CHAPTER
II.

ELIZ.

A.D. 1559.

own subjects; and they, with all their faults, were loyal and sound at heart. It was pitiful to see, as years passed on, the mistress of an empire setting herself in stern displeasure against scrupulous consciences. Foreigners could not understand that she who was the champion of the principles of the reformation wherever they shewed themselves abroad, should be so nervously sensitive to their most trifling excesses in England. It is beyond dispute that she owed much of her reputation in civil affairs to the singular wisdom of her various counsellors. Had she in the first instance deferred to her spiritual counsellors; had she not set at nought the wishes of such men as Jewel, Horn, and Parker, the history of the puritans would have been written, if written at all, more to her advantage. Her accession afforded an opportunity, such as rarely presents itself, for an oblivion of the past, and a firm union for the future. Unhappily the golden opportunity was lost. Scarcely an attempt was made to conciliate prejudice, or disarm suspicion. At present no venerable usage gave to the obnoxious forms and vestments its mysterious sanctions. A great revolution had just occurred. The church of England must be remodelled. The question of its services and vestments came beneath review of necessity; and might have been decided, even had the queen yielded up her wishes, without exposing her to the humiliation of defeat. At no subsequent period could this state of things return. The question would soon involve the disgrace of one of the contending parties; for those who are compelled by acts of force, or arbitrary laws, to give up the usages which have become habitual in matters of religion, will always feel themselves aggrieved.

8. The act of uniformity, which passed in the first year of Elizabeth, may be considered as the point of time at which the battle was at length joined, and each of the two parties, the puritans and prelatists, assumed its definite position. The act embraced two vital questions : the revisal of the prayer-book, and the compliance hereafter to be rendered to the forms and ceremonies. With regard to the book of common prayer, it remained in substance the second of two prayer-books is- sued by king Edward, namely, that of 1552. The few alterations in it, did not relieve the puritans, nor were they meant to do so. With regard to the vestments, they felt themselves injured afresh ; for they were compelled by a rubric in the revised book to retain " all such ornaments of the church and ministers as were in use in the second of king Edward," the year in which his first imperfect prayer-book was put forth, abounding as it did with the traces of superstition : whereas the second prayer-book of 1552, insisted only on the use of the surplice. This was much to be deplored ; not because the difference is important between a surplice and a cope, but because it shewed an un- yielding temper. Still it was for a time uncertain how far conformity would be rigidly enforced. On the side of the puritans there was a disposition to

CHAPTER II.

ELIZ.

A.D. 1559.

receive the prayer-book as a general directory for public worship, guiding but not absolutely restraining them. So far they were disposed to yield; but if it were to be in every point literally enforced, they held that in some of its details it was inconvenient and oppressive, and in others superstitious. As its enactments were successively urged upon them, their discontent increased. Each attempt to reduce them to an uniform submission only provoked a fresh resistance. Mutual exasperations followed; and the puritans discovered fresh grievances as the contest was prolonged. When at last they drew up a formal statement of their principles, and made in turn their own demands, the prospect of a reconciliation was more remote than ever. At this early period a few concessions would have satisfied them, or placed them so clearly in the wrong that their cause would have been undermined and lost. Twenty years later their terms were unreasonable; they were such as men offer who are sure of success, or abandoned to despair. But for this violence the queen and her advisers are to a great extent responsible. Gentleness had not been tried; the puritans were goaded to desperation, and as their power increased, they began to demand concessions which it was impossible to grant, in a temper which it was impossible to pass unnoticed. They too, in their turn, forced upon their opponents the alternative of conquest or submission; and if vanquished, it was not likely in those rugged times that they should be treated with much for-

bearance. A deeper spirit of piety would have CHAPTER
produced more forbearance on both sides; but it   II.
is one of the painful lessons of this whole history, ELIZ.
that men may be much in earnest in defending A.D. 1559.
the cause of religion and of God, and at the same
time display an evident want of the Christian
virtues of meekness and forbearance.

9. The act of uniformity was passed in May,
and came into effect on the 24th of June 1559,
though not without a protest from Heath, archbishop of York. It not only enacted a rigorous
conformity in the conduct of divine worship and
in the habits worn by the minister, but further
empowered the queen, by the advice of the commissioners or metropolitan, to ordain and publish
at their pleasure further rites or ceremonies, with
no other limitation than these words convey;—
"as may be most for God's glory, the edifying of
his church, and the due reverence of Christ's holy
mysteries and sacraments." The rigorous press-
ing of this act, says the great chronicler of puritanism, was the occasion of all the mischiefs that
befel the church for above eighty years.* It is
certain that every disposition was shewn to enforce
the law, and that too little allowance was made
for the scruples of a large body of dissentients,
numbering amongst them not a few of the brightest ornaments of the church. The evils which it
was meant to remedy were no doubt both real and
extensive; but the measure was violent. And it
fared with it according to the disastrous law which

* Neale 1. iv. 110 et seq.

ever governs such proceedings ; what was conceived with rashness was carried into effect with obstinate severity.

10. A convocation of the church was opened at St. Paul's on the 13th day of January 1562, in the third year of the reign of Elizabeth. The articles of the church were then agreed upon, although they did not become law till some years afterwards : and the rites and ceremonies of the church came again under consideration.

11. The state of parties, and their relative strength, at this important crisis, is clearly shewn by the records of this assembly.

12. Bishop Sandys (afterwards archbishop of York) proposed that private baptism, and baptism by women, should be discontinued ; that the use of the cross in baptism should be disallowed as both needless and superstitious ; and that commissioners should be appointed to reform the ecclesiastical laws.

13. Another paper was presented to the house, containing the following demands : that the psalms should be sung distinctly by the whole congregation, and that organs be disused : that ministers only should baptize, and that without the sign of the cross : that at the ministration of the Lord's supper the posture of kneeling should be left indifferent : that the use of copes and surplices be abolished, so that all ministers should use " a grave and comely side garment," or preaching gown : and that they should not be compelled to wear such caps and gowns as the Romish

clergy : that the punishment of those who did not CHAPTER in all things conform to the public about cere- II. monies should be mitigated: and lastly that saints' ELIZ. days and festivals in honour of a creature should A.D. 1562. either be abolished, or observed without superstition ; so that after a morning service all men might resume their daily pursuits.

14. This overture bore the signatures of five deans, the provost of Eton, twelve archdeacons, and fourteen proctors or representatives. But it was not approved.

15. Another motion followed immediately. It was to this effect. That all Sundays, and the feasts which commmemorate the events of the Saviour's life, be kept holy; and that all other holydays be abolished, that in all parish churches the minister in common prayer should turn his face towards the people, and there read the service distinctly ; so that the people may hear and be edified. That the cross in baptism be omitted; that kneeling at the sacrament of the Lord's supper be left to the discretion of the minister ; that organs should be removed; and that it should suffice if the minister wore the surplice once, provided that he ministered in a comely garment or habit.* Unhappily these moderate proposals were once more rejected.† Of the members of convocation present there was a majority ; the numbers being forty-three in favour of the resolutions, and thirty-five against them.

* Strype, Annals, 337. Burnet, Ref. III. 444.
† Heylin, Hist. Reformation II. 391. Ecc. Soc. Edit. He however praises the moderation of the convocation.

CHAPTER
II.

ELIZ.
A.D. 1562.

The name of Nowel, dean of St. Paul's, the pro-locutor, or speaker of the convocation, appears in favour of this as well as of the previous motion. His reputation, which even then was great, has suffered no decay. His catechism (though in part compiled from that of Calvin), sanctioned by convocation, and commended by cotemporary prelates to the daily study of the clergy, places him high amongst the divines of England and the defenders of its church. But the proxies turned the scale, though by the narrow majority of a single vote —the vote of one, it was remarked, who was not present during the discussion. From so trivial a cause arose momentous consequences. Never was a casting vote of more grave importance.

16. Parker, now archbishop of Canterbury, pushed his slender triumph to the utmost. On his part no pains were spared to produce an exact obedience : and the disorders which prevailed in the church afforded a man not indisposed to wield despotic power frequent occasions to interfere. A paper was laid before the queen which describes the various irregularities which at once provoked his severities and eluded his authority. They were such as to demand a remedy, had that remedy been applied with judgment. But they were not vital : they touched no doctrine ; they approached the confines of no heresy. And since gentleness was never tried, it is impossible to deny that gentleness might have availed where force was foiled. Some perform the divine service,* so runs

* Strype. Life of Parker, 152.

the document, in the chancel; some in the body of the church, some in a seat, some in a pulpit with their faces to the people; some keep to the order of the book, some intermix psalms in metre, some say with a surplice, and some without one. The form and position of the communion-table was a frequent scandal. In some places the table stands in the body of the church, in some places it stands altar-wise, in others in the middle of the chancel placed north and south : in some places the table is joined, in others it stands upon tressels : sometimes covered with a cloth, in other a naked board. The administration of the Lord's supper was no less irregular. Some administer the communion with surplice and cap; some with surplice alone; others with none. Some with unleavened bread (the lingering remains of popery), and some with leavened. Some receive kneeling, others standing, others sitting. Baptism was variously administered. Some baptize in a font; some in a bason. Some sign with the sign of the cross; others sign not. And the habits of the ministers were as motley as their conduct. Some minister in a surplice, others without; some with a square cap, some with a round cap; some with a button cap, some with a hat; some in scholar's clothes, some in others. The queen upon this issued a letter to the two archbishops directing them to confer with the ecclesiastical commission; to inquire what diversities existed among the clergy in doctrine, rites, and ceremonies; and to take effectual methods to

CHAPTER reduce them to an exact order and uniformity.
II.   So far as external rites and ceremonies were con-
ELIZ. cerned, uniformity was at once secured by the
A.D. 1564. stern command that none hereafter be admitted
to any ecclesiastical preferment who were not well
disposed, and would not formally comply with the
common order.* The ejection of many good men
immediately followed.

17. One of the first sufferers was Miles Coverdale, bishop of Exeter in the reign of Edward
VI. On the accession of Mary he was imprisoned,
and escaped the flames only through the intercession of the king of Denmark, to whose territories he fled. Returning at Elizabeth's accession he assisted at the consecration of archbishop
Parker; but as he disliked the ceremonies and
habits, his bishoprick was not restored : and the
venerable translator of the bible was suffered to
fall into neglect and poverty. When old and poor
he was presented by Grindal bishop of London
with the small living of St. Magnus near London-
bridge. He had scarcely held his preferment two
years, when he was driven from his parish by the
stringent demand of a rigorous conformity, with
which he could not comply. He died soon after
in 1567, at the age of eighty-one :† vast crowds
attended his funeral at St. Bartholomew's near the
Exchange; from whence, with almost equal reverence, his bones were lately carried (the church
being taken down) by a posterity not more sensible

* Neale's Puritans I. iv., 147.   † Strype, Ann. 405.

of his illustrious worth than ashamed of the barbarous and worse than useless severity which
brought his gray hairs with sorrow to the grave.
18. Sampson, dean of Christchurch, was one
of the proscribed; a man of whom Grindal and
Horn attest* that his learning was equal to his
piety. Of the former few traces exist; of the
latter an affecting evidence appears in his own
letter to Peter Martyr, on declining the see of Norwich. His friend Parkhurst, on his own refusal,
had been elevated to the post of honour, and thus
the danger of an improper person obtaining the see
was, as he remarks, well provided against. "To God
Almighty," he exclaims, " be the praise." Then,
after a modest allusion to " his own unfitness,
which he had well considered,"—" I scarcely know
how to be sufficiently thankful to the Lord God.
Do you, my father, praise him, and do not cease to
pray for me." But it was now thought necessary
to deprive him of his deanery for the old offence.
He disliked the habits. And yet of the moderation of the party he led, (and of which Lawrence,
Humphrey, and Lever were chieftains likewise),
it is to be noted, that the ultra-puritans, of whom
some account is given at the conclusion of this
chapter, regarded them as semi-papists, and would
not permit their followers to attend their preaching. These proceedings greatly distressed the
friends of the reformation abroad. Bullinger
especially wrote in the language of earnest expostulation, on behalf of Gaulter and himself, ad-

* To Bullinger and Gaulter, February 6, 1567.

CHAPTER II.

ELIZ.

A. D. 1566.

dressing his letter to bishops Horn, Grindal, and Parkhurst, with a request that it might be communicated to Jewel, Sandys, and Pilkington. The letter is short, but full of deep feeling. "We exhort you, reverend sirs, and very dear brethren, to have respect to faithful ministers and learned men. They have their own feelings : whence the apostle has instructed us to bear one another's burdens. Your authority can effect much with her most serene highness the queen. Prevail on her majesty to grant that these worthy brethren may be reconciled and restored.* * Farewell, reverend sirs, and may the Lord bless both you and your labours,* * again and again farewell." At the same time the Scotch ministers remonstrated on behalf of " divers of their dearest brethren in England, who are deprived and forbidden to preach" on account of the vestments. Their letter contains some sharp expressions about the " Romish rags," the " vain trifles," and the " dregs of the Romish beast." Still they deplore, they say, the vehemence with which the dispute was carried on on both sides, and entreat the bishops and pastors to whom they write to shew more forbearance.* The church in Scotland was now assuming its presbyterian form, and it is honourable to the Scottish clergy that, surrounded as they were with danger and perplexity, they had sympathy, if nothing more, for their brethren in England.

19. The church of England could ill spare such men at any time. Nor were these the only victims.

---

* The letter is printed by Neal, Appendix, Vol. i.

The venerable John Foxe shared in Coverdale's CHAPTER disgrace. He too had narrowly escaped the flames II. by a voluntary exile. But he lived to return. He ELIZ. placed the church of England under greater obli- A. D. 1566. gations than any writer of his age, and had his recompence in an old age of poverty and shame.* It would be no exaggeration to affirm that his immortal work, the acts and monuments of protestant martyrs and confessors, has done for three hundred years more and better service in our conflicts with the papacy than the countless volumes of all other writers, great as their worth may be. Nor were his writings undervalued even then; they were commanded to be chained up in churches by the side of the homilies and the English bible, that all might learn the ground of their secession from popery as well as the doctrines of the true faith; thus the book of martyrs stood amongst the high, authentic records of our church, while its venerable author yet lived. Perhaps no historian since the revival of letters has gained a popularity so sudden and yet so extensive and so enduring. Elizabeth herself, it is said, held him in high esteem, and spoke of him with affection as "her father Foxe." Still his offence was unpardonable. He "scrupled the habits,"—a significant expression then common—and was reduced to poverty. In his old age he complains even of want of clothes. At length he was presented to a small prebend in the cathedral church of Salisbury, in possession of which he died.

* Fuller, Ch. Hist. II. 475.

CHAPTER II.

ELIZ.

A. D. 1566.

20. Whenever extreme counsels are adopted, one sure consequence is that not only the timid but the aged, that is, the wise and thoughtful, retire from the scene of tumult. It was thus with the fathers of the reformation as the conflict with the puritans increased. They were amazed to find in their old age, that amongst the children of the reformation and in their own countrymen, lay their greatest trials. Assailed by popery on the one hand, and by the ultra-puritans upon the other, and obliged to defend from the pulpit cere- monies to which he was known to be averse, Jewel would gladly have resigned a mitre, and retired once more a willing exile to lay his bones in a foreign land. Other bishops express in con- fidential letters the same distress. They were ready to abandon all, they said, but the gospel, for the sake of peace.

21. Amongst the puritans, a similar change took place. New men appeared upon the stage, the advocates of principles hitherto scarcely known in England. The infection spread ; a spirit violent and discontented, " a zeal for discord," seized the multitude. They no longer asked for a compre- hension ; or sought for toleration. Their demands extended to an ecclesiastical revolution, and that of the most sweeping character.

22. The violence of some of the early puritans, adopting a view of the subject most favourable to themselves, is to be thus explained. Just es- caped from the iron grasp of popery, they had yet to discover the terms and true conditions under

which freedom can be enjoyed. If tyranny has CHAPTER
its dungeons, even liberty has her cautions and II.
restraints. Freedom is not licentiousness, nor in- ELIZ.
dependence the right of incessant outrage upon A. D. 1566.
institutions which the majority respect. But these
familiar lessons they had yet to learn; for experience alone teaches them, and experience they
had none. Their triumphs and virtues were their
own : their excesses they shared in common with
every party, civil or religious, who, after long
oppression, rise upon a sudden to the possession,
or even the prospect, of unbounded power. However just the occasion of it may have been, every
great revolution in the history of mankind repeats
the warning that excess and violence, and the
madness of the people, will, for a time, succeed to
the forced repose of despotism, as the thunder-
storm follows the deep silence in which all nature
had mourned the oppression of intolerable heat.
The severity of the church party finds its excuse
in the same considerations. It was taken by
surprise. Its leaders were wise and learned, and
the page of history was familiar to them; but
they had overlooked this important lesson, and
were unprepared for the crisis when it arrived;
as, in one form or other, arrive it must. They
were alarmed; and no severity equals that of men
who are themselves afraid. And they are entitled
to the benefit of this further consideration; they
had been brought up in a school of hardship : and
suffering engenders impatience. The doctrines of

the church of Rome they had repudiated : its intolerant spirit neither they nor their opponents
had yet unlearned.

23. Under the common name of puritans were
comprised, at this time, all those except the Romish party who were dissatisfied with the state of
things in the church recently established. Thus
the most discordant principles were ranged together under the same banner ; for it is the misfortune of a new party that its boundaries are not
yet defined, and that agreement upon a few leading points is received with too much readiness as
a test of general fidelity. In time, however, this
motley host, by successive desertions, fell away
and dissolved itself ; and puritanism became the
title of one section only, but still the most numerous and powerful of the body of which it had
previously been composed. The seceding mino-
rities became dissenters from the church. The
puritans, properly so called, remained in communion with it till the unhappy days of Charles I.
and archbishop Laud. It is necessary to bear
these distinctions in mind, not less for the sake of
truth, than that the history of the puritans may
be clearly understood. It is not by any means the
history of English dissent with which it has been
generally confounded ; although it is true that the
origin of our early non-conformity is closely connected with it, and will frequently demand attention.

24. The extravagance displayed by some who

still bore the name of puritans, almost defies exaggeration. Every form of church government,
and every distortion of christian doctrine, had for
a while its boisterous advocates. Some would
have rejected all those orders in the ministry which
had been known in the church of Rome, as well as
their names or titles. Others were for the demo-
lition of all parish churches, not to mention abbey
churches and cathedrals ; for they had been pol-
luted with idols and were unclean places. Many
passed through enthusiasm to unbelief and atheism,
or back again to the church of Rome. Others rejected all authority—save only what was self-
imposed.

25. Of the more sober of this extreme class of
puritans, various congregations were formed from
time to time and upon different models. In the
year 1568 four or five ministers openly separated
in London, and became the pastors of a considerable flock. They assembled stealthily at first in
private houses, in the fields, in ships upon the
river. They administered the sacraments, ordained
elders and ministers, and excommunicated delinquents of their own body. The queen in vain
threatened them with the loss of the freedom of the
city, a severe penalty amounting to civil excommunication in those days, for the first offence, and
severer punishment afterwards unless they returned to their parish churches. They still assembled, and gaining courage with the increase of
their numbers, they hired the Plumber's Hall.
Here the sheriff surprised a body of a hundred, and

carried them to prison. The next day they were brought before the lord mayor, Grindal bishop of London, the dean of Westminster, and others. A long and angry discussion took place in the court. Grindal spoke with kindness, and the lord mayor endeavoured to conciliate. " You go," said one of the prisoners to the bishop (habited) " like a mass priest." " You see me wear a cope or a surplice," answered Grindal, gently, " at Paul's. I had rather minister without these things, but for order's sake and obedience to the prince." " Your garments are accursed," was the reply of Nickson, another of the party. " Good people," said the lord mayor, " I cannot talk learnedly with you, but I will persuade you the best I can. The queen hath not established these things for any holiness' sake, but only for civil order and comeliness ; as aldermen are known by their tippets, and judges by their gowns." " Even so, my lord," answered Nickson, " as the alderman is known by his gown and tippet, so by this apparel, that these men do now wear, were the papist mass priests known from other men." The business ended with the committal of a considerable number of both men and women to Bridewell. Here they lay a year and upwards, glorying in their cause ; and diffusing their principles among those who now viewed them with the reverence due to martyrs and confessors, by means of circular letters which they addressed in apostolic form " to all the brethren that believed in Christ." At length they were released,

—twenty-four men and seven women,—through the bishop's intercession, by an order from the lords in council. As a punishment or as a caution, this act of despotism, for it was a rigour beyond the law, was equally impolitic.*

26. The demands of the extreme puritans are thus summed up by Sandys, bishop of London, in a letter to Bullinger dated at London, August 15th, 1573 :—

" New orators," he says, "are rising up from among us ; foolish young men who despise authority and admit of no superior. They are seeking the complete overthrow and uprooting of the whole of our ecclesiastical polity ; and striving to shape out for us I know not what new platform of a church. That you may be better acquainted with the whole matter, accept this summary of the question at issue, reduced under certain heads.

i. The civil magistrate has no authority in ecclesiastical matters. He is only a member of the church ; the government of which ought to be committed to the clergy.

ii. The church of Christ admits of no other government than that by presbyteries : viz., by the minister, elders, and deacon.

iii. The names and authority of archbishops, archdeacons, deans, chancellors, commissaries, and other titles and dignities of the like kind, should be altogether removed from the church of Christ.

iv. Each parish should have its own presbytery.

* Strype's Life of Grindal, p. 135.

v. The choice of ministers of necessity belongs to the people.

vi. The goods, possessions, lands, revenues, titles, honours, authorities, and all other things relating either to bishops or cathedrals, and which now of right belong to them, should be taken away forthwith and for ever.

vii. No one should be allowed to preach who is not a pastor of some congregation ; and he ought to preach to his own flock exclusively, and no where else.

viii. The infants of papists are not to be baptized.

ix. The judicial laws of Moses are binding upon christian princes, and they ought not in the slightest degree to depart from them."

27. This concise statement, which we have chosen for its brevity, agrees with various documents and manifestoes issued from time to time by the ultra puritans themselves, and may be received as a veracious record of their intentions.

28. Whatever might be the merits of the presbyterian form of church government, it is evident that it could have been introduced at this time into England only through the direful process of a revolution, attended probably with civil war. The presbyterian church was not to be supplementary to the episcopal. It was to sweep it from the nation, and to erect itself upon its ruins. The scheme was, to overthrow the church which then existed in the land, and to supplant it with

another : for the puritans, even those of the most
extreme opinions, clung to the principle of an
established church with as much devotion, and
far more unanimity, than they clung to the
model of a presbyterian one. On the latter point
there were already many shades of difference;
on the former there were none. In thus asserting the claims of presbyterianism, not as a
system to be tolerated, but established and made
national, they placed themselves in an attitude
of defiance to the law : and they invoked the
hostility both of laity and clergy, whose rights
and property they proposed to treat with so
little respect. Patrons of livings, and corporate
bodies, were of course alarmed ; and their hostility was soon inveterate. It was now a mixed
question, partly religious, but in many of its
bearings secular and political. Thus it came
to pass—and very much, it must be admitted, from
their own extravagance—that the puritans were
regarded in the court of Elizabeth, not as men of
scrupulous minds, but as a party ill affected to
the state. And in fact the triumph of their principles was at length fatal to the constitution,
as, in its recoil, it was fatal to themselves.
The misfortune was that the whole body of the
puritans was involved in the disgrace which belonged only to a few. Under one name all were
included ; Foxe and Nickson, Jewel and his revi-
lers ; although they had nothing else in common
than a dislike to a few ceremonies of the church.

29. The last article, in which the judicial laws

CHAPTER of Moses are maintained as binding upon christian
II. princes, was pregnant with vast and perilous re-
ELIZ. sults. As a theological dogma, it was utterly un-
A. D. 1568. tenable by a party who held, and justly gloried in,
the evangelical doctrines of the new testament.
But it took deep root in the minds of the puritans;
and when for a time they seized the reins of
government in the succeeding century, they applied it with terrible effect. In peaceful times it
was a dry question of theology—a discussion for
divines and casuists: but in civil war it was the
shrill clang of a trumpet which summoned armies
of enthusiasts to the work of unrelenting slaughter.
It was this mistaken notion which sanctified crime
and made revenge appear a christian virtue.

CHAPTER III.

1. In 1572 a presbyterian church was formed, and a meeting house erected, at Wandsworth in Surrey.* Field, the lecturer of Wandsworth, was its first minister ; and several names of consideration with the puritans, including those of Travers and Wilcox, were amongst its founders. The step was a decisive, and under all the circumstances, a daring one. The court resided in the adjoining parish of Richmond, and would not fail to regard the proceeding with indignation ; while the river Thames, on the banks of which Wandsworth stands, and which was at that time the highway of communication even for the higher classes of society, brought it under the immediate observation of the metropolis. The bishop of London gave information to the government, and the queen issued a proclamation enjoining compliance with the act of uniformity. The conventicle—for by this obnoxious term such assemblages were designated—was immediately suppressed ; though

CHAPTER III.

ELIZ.
A. D.
1565—75

* Neal i. 237.

CHAPTER III.

ELIZ.
A. D.
1565—75.

after a while it re-appeared ; and in a retired court-yard in this suburban village there yet stands a meeting-house, the representative of the modest structure which once gave note to England that a division had taken place among her sons which, alas, was never to be healed.

2. Other presbyteries were formed in other parts of the kingdom ; and numerous secret meetings were held besides in private houses, which gave more alarm to the government, or at least a stronger pretext for severity. The Romish party who still thronged the court did not lose their opportunity. They insinuated into the ear of the queen that these troubles were merely the legitimate fruits of the reformation, and such as they had all along foreseen. Even moderate men began to express anxiety. And to meet the danger the high court of commission was put in motion.

3. This tribunal, which proved so disastrous both to church and state, had been created by a clause in the act of supremacy in the first year of Elizabeth. It empowered the queen and her successors, by their letters patent under the great seal, to authorize, whenever they thought fit, and for as long a period as they pleased, a commission of persons, lay or clerical, to exercise all manner of jurisdiction under the queen and her successors in spiritual things ; namely, "to order, visit, reform, and redress, all heresies, errors, schisms, abuses, contempts, offences, and enormities whatsoever." The only limitations were, that the commissioners must be born subjects of the realm, and that in the exercise of their functions they

should have no power to determine anything to CHAPTER
be heresy but what had been adjudged to be so by III.
the authority of the canonical scripture, or by the ELIZ.
first four general councils, or any of them, or by A. D.
any other general council, wherein the same was 1565—75.
declared heresy by the express and plain words of
canonical scripture. These were ample powers,
and capable of being used with terrible effect.
But another clause extended their jurisdiction to
the restraint of heresies not yet defined, possibly
not yet in existence ;—namely such as parliament
with the consent of the convocation might hereafter in their wisdom place in the dark catalogue
of spiritual felonies.

4. Of this commission, as of its twin sister,
the star chamber, it is difficult to determine
whether it inflicted more suffering on the puritans
or infamy on their opponents. One of its first
acts was the violent suppression of the presbyterian
meeting at Wandsworth. Its subsequent labours
were of the same character. It always proceeded
upon the principle that the conscience might be,
and ought to be, coerced by the dread of punishment; that the inner man would yield its independence to the tyranny of pain and torture ; a
suicidal principle in any state into which the
first gleam of light has once penetrated ; and
fatal to all integrity in the subject, because it
places him in the alternative of slave or rebel. It
implies conditions under which rational government can as little exist as christian liberty or integrity of mind and conduct. An Italian brought

up in dread of the inquisition, may be an honest papist ; but his honesty has not been tried ; he has never dared to think and to inquire : it is the honesty of ignorance, if not of fear. The opinions of such a man are of no importance. It is impossible to say that if he were not a papist he would not be an atheist. He is a son of the church because he is unenquiring and a slave. Such is the conformity that severity can effect. And yet the high court of commission was not looked upon at first with the indignation it deserved ; nor were its ill consequences foreseen. The limits assigned to its power point out the intention of its authors; and had it been possible to confine its operation within them, it would have presented nothing more obnoxious than many other legislative enactments of the same age. It would have been inquisitorial and arbitrary, but not more so than the spirit of the times allowed. Many statutes of the sixteenth century might be produced, which are drawn up in the same spirit : and by comparison with these it would seem that no intentional injustice or oppression was designed. Carelessness in the statement of principles, and a pedantic accuracy in unimportant details, was the characteristic of an age just bursting into the first life of free institutions. But after these admissions the painful truth remains untouched : the high court of commission aimed, whether with design or otherwise, a deadly wound upon our civil and religious liberties ; and while it existed it was equally inconsistent with both.

5. It was impossible that a body of commissioners so chosen, and armed with despotic power,
should long be restrained within the proposed
limits,—the precincts of holy scripture, or the
wider range of the first four general councils. If
the appeal were to scripture, who must decide the
meaning of a doubtful text but themselves ? if to
one, or all, of the councils, who but they must challenge the true construction of its decrees ? and
with regard to heresy when the scriptures and
the councils had been consulted, and still a doubt
remained, (as in the breast of one of the two parties, the judges or the accused, it must always remain), who but the court itself was to determine
the nature and boundaries of the crime ? Heresy
is the denial, not of the authority of any particular church, but of the truth on which the catholic
church is built, and upon which salvation depends.
Yet, in the judgment of the church party and
of not a few of the puritans, anabaptists were
heretics of the worst kind, and those who denied
the necessity or validity of infant baptism, however orthodox on other points, are constantly
classed by writers of this period with donatists,
infidels, and atheists; while, in return, deadly
superstition,—something worse, if possible, than
heresy itself,—is charged by the anabaptists against
the church and prelates. Both sides then appealed
to holy scripture, and both admitted that the first
four councils threw but little light upon a controversy which was indeed of a much later date. It
was therefore impossible that the anabaptist could

acquiesce in the justice of the court; for the meaning of the text of scripture, on which he was condemned, was the very point at issue. If the high commission could indeed convince him that its interpretation was right, he ceased to be an anabaptist; if it failed in this, he could only regard himself as a martyr. And were the voice of the councils ever so explicit, still the spirit of reverential confidence in God's word, which the reformation had diffused, had already brought their authority into question even with the learned. "General councils," so taught the episcopal divines in their own article of the church, recently set forth, "may err and have erred." How preposterous then to appeal to their decisions, as final on a question affecting the conscience, nay the life of a fellow citizen; and the more so as their aid would chiefly be invoked when the voice of holy scripture was felt to be insufficient! Besides, when controversialists are inflamed with passion, it is ever to be dreaded that each side will deal in these bitter exaggerations. And thus the lesser fault of schism is, by the opposing party, magnified into heresy; and those whose worst crime is ignorance or obstinacy, are punished as heretics, with unreasonable severity.

6. To these objections the high commission was open from the first; and as if no means were to be neglected of bringing its proceedings into discredit, it made itself infamous by the mode in which its judicial examinations were conducted. Delinquents were put upon their oath, and then

compelled to criminate themselves. Numbers suffered thus ; convicted solely upon their own extorted evidence. Others refused to take the oath; but these again were punished for contempt. From the meshes of this detestable inquisition there was no escape.

7. Notwithstanding these severities, or perhaps in no small degree as their consequence, puritanism continued to increase ; for the persecution which does not exterminate a religious party, never fails to strengthen it. The universities had not yet forgotten the lessons or the examples of their great professors, Bucer and Peter Martyr. At Cambridge their principles made great progress. The surplice question was revived, and the university was distracted. A university is a mimic state : and plunging into the discussion of great questions, it seldom fails, with more learning, to bring less practical good sense and temper to the consideration of them ; the field is too narrow, and the vehemence too much compressed. Oxford in the previous century had been convulsed with metaphysical tumults. Nominalists and realists contended at first with syllogisms, then with blows and bloodshed; and Cambridge was now to be scarcely less disturbed, though, on a question, it must be owned, of far greater moment. St. John's college was at that time the most flourishing in the university, and it was warmly attached to the principles of the reformation. On the accession of queen Mary, the master and twenty four fellows with several scholars resigned, rather than con-

CHAPTER form to the renovated superstitions. On the ac-
III. cession of Elizabeth, Dr. Pilkington was chosen
ELIZ. master, and soon afterwards he was raised to the
A. D. bishopric of Durham. His works testify, at once
1565—75. to his detestation of Romish superstitions and his
wisdom and piety : in his will he desires to be
buried " with as few popish ceremonies as may be,
or vain cost." He had been one of the exiles at
Zurich and Geneva, and on his return to England
assisted in the revision of the book of common
prayer ; and when a solemn commemoration was
held at Cambridge, in memory of Martin Bucer
and Paulus Fagius, to obliterate the indignities
offered to their remains, which had been dug up
and burnt in the reign of Mary, he pronounced
the funeral oration. His latest biographer sums
up his character in few but weighty words : "A
zealous protestant, bishop Pilkington possessed in
an eminent degree that rare judgment and moderation which are the characteristics of our early
English reformers."*

8. It was in this college that a resolute opposition first appeared against the imposition of the
vestments. In the absence of the master Dr.
Longworth, Dr. Pilkington's successor, the stu-
dents and fellows to the number of three hundred
laid aside their hoods and surplices. In Trinity
college the example was followed with but three
exceptions ; and the smaller colleges were preparing to act in the same manner, when a violent
storm arose, and Cecil, the queen's secretary, ad-

* Prof. Scholefield : Life prefixed to Pilkington's Works, P.S. Ed.

monished them in no gentle terms to resume the discarded habits. Cecil was then chancellor of the university.

9. The university remonstrated. A letter was addressed to Cecil by the heads of houses and professors, imploring him to intercede with the queen. It was dated November 26, 1565. "A report," say they, " has reached us that, for the future, all scholars of this university will be forced to return to the old popish habits. This is daily mentioned to us by a great multitude of pious and learned men, who affirm in their consciences that they think every ornament of this kind is unlawful; and, if the intended proclamation is enforced, they will be brought into the greatest danger. Lest our university should be forsaken, we think it is one of our first duties to acquaint you with this condition of ourselves and of our brethren. And by these letters we most humbly beg, as well from your wisdom as from your credit and favour with the queen's majesty, that you would intercede with her to withhold a proclamation of this kind. For, as far as we can see, there can be no danger or inconvenience in exempting us from this burden: but, on the contrary, we very much fear that it will prove a hindrance to the preaching of the gospel and to learning."*

10. This letter was signed, amongst others, by the masters of Trinity and St. John's; by Hutton, master of Pembroke hall, and afterwards archbishop of York; and, which more concerns the

* Strype, Life of Parker, Appendix.

reader who would trace the conduct and motives
of the chief actors in the story, by John Whitgift,
then Lady Margaret's professor of divinity, soon
afterwards successively master of Pembroke hall
and Trinity college, and at length, on the death
of archbishop Grindal, successor to the see of
Canterbury.

11. A spirit so anxious and dissatisfied and yet
so powerful, was not likely long to want a leader.
It soon found one in all respects equal to the
task ; a man whose name belongs to history ; and
to whose importance in the events which we are
about to relate, an equal testimony is given in the
unbounded eulogy of his admirers, and the less par-
donable rancour of his foes. JOHN CARTWRIGHT,*
of whom we speak, is one of the few men whose
life and personal character still interest posterity
after a lapse of nearly three hundred years, and
angry writers have not yet ceased by turns to defend
and assail his memory. The heroes in Homer did
not contend more fiercely for the dead body of
Patroclus than the authors of each succeeding
age, themselves the representatives of great principles and powerful parties, for the reputation of
this great puritan divine. Cartwright was a scholar
of St. John's, diligent and successful ; when the
accession of queen Mary and the apprehension of
coming danger dispersed that learned and heartily
protestant body, he retired into obscurity and

---

* The facts of Cartwright's life are chiefly taken from Brooke's
Life of Cartwright : from the opinions of this writer I find reason to
differ on many points. The facts are collected with great care.

entered upon the study of the law. On the death
of Mary he returned to St. John's. Dr. Pilkington, the new master, esteemed him highly, and
promoted his advancement ; for which an amusing
old writer reviles him as " a zealous puritan out
of whose school proceeded Cartwright and others."
But the master of St. John's was not peculiar in
his regards. The year after his re-admission he
was chosen fellow, and so rapidly did his reputation grow that in three years he removed to the
recent, but already magnificent foundation of
Trinity college, the princely rival of St. John's,
and here he was at once elected a senior fellow.

12. The young queen had paid a visit to the university in 1564, where she was entertained in the
morning with scholastic exercises, at night with
comedies and plays. The most learned men were
selected to dispute before her in the schools ; and
Cartwright was chosen to sustain a leading part.
The queen took leave of the university in a latin
speech. She approved of all the disputants, but
most of Dr. Preston, who is said to have been a
man of elegance and taste, while Cartwright is described as unhewn and awkward. It would be an
amusing, were it not a painful, instance of the
asperity of Cartwright's opponents, that to this
trivial circumstance (and yet one so natural to
a young and accomplished lady), they have as-
cribed, without pretending further evidence, his
estrangement for the remainder of his life from
the church party. He became a puritan to avenge
himself on doctor Preston !

13. In 1569, Cartwright was chosen Lady Margaret's professor of divinity, and gave lectures on the Acts of the apostles. They created the greatest interest, and were listened to with admiration : when he preached at St. Mary's church the windows were removed for the sake of the crowds who were compelled to stand without. The university of Cambridge must have been strangely unlike itself, if such a reputation could be made, much less sustained, by one who possessed none but superficial acquirements. The taste of the age was, it is true, theological. Divinity was a science in which all endeavoured to excel ; among courtiers and gentlemen it was an accomplishment ; with divines a profession ; at the bar a collateral branch of law. This may explain the extent and enthusiasm of Cartwright's triumph; but it suggests too the difficulty of achieving it.

14. His sentiments as a puritan were not concealed in his divinity lectures and sermons. The opposition which he must have foreseen, even if he did not court it, soon arose; and Whitgift was his earliest antagonist. What Cartwright preached before the university on one Sunday, Whitgift from the same pulpit refuted on the next. Each of them is said to have been listened to with vast applause; if so, we can easily infer the tumult and insubordination which prevailed at Cambridge ; and the uneasiness of those in power. Whitgift had now abandoned his early principles; which, as we have seen, leaned in favour of the puritans. This has been an unpardonable crime

with some historians. But those who are not CHAPTER III. satisfied that history should be the drudge of fac-
tion, will not be displeased with the suggestion ELIZ. that young men of ardent minds are not to be too A. D. harshly dealt with if they live to repudiate some 1565—75. of the sentiments they avowed when first entering upon public life. Through a long career Whitgift was consistent afterwards; and we find no difficulty in admitting that, in such times, he may have had what appeared to him, at least, sufficient reasons to justify his conduct. It is true, that his course led to high preferment, and Cartwright's to a life of suffering; a difference which compels us to give our sympathy in Cartwright's favour, but not our judgment; unless indeed it could be shewn that Whitgift was influenced by dishonourable motives. Archbishop Grindal too appears amongst his opponents. He was for dealing with " this unhappy faction," he says, " with all expedition, as people fanatical and incurable." Whether his scheme for their recovery were wise or not, it was not wanting in decision. "In my opinion, under your lordships' correction," writing to the lords of the council, " it were not amiss that six of the most desperate of them should be sent to the common goal at Cambridge; and six likewise to Oxford, and some others of them to other goals, as to your wisdoms shall be thought expedient !" *

15. We remark with pain, in reviewing these events, the facility with which men who espoused

* Remains 319. P.S. Ed.

a fresh party turned their keenest weapons upon that from which they had just withdrawn. It seems as if no sense of shame existed; or as if the remembrance of the past was obliterated with every change of principle. But it was still a barbarous age; and the restraints of civilized life were but imperfectly acknowledged. It is strange that Whitgift and Grindal should have behaved with severity to Cartwright, since they themselves had deeply shared in his early scruples, and to a recent period had been his associates in disgrace. But they were not singular. We have seen that Cranmer and Ridley had consented to Hooper's imprisonment, upon a difference so trifling that they were ready on his release to admit him forthwith to a share in the episcopate itself; and lord Bacon, at a still later period, coarsely reviled his benefactor the earl of Essex at the tribunal before which he was vainly pleading for his life. Such was the habit of the times. The delicacy of feeling which belongs to a refined state of society, and a lofty standard of private morals, was then, and long afterward, almost unknown.

16. Archbishop Grindal applied to Cecil, as chancellor of the university, to exert himself that Cartwright should either be silenced or expelled. The matter was laid before the vice-chancellor and the heads of houses, and the immediate consequence was the refusal of his doctor's degree; then his suspension from the professorship of divinity. The chancellor seems to have behaved with great moderation. Having considered the affair with

much " deliberation and meekness," his conclusion was that Cartwright, " not from arrogance or
any ill design," but as " the reader of the scriptures,
had given notes, by way of comparison, between
the orders of the ministry and the times of the
apostles, and the present times of this church of
England." He therefore thought it sufficient to
prohibit him from reading on those " nice questions," and he also wrote to him a kind letter of
caution and advice.

17. Cartwright, however, was deprived of his
professorship, and forbidden to preach in the university, through the influence of Dr. Whitgift, now
vice-chancellor.* And against this proceeding,
severe as it was, there is little to object, except
the unseemly haste and superfluous bitterness displayed by Whitgift and his friends. They have
been severely blamed,† because, without appealing
to the authority of the scriptures, they thought
it sufficient to assert that Cartwright's doctrines
were contrary to the religion established by public
authority, and on that account alone to demand a
recantation of them. Had the university been
nothing more than an open arena of political and
theological controversialists, where all comers
were at equal liberty to maintain their sentiments,
their conduct would indeed have been unjust. But
this was not the case. And in what country could
such a community exist with safety ; or what could
such a university become even in quiet times,
except a school of uproar and sedition ? The

* Paul's Life of Whitgift, 16. † Brooke's Cartwright passim.

CHAPTER
III.

ELIZ.
A. D.
1565—75.

nation had determined upon a certain ecclesiastical constitution, with respect to which the duties of the universities, and more especially those of their theological professors, were perfectly well defined. They were to educate the youth of England in accordance with its laws,—its fundamental constitution,—both in church and state. However imperfect the church established by law might be, and however wise and perfect Cartwright's project of reformation, it was still impossible that any corporate society which was not already quivering on the verge of revolution, or profoundly wanting in self-respect, could tolerate a professor who lectured upon the duty of overthrowing the church whose sons and members he had undertaken to instruct. What church, what party, not utterly indifferent to all truth and all fixed opinions, has ever tolerated such a proceeding? Cartwright, if dissatisfied, should have at once retired, and challenged other hearers than his pupils, and upon some other tilting ground than the fenced enclosures of a university. If there was a want of forbearance in his opponents, we must admit in this instance the want of high integrity in Cartwright.

18. His sentiments, committed to writing by himself, and submitted to the university in his own defence, included the following propositions. That the names and functions of archbishops and archdeacons ought to be abolished. That the existing ministers of the church, namely, bishops, priests, and deacons, ought to be reduced to the apostolical

institution, (meaning that bishops, as a third order in the church, should be abolished) and that presbyters only should remain to preach the word of God, and to pray ; and deacons to be employed in taking care of the poor. That every church ought to be governed by its own ministers and presbyters. That no man ought to solicit, or be a candidate for, the ministry. And that ministers ought to be openly and fairly chosen by the people. "To effect this reformation," he concludes, " every one ought to labour in his calling; the magistrate by his authority; the minister by the word, and all by their prayers."*

19. But how was this reformation, granting that it were one, to be accomplished ? His opponents were no less in earnest than himself. They believed that episcopacy was ordained of Christ or his apostles ; that of all forms of church government it was the wisest and the best. They had suffered much to bring about the reformation now so decried ; nor was it likely they would abandon, without a determined struggle, a cause so dear to them, for the sake of a mere experiment ; for the presbyterian churches established at Geneva and elsewhere were of too recent a growth to claim the respect which is due to long enduring and well tried institutions. A church upon Cartwright's model was a novelty ; and all of his opponents thought no doubt the scheme impracticable, while not a few of them, viewing it as unscriptural and wrong, would have passed through another persecution

* Strype's Whitgift. Appendix.

such as that from which they had escaped, rather than submit to it. For this was the alternative, submission or resistance. Cartwright and his friends asked, not for the toleration of their opinions but for their endowment; not that they might be permitted to hold them unmolested, but that they might throw down the existing church in order to establish them. A presbyterian church, occupying the place of the present establishment, and appropriating to itself its funds and dignities, was the meaning of Cartwright's propositions. It is true that he repelled with the indignation, and no doubt with the sincerity, of one much aggrieved, the charge of intending to bring about by force the reformation he was planning : but to his opponents this appeared as an inevitable consequence ; a consequence at least only to be avoided by their unconditional submission. And there were those among them, inconsiderable neither for their numbers nor for their moderation and piety, who would have decided that the episcopal church was cheaply defended at the cost, if necessary, of their own lives, and all the hazards of a civil war.

20. It may seem severe to charge Cartwright and his party with consequences which, in their judgment, would either not arise at all, or only from the ignorance and obstinacy of their antagonists. But such apologies, though specious and plausible, must always fail to have the slightest weight with the opposite party. They who set themselves to the subversion of principles which

others cling to, as to life itself, must be prepared to take their full share of responsibility in the terrible collisions which will certainly ensue.

21. Still Whitgift's severity was impolitic, and quite unworthy of his christian character, even after making a large allowance for the barbarism of the times. He threw the sympathies of pious men, including the chancellor Cecil, lord Burghley, himself, and the great earl of Leicester, warmly into Cartwright's favour. He contributed to force a large party into desperation; and he made Cartwright its martyr and its hero.

22. On the pretext that Cartwright had not taken priest's orders, he charged him with perjury, and procured the forfeiture of his fellowship; which, according to the statutes of his college, required that he should be in holy orders. Cartwright, who was in deacon's orders, maintained that he had complied with the spirit, if not with the very letter, of the statutes, of which the meaning was no more than this; that the senior fellowships should be held by spiritual men for the guidance of the college, to the exclusion of the other professions, law and physic; and that as reader of divinity and a preacher in the university, he had fulfilled the conditions with accurate fidelity. There appears no ground to charge him with the revolting crime of perjury. But even this was not sufficient; he was soon afterwards expelled. In a letter addressed to the chancellor, dated 17 October 1571, he mentions his expulsion, first from the college and then from the university; and implores very

CHAPTER
II.

ELIZ.
A.D.
1565—75.

humbly that the affair may be reheard. " I would write," he says, " a full account of the matter, but I am afraid of perplexity. I would rather state the affair in your presence, which would enable me to be more brief and distinct. Behold a new and cruel device of the most unjust of men, who omit nothing to consummate my wretchedness; since both water and fire are forbidden me. They seem to want nothing but a sack that they may destroy me like a matricide. I hear also that I am accused of seditious and schismatic practices; O baseness!" Cartwright went abroad, where he was received with the greatest attention by the leaders of the reformed churches; but at the solicitation of his friends, among whom were Foxe and the learned Fulke, now as well as himself, and for a similar cause, deprived of his fellowship, but afterwards master of Pembroke hall, he returned to England. His reputation was yet untarnished. Cecil, as lord treasurer, solicited his opinions upon an affair of state in a manner which shews that he was not regarded as a time server. The queen contemplated marriage with the duke of Anjou, a Roman catholic; and the lord treasurer himself was thought to favour the match. The question he proposed was this, " Whether it was lawful for one professing the gospel to marry a papist ?" Cartwright's answer was explicit. " I am fully persuaded for my part that it is directly forbidden in scripture." Happily for the nation the marriage was broken off.

23. The remainder of Cartwright's life is inter-

woven with the ecclesiastical history of the times. It presents us with the records of a man of high attainments, fervent zeal, and unwearied resolution, devoting himself to suffering and disgrace, in the long endeavour to achieve, as he believed, a second and a better reformation. Such examples deserve to be recorded for the reverence of future ages; and happily the time has appeared when we no longer hesitate to acknowledge exalted worth, though in alliance with principles and opinions we condemn: and such respect at least is due to the memory of Cartwright.

24. The year 1572 was memorable in the history of the puritans. Many severities had been exercised, many of their ministers degraded, silenced, and imprisoned. The church party and their opponents had both alike become stern and unforgiving. Despairing, as they said, of reformation beginning elsewhere, two of the puritan leaders, Field and Wilcocks, published "An admonition to the parliament for the reformation of church discipline." Beza had addressed to the earl of Leicester, the friend and patron of the puritan cause, a letter, in which he urged the necessity of a further reformation in England, and of more forbearance to the discontented party. Gaulter had written to bishop Parker in the same spirit. These letters were printed with the admonition, and contributed not a little to its marked effect. The petition itself exposed the splendours of the hierarchy, and the proceedings of the bishops; and prayed that a church might be established by

CHAPTER law more consonant with God's word; that is,
III.   upon the presbyterian model. It was presented
ELIZ.   to the house by its authors, Field and Wilcocks;
A. D.   a proceeding for which they were immediately
1565—75. committed to Newgate; where their sufferings
gave a fresh impulse to their cause. They were
visited by the leaders of the party, amongst whom
occur the names of Fulke, Humphrey, Wyburn,
and Cartwright; and although every effort was
made to suppress the pamphlet, three or four
editions were published in as many years.*

25. Whitgift was summoned by the voice of the
church party to answer the admonition, and he
is said to have been assisted by archbishop Parker
and other eminent divines. His opponents still
admit that his method was fair and unexception-
able; and his admirers then claimed for his work
much higher praise, as an unanswerable defence of
the reformed church of England. Its merits are
great no doubt; and it would probably still have
been a popular treatise upon the subjects it dis-
cusses, notwithstanding its many antiquated allusions and personal asperities, had not Hooker
soon afterwards won for himself an immortal
reputation as the sole champion of our English
church; casting into the shade whatever had been
done before him, and leaving nothing to be accomplished on this arena by those who should come
after. Yet Hooker appears to have been himself

---

* Strype's life of Parker, 413. The 'admonition' has been frequently but erroneously attributed to Cartwright himself. Brooke's
Cartwright, p. 97.

indebted to this famous controversy for something of his method, and for many of his arguments.

26. Cartwright now came forward in reply, and braving the certain penalty that must follow, published " A second admonition to the parliament." It opened with an address to his readers, in which he says, " We have cast our accounts, who bend ourselves to deal in these matters, not only to abide hard words, but also hard and sharp dealings for our labour ; and yet," he adds, " we shall think our labour well bestowed, if by God's grace we attain but to give some light of that reformation of religion which is grounded on God's word, and to have somewhat opened the deformities of our English reformation, which highly displeaseth God." He then proceeds to state and defend at large the puritan demands,—or rather the demands of those of the puritans who had now decided in favour of an entirely new platform of church government.

27. Whitgift replied to Cartwright, and Cartwright again answered Whitgift ; while a host of inferior writers took up the question on both sides ; and swelled the tide of battle, and increased the uproar, without adding materially to the force engaged. Thus arose a controversy which, while it lasted, occupied the attention and absorbed the sympathies of all the reformed churches; and which has ever since been referred to as containing within itself the germ of almost every important argument which either party has been able to advance. We interrupt our narrative for a time,

CHAPTER that we may attend to this remarkable discus-
III.   sion.

ELIZ.   28. The demands of the admonition, as it was
A. D.   afterwards defended and explained by Cartwright
1565—75. and others, resolve themselves into two great
heads. The first of these concerns the constitution of a church. The second relates to the abuses
then existing in the church of England. On the
latter point, large concessions might have been
made without abandoning any one principle of the
least importance. And if so, they ought to have
been made at once,—cheerfully and without hesitation,—were it only on the principle of yielding
things indifferent to the scruples of weak consciences; an apostolic principle, and of the greatest
moment, though for the most part held in great
contempt in religious controversy. The cross in
baptism, and the ring in marriage, once parted
with, would scarcely have been regretted, and very
soon forgotten. The use of organs was not essential to public worship; nor choral chanting;
nor were square caps or surplices. All these were
grievous to the puritans. But the wrong done
to them, and the mistake committed, lay in this :
not that the church party retained these peculiarities, but that it insisted on them, and chained
them on the necks of others. A compromise
ought to have been attempted. It would in all
probability have succeeded perfectly ; for such is
human nature that indulgences which are no
longer denied are seldom asked for ; and had the
ceremonies so fiercely contested been left as things

indifferent, uniformity would have crept on by
slow degrees ; or a mutual forbearance, (in things
indifferent a greater blessing oftentimes than uniformity itself) would have healed the division and
produced, if not uniformity, at least a real unity, at
last. For instance, the anabaptists of modern
days, the legitimate successors of the extreme
section of the puritans, neither reject an organ
nor think it superstitious : and in every class of
modern dissenters there is a perceptible tendency
to revert again to those sober and now well-tested
forms of the church of England, against which their
puritan ancestors would never have contended so
much in the spirit of martyrs, had it not been
that they were threatened with a martyr's fate.

29. Nor were their demands altogether unreasonable. The abuses then prevailing in the
church were such as to shock, if they do not
amuse, by their extravagance. Pluralities may
have admitted of some excuse ; for able ministers
were but few in number ; and vacant benefices
were better disposed of, it might be contended, by
placing several in the hands of one able person,
than either by leaving them void, or bestowing
them upon the incompetent. Whitgift was rector
of Feversham, master of Trinity college, prebend
of Ely, and dean of Lincoln. And his case was
not a solitary one : other favoured individuals
were loaded with preferment. This, however justified, was an evil precedent, and productive of unhappy consequences. But what defence can be
offered for the splendours of the hierarchy ? In
an age of state and pageantry, archbishop Parker

CHAPTER
III.
——
ELIZ.
A. D.
1570—75.

exhibited a model of almost regal magnificence. Whitgift, shortly afterwards raised to the primacy on the death of Grindal, surpassed even Parker in stateliness. It is recorded of him by one of his biographers that he travelled with a retinue of a hundred servants, including forty gentlemen in chains of gold. And that nothing might be wanting, he kept " a good armoury for the exercise of military discipline, and a fair stable of horses ;" insomuch that he was able at all times to equip both horse and foot, and frequently mustered a hundred of the former and fifty of the latter, "his own servants, trained and mounted."* No wonder that prelacy, with its pomp and pride, was the favourite mark for the keen shafts of the puritans!

30. But the admonition and its defenders had wider views, and aimed at something far beyond the amendment of the existing institutions. They repeated their demands for a national church fashioned after the presbyterian model. This, they affirmed, and only this, was agreeable to scripture and the will of heaven, and nothing less could satisfy them.

31. They demanded a national church, endowed with tithes and ecclesiastical emoluments; for this, they said, was in accordance with the will of God as expressed in the law of Moses : yet they rejected the spiritual headship of the sovereign, although it prevailed in the jewish church, because, they affirmed, it was inconsistent with the new testament. They assumed it as an unquestionable

* Paul's Whitgift, 97. 105.

truth that the constitution of the christian church was traced out, and the duties of its several officers assigned in scripture, with as much, if not more, clearness than the instructions for building the tabernacle, and regulating the daily service of the temple. If the jew had an exact directory from God in all that concerned his mode of worship, much more the christian; the christian dispensation was in this, as in all points, clearer than the jewish. From whence it followed that to introduce an office into the church, unknown in scripture, was a grievous sin. It was only to be compared to the effrontery of Uzzah, who touched the ark and died.

32. The assault of the extreme puritans fell heavily on archbishops and high dignitaries; for whatever were their weaknesses the want of candour or of courage, was not one of them. " In the tabernacle," says Cartwright, " the church is expressly set forth. As the temple was nearer the time of Christ (than the tabernacle), so it is a more lively expression of the church of God that now is." He then proceeds to shew that both in the one and in the other every thing was done as God prescribed; and he adds, with sarcastic indignation, " Is it likely that he who appointed, not only the tabernacle and the temple, but their ornaments, would not only neglect the ornaments of the church, but that without which it cannot long stand? Shall we conclude that he who remembered the bars there, hath forgotten the pillars here? Or he who there remembered the pins,

CHAPTER here forgot the master builders ? Should he there
III.   remember the besoms, and here forget archbishops,
ELIZ.   if any had been needful ?   Could he there make
A. D.   mention of the snuffers, to purge the lights, and
1570—75. here pass by the lights themselves ?"*

33. This is the clue to the whole argument; which descends into all the details of church government, and condemns whatever has not the express sanction of scripture. Whatever is not written is erroneous. Upon the other hand, the acts of the early church in the new testament, are not less binding upon other christian churches, in matters of discipline, than its teaching in matters of doctrine. If it be heresy to pervert the doctrines of the bible, it is popery and gross impiety, he contends, to add anything to its precedents of church government and discipline : for this is to charge its author with having given an imperfect revelation.

34. The theory is plausible: its evident simplicity, and the reverence which it seems to pay to the word of God, will always commend it to many admirers.   It has never ceased to be urged, from time to time, upon the attention of the christian church ; though it has seldom found in after years an advocate to be compared with Cartwright ; whose mingled wit and wisdom, whose vehement declamation and logical precision, and whose nervous style and manly courage, the expression of a profound sincerity, will ever give his writings, apart from all other considerations, a distinguished place in the literature of his country.   Cart-

* Cartwright's Reply, 82, &c.

wright was the Hooker of non-conformity : his equal in acuteness, though not in penetration ; in eloquence, though not in learning his superior : his inferior perhaps only in that profound dexterity and skill in argument which, mingled with an awful reverence for truth, scorns or dreads to take advantage of an adversary's weakness. For, in these high polemic virtues, Hooker is without an equal.

35. Whitgift replied in a tone equally disdainful, (for the meekness of christian polemics, was sorely wronged on both sides), but with a depth of learning and of patient thought which was a greater tribute to Cartwright's prowess, than the loudest acclamations of his own party. It was evident that the reformation was put upon its trial, and that its friends were conscious of the greatness of the crisis. All the warmth of enthusiasm, all the energy of hope or of despair, was on the side of the assailants. To retain an empire kindles less excitement than to storm a battery. The prelates, if courtiers and men of this world, could only wish for peace ; if saints and men of apostolic holiness and zeal, they could still have no other ambition. They had accomplished a reformation the greatest, and, as the results have shewn, the most abiding the church has ever seen : if slothful, it was reasonable they should wish to enjoy its fruits ; if zealous for God, to dispense its blessings. But it was difficult to revive in their favour the popular zeal. They had now to control, and not to stimulate, the ardour of the multitude : to repress the desire of change and inculcate submission. And this task, always difficult, is doubly so

CHAPTER III. in the hands of those who have been once known as the leaders in a popular movement. They seem ELIZ. inconsistent as soon as they become practical. A. D. 1570—75. When they no longer innovate, they are charged with a desertion of their principles.

36. Whitgift, however, asserted a principle which, if true, was destined to unfold a degree of liberty far beyond the aspirations of the most zealous puritan. He maintained the right of christian churches to determine their own forms of government.* His statements, if pushed to an extreme, would seem to warrant the conclusion that he thought that church government was in itself a thing indifferent ; that it was a wise and cautious step to consult the scriptures, and to adhere to the examples of the ancient church, but that no absolute command required even this degree of deference, whether paid to the scriptures or the fathers of the church. It was enough for him that an office was useful ; it was not necessary that it should be scriptural. He regarded the end of the institution, namely a good and useful government as the only consideration of primary importance ; and he thought that true wisdom led us to seek for this, not in a servile imitation of what existed at Corinth or Philippi in the days of St. Paul ; nor in the usages of the African church in the days of Cyprian : but in a judicious adaptation of the precedents contained in scripture and in the fathers, to the wants of an English church in the sixteenth century.

* Whitgift's Answer to a certain libel entituled An admonition to the Parliament, 1572, and " Defence of the Answer &c.." 1574.

37. He replies to Cartwright's attack upon the office of an archbishop thus. "It is manifest," he says, and a more liberal foundation could not possibly be laid, " that Christ hath left the government of his church, touching the external policy, to the ordering of men who have to make orders and laws for the same, as time, place, and persons require ; so that nothing be done contrary to his word. We make not an archbishop necessary to salvation, but profitable to the government of the church, and therefore consonant to the word of God." Again : " We are well assured that Christ in his word hath fully and plainly comprehended all things necessary to faith and good life, yet hath he committed certain orders of ceremonies and kind of government to the disposition of his church ; the general rules given in his word being generally observed ; and nothing being done contrary to his will and commandment."

38. The utility of an office, then, justified its introduction, and Whitgift was not anxious, indeed he thought it impossible, to go higher. Christ willed the government of his church in willing its existence ; for without government, social or corporate, existence is impossible. He had laid down no precise law, like that of the old testament, by which one uniform, unbending, government could be framed. The church, therefore, was at liberty to make its own choice ; the honour of God being its sole aim, and to do " nothing contrary to his word," its single limitation. " What," he adds, " if the name of an arch-

bishop was not in St. Paul's time? doth it therefore follow that the thing signified by the name was not in his time? The authority and thing whereof the archbishop hath his name *was* in Paul's time; therefore the name is lawful; and if it had not been in his time, yet were both the name and office lawful, because it pertains to the external policy and government of the church."*

39. It belongs to a treatise of ecclesiastical polity to determine the merits of this great and anxious question. We must be contented to remark, that Cartwright failed by an overstatement of his premises, while Whitgift was in practise inconsistent with his own conclusions.

40. Few intelligent non-conformists would now choose to embarras themselves with Cartwright's bold assertion, that the new testament contains the exact delineation of a christian church. Nor would they affirm that the precise admeasurements and other minute directions which were given to Moses for the construction of the tabernacle, and the ordering of its ritual, find a counterpart in the confessedly few and general precedents to be gathered from the new testament, on the subject of church polity. The history of three centuries has brought, at last, some healing lessons of moderation with it. Amongst the jews, no schism found a place; so clear and comprehensive their instructions. And when the ten tribes revolted, they were soon compelled to reject some portions of the law, in order to conceal the

* Defence of Answer, 301—470.

schismatic character of their rival temple on mount Gherizim. But no community of christians has yet presumed to claim, as exhibited in its own practice, the precise institutions of a new testament church,—perfect and unaltered,—without calling up a host of opponents eager to deny its claims and challenge its proofs. And every such body has been in turn compelled to decline the contest, or to abandon something of its high pretensions, and confess that the utmost it has been able to accomplish, is but a feeble imitation of the primitive examples of the new testament : an adaptation, but not a transcript.

41. It is a question, which the learning and ability displayed on both sides has not entirely set at rest in the minds of many sincere and intelligent christians, whether the new testament bishop was merely a presiding presbyter, *primus inter pares*, or a minister of a superior order, and of a higher rank. Cartwright would have revolutionized the church of England upon this single point. All ministers were equal. Every church was independent. The right of choosing ministers lay exclusively with the congregation. These were first principles, to be maintained at whatever cost.

42. Whitgift, on the other hand, and the powerful party whom he represented, were unreasonably tenacious. Their own argument condemns their conduct. The weapons which wound their reputation most, were sharpened by themselves. For if the constitution of a church were, to so great an extent, committed to their own discretion ; if no

sin, no disrespect to scripture, were involved in
making those alterations from time to time which
fitted it for usefulness; adapting it to altered
times and circumstances; why did they resist all
change? Why did they oppose a stern and iron
front to the demands of their own brethren—not
of a few capricious minds, unstable and self-willed;
but of hundreds of good men,—of learning scarcely
inferior to their own, and in zeal and piety, not a
whit behind them? Because some of Cartwright's
demands were unreasonable, why should every
puritan be treated with contempt? With regard
to many of the points at issue, they pleaded, not
conscience, but mere convenience. Of that convenience why should not their brethren be sometimes allowed to judge? Why crush a large and
earnest minority, whose number, combined with
their acknowledged zeal and piety, was a sufficient
indication that some deep grievance did really
exist beneath a surface too much ruffled, it is true,
by tumultuous discontent?

43. There is one consideration which, had it occurred to either party, would have abated something of its warmth by placing the subjects of contention in a far less important light. We mean
the tendency of all institutions to mould themselves in practice, so as to accord with the genius
and disposition of those amongst whom they
flourish. An exact transcript of the primitive
churches of the new testament, were it possible to
be revised, in London for example or New York,
would grievously disappoint the expectations of

its ardent votaries. Names and offices would
remain as they were from the beginning, and probably the likeness would be traced in nothing
else. The national character could not fail to
act with irregular and unequal force upon the
different parts of an ancient and foreign institution ; and long before it had begun to perform its
work with ease, it would in fact have been remodelled. Had the puritans remained within the
national church, they would have possessed a vast
and salutary influence. Had their zeal and united
energies been wisely directed, not to the attainment of doubtful and speculative theories, but to
the diffusion of piety, the earthly splendours of the
hierarchy which withstood their arguments, would
soon have confessed their presence. Worldly-
minded prelates would have been compelled, in
self-defence, to assume a modest bearing ; and
needless pomp would have been discountenanced.
The middle classes, the bulk of every parish,
though not formally admitted to elect their pastors,
would, if educated in christian piety, have exercised a wholesome restraint upon the rights of
patrons. Without the name or authority of
rulers, they must have soon possessed a power,
which the most imperious are compelled to respect ; the power of public opinion, rightly
directed and temperately expressed. The democratic disposition would have worked well and
safely in the presence of a legitimate controlling
authority. On the other hand, a wise episcopate,
though somewhat reduced, and liable to be always

checked when its pretensions were unreasonable, would have experienced no real danger ; and, after a time, its learning, calmness, and high position, remote from clamour and transient excitement, would have led all but the restless and visionary to confess its worth. The church of England might then have borne a closer resemblance to her civil constitution ; where the various elements meet, not in ceaseless conflict, but in well blended proportions, and in joint control ; and therefore in harmonious and successful action.

CHAPTER IV.

1. THE great leaders of the reformation were
now hastening from the scene, and their places
were filled in succession by other men who were
often strangers alike to their sufferings, their simplicity, and their triumphs. A single year, 1575,
proved fatal to Parkhurst bishop of Norwich, Pilkington bishop of Durham, Matthew Parker archbishop of Canterbury, and Bullinger the great reformer of Zurich. Peter Martyr, and the wise
and saintly Jewel bishop of Salisbury, had already
entered into a world of peace. Bishop Horne
soon followed, with many others. Thus the cause
of the reformation, and of the church of England, was transmitted to another generation.
Grindal succeeded Parker in the primacy, and
if any argument were wanting to convince the
ultra-puritans that an archbishop might ex-
hibit the loftiest virtues, and discharge with exemplary wisdom, zeal, and meekness the most
painful duties of the ministry, they had for nine
years a conclusive one in the life and example of
archbishop Grindal. But the current of the times

CHAPTER IV.

ELIZ.

A.D. 1575.

bore hard against him. He was thwarted and borne down by an imperious sovereign, whose piety had now visibly waned before the splendours, the adulation, and the unbounded power which few women ever coveted more passionately, and none perhaps ever so abundantly possessed. The English reformation had reached its zenith. From this time new men and new principles begin to appear, and the relative position of puritans and churchmen insensibly alters; and two questions appear in the distance which are by and by to absorb the whole attention of either party; though to this period, the one in our church had no existence, and the other had gained but little notice. The first of these embraced those great points of christian doctrine which afterwards assumed the form of the Calvinistic and Arminian controversy, including the nature of the sacraments and the method of justification. The other was the political question; already opened in fact, though incidentally, by Cartwright and his party; namely, the rights of a sovereign in matters of religion, and those of a christian church in civil government. Into these two channels the overflowing waters of strife soon found their way; and along them they have never ceased to flow.

2. The state of England in regard to moral and religious culture was at this time deplorable. When we read of the thousands who assembled at Paul's cross to listen to the stirring eloquence of Latimer, or of the five thousand voices at the same place, rising like the sound of many waters,

in one tuneful psalm of praise ; we are apt to infer
the existence of an amount of scriptural zeal and
knowledge in other parts of the kingdom, painfully at variance with the real facts of history.

3. The number of the Romish clergy who had
resigned their preferments at the reformation, appears almost incredibly small. Including bishops,
abbots, heads of colleges, and other dignitaries,
as well as the beneficed clergy, no writer can
muster up two hundred and fifty : bishop Burnet
reduces them to one hundred and ninety-nine; and
D'Ewes's journal, a still better authority, to one
hundred and seventy-seven,—a number altogether
insignificant when distributed among the ten
thousand parishes of England and Wales. It
would be something more than charity to suppose
that such numbers of the Romish clergy accom-
modated themselves at once to a change so great
and sudden without violence to their consciences;
or, which is more probable, without an utter scorn
and contemptuous disregard of all religious principle. From such incumbents the reforming
bishops had little to expect. To restrain their
popish sympathies, and to insist upon a few decent
observances—such as public prayers in English,
and the reading of the scriptures—was probably
all they could attempt ; and without a just severity, even this was often more than they could
accomplish.

4. The christian ministry in Romish countries
is not an object of ambition. The priests and
friars of Italy are chiefly drawn from the lower

CHAPTER ranks of life; and this is still more visible in
IV. remoter nations, where the great prizes of their
ELIZ. church are fewer, and out of sight. A slavish
A.D. 1575. life, busied with a succession of fretful observances,
has no attractions. The wise and good recoil
from it. But a low and ignorant ministry had so
long prevailed that it gave but little offence; and
this is to be borne in mind when we read of the
meanness of those from amongst whom the ministry of the church of England was at first re-
plenished. When archbishop Parker made the
primary visitation of his diocese, some of the
beneficed clergy were mechanics, others Romish
priests disguised. Many churches were closed.
A sermon was not to be heard in some places
within a distance of twenty miles. To read, or
at least so to read as to be intelligible and impres-
sive, was a rare accomplishment. A homily was
not read for months together in many parishes.
Even in London many churches were closed for
want of ministers; and in the country it was not
easy to provide a minister competent to baptize
infants and inter the dead.* Bishop Sandys of
Worcester, preaching before the queen, tells her
majesty (with a solemn intimation that "their
blood will be required at somebody's hands,")
that many of her people, especially in the north,
were perishing for lack of knowledge. "Many
there are," he said, "that hear not a sermon in

---

* Neal, vol. I. Ch. iv, p. 137-8, and Ch. vi, 287, from a manuscript, he says, in his possession. See too Strype, Life of Parker,
p. 224, &c.

seven years; I might say in seventeen." The
bishop of Bangor had but two preachers in all
his diocese. In Cornwall there was not a single
minister, says Neal, the historian of the puritans,
capable of preaching a sermon. The universities
afforded little assistance. In 1563 the university
of Oxford had but three preachers; and these
were chief men amongst the puritans; Humphreys,
Kingsmill, and Sampson. There was yet no succession of young men in the universities who had
been piously brought up in the protestant faith.
This evil had been foreseen by Latimer and the
fathers of the reformation, and was indeed
amongst their chief anxieties. The indiscriminate plunder of church property, which still continued in the reign of Edward VI., was one great
cause. The rapacity of those who should have been
the church's guardians, is frequently denounced
in the sermons of the reformers. Ridley deplored
the lack of " yeomen's sons" as candidates for the
ministry. But they did not live to carry into effect those measures of redress on which they were
earnestly intent, and which might have prevented
the dishonour of the reformation, and the calamities of a future generation. Thus, the want of
endowments hindered many; and the terms of
subscription, and the rigid conformity, which was
enforced with needless severity, was a still greater
obstacle to many more who might have adorned
the ministerial office.

5. Not only schoolmasters and law clerks, but
others of a much inferior class, serving men,

CHAPTER traders, and mechanics, scarcely possessing the
IV.
first rudiments of learning, were admitted into

ELIZ. holy orders. They wanted the only qualifications
A.D. 1575. which can render such a ministry useful, or even
tolerable; fervent piety and self-denying zeal.
They merely debased the ministry without extending its efficiency.

6. This was a state of things which the queen
regarded without much uneasiness. Preaching
at least seemed to her a sort of spiritual luxury
which she was always at liberty to withhold.
This was the dogma of the Romish church; and
it was one of several points in which the bias of
her mind appeared from time to time in a lingering fondness for the religion of her fathers. In
the first year of her reign all preaching was forbidden for a time. The unsettled state of men's
minds; the uncertainty and contradictoriness of
the doctrines taught in the same place, and from
the same pulpit; the necessity of proceeding with
caution; above all, the mischievous introduction
of state affairs into these popular harangues,
threatening the safety of the country and the
stability of her throne; these were reasons which
may for a short time have justified even so violent
a measure. But it was evidently one to which
no christian church could long patiently submit.
Preaching is the ordinance of Christ himself: it
is the great commission which he gave his ministers,—to go into all the world and preach the
gospel to every creature. The reformers well
knew where their strength lay. Bishop Latimer

had, at an early period of the reformation, turned
the tide of popular feeling against the Romish
bishops, those "unpreaching prelates;"—holding up their incapacity in the pulpit to the deri-
sion of the thronging multitudes who now first
learned, from this great father of English eloquence, how powerful an engine the preaching of
God's word was to become henceforward. But
Elizabeth had no Latimer to guide, or with dauntless courage, to reprove her. Her dislike of preaching continued to increase. One or two preachers
in a diocese, she said, were quite enough. Let a
homily be read, and the young catechised. The
craving for sermons was by no means to be
encouraged. Unhappily her notions obtained a
mischievous currency, and continued to infect the
church of England long after she had ceased to
wield a sceptre.

7. At once to meet the necessity of the times
and to "make full proof of their ministry," by
exercising it in the most effective manner, the
puritans instituted their famous prophecyings.
The word must be understood as it is used by St.
Paul in the new testament; to prophesy, being
synonymous with, to preach. It was in this sense
only that they used it to designate the character
of their assemblies; a remark which, obvious as
it is, has often been overlooked, to the serious hurt
of the puritan cause and character. Hence they
have been described as idle fanatics, who gravely
assembled at stated seasons to compound a pro-

phecy, or denounce future woes upon individuals whom they happened to dislike.

8. Of these prophecyings one of the first and most considerable was formed at Northampton.* It had the approbation of the bishop; and was of sufficient local importance to ask, and to secure, the sanction of the mayor of the town, and the co-ope-ration of the county magistrates. The laws of the association were drawn up with care under three heads: the first contained an outline of the discipline which those who joined in the undertaking imposed upon themselves; the second regulated the method of proceeding in their public meetings; the third was a short confession of their faith.

9. The code of discipline, if reasonable allowance be made for the circumstances of the party and the manners of the age, presents none of those austere features which are generally supposed to have marked the habits of the puritans. It is true " the playing of organs in the choir" is denounced, and singing (or choral chanting) is to "be put down;" and Calvin's catechism is appointed for the examination of the young on the Sunday evenings, to be followed up with a catechetical lecture for an hour on the same thesis;—but beyond these peculiarities there is little in the " rules for discipline" enacted by the Northampton puritans, to which an earnest christian of any scriptural church would refuse his consent; and much which, if carried into effect, would contribute, even now,

* Neal I. Ch. v. 215.

to the spiritual welfare of our towns and parishes.
Sunday was not to be profaned by walking abroad,
or sitting idly in the streets, in the time of divine
service ; nor by " excessive ringing of bells ;"
but after hearing morning prayer, and singing a
psalm in their own parish churches, the people
were to resort to the chief church to hear the sermon, except on those rare occasions when there
was a sermon in their own. Once in each quarter of a year there was a general communion in
every parish, together with a sermon. And previous to these, the minister and wardens undertook to go from house to house to take the names
of the communicants and examine into their lives.
After the communion, the minister visited every
house to learn who had not received the communion, and the reason of his absence. The day
of the administration of the eucharist was one
of more than usual solemnity. It was celebrated
twice in each parish church ; first at five in the
morning, with a sermon of an hour, the service
concluding at eight : this was particularly designed for servants : and again from nine to twelve
for masters and dames. Every Tuesday and
Thursday a lecture was held ; and on holidays, a
sermon was delivered.

10. Their prophecyings were conducted in imitation, they maintained, of the primitive church,
and in close compliance with the apostolic rule :
" ye may all prophesy one by one, that all may
learn and all be comforted." (1 Cor. xiv. 31.) The
congregation being assembled, the first minister

CHAPTER began with prayer, and explained a text of scrip-
IV. ture. He was to confute foolish interpretations,
ELIZ. and make practical reflections; but was especially
A.D. 1575. charged not to run out into common-place remarks; he was to conclude with prayer, and
within three quarters of an hour. He was followed by another minister, who might add what he
thought deficient, or explain what had been left
obscure; but he was forbidden to repeat what had
been said already, or to oppose his predecessor,
unless he had spoken contrary to the scriptures.
He again was followed by a third, who spoke under the same conditions as the second; and neither
of them was to exceed a quarter of an hour. A presiding moderator always concluded the exercise,
which lasted from nine to eleven o'clock. There
was here a close resemblance, it must be owned,
with St. Paul's directions to the Corinthian church:
" let the prophets speak two or three, and let the
other judge." The whole proceeding was conducted with great solemnity: if any person caused interruption or disorder, the president (say
their orders) shall command him, in the name of
the eternal God, to be silent; and after the exercise he shall be reprimanded. When the public
meeting had closed, the clergy remained in conference on the subjects which had been discussed.
The next preacher was appointed, and his text assigned. These prophecyings were occasional, and
do not seem to have interfered with the regular
services of the Lord's-day. Nor does it indeed
appear that they were held upon the Sunday.

11. Their confession of faith is a remarkable document, comprehensive, clear, and forcible, and is entitled to a place in the pages of their history. It was subscribed by each member, and was to this effect :*

—That they believed the word of God, contained in the old and new testament, to be a perfect rule of faith and manners ; that it ought to be read and known by all people ; and that the authority of it exceeds all authority, not of the pope only but of the church also ; and of councils, fathers, men and angels.

—They condemned, as a tyrannous yoke, whatsoever men have set up of their own invention, to make articles of faith, and the binding men's consciences by their laws and institutes. In sum, all those manners and fashions of serving God which men have brought in without the authority of the word for the warrant thereof, though recommended by custom, by unwritten traditions, or any other names whatsoever ; of which sort are the pope's supremacy, purgatory, transubstantiation, man's merits, free-will, justification by works, praying in an unknown tongue, and distinction of meats, apparel, and days, and briefly all the ceremonies, and whole order of papistry, which they call the hierarchy ; which are a devilish confusion established as it were in despite of God, and to the reproach of religion.

—And they content themselves with the simplicity of this pure word of God and doctrine thereof,

* Neal I. Ch. v. 216.

a summary of which is in the apostles' creed, resolving to try, examine, and judge all other doctrines whatsoever by this pure word, as by a certain rule and perfect touchstone. And to this
word of God they submit themselves and all their
doings ; willing and ready to be judged, reformed
or further instructed thereby in all points of religion.

12. A slender acquaintance with ecclesiastical
history, or with human nature, may suffice to conduct us at once to the conclusion that the prophecyings would certainly be popular and might possibly be mischievous. But a deeper thought and
a larger wisdom is required before we are in a
condition to decide as to the course which ought
to have been taken by the rulers of the church
with respect to them. The future character of the
church of England was the real question at issue.
Should the reformed church of England expand
itself, and generously—or rashly it might be—cast
itself on the affections of the people, and adapt
itself to the growing passion for religious teaching;
a passion which it might hope to lead, and which
it was equally wicked and insane to attempt to
quench ? This was one alternative. On the other
hand, should it risk all hazards, resist every innovation, and subdue by authority rather than conciliate by gentleness and love ? In a word, should
the church be made more popular or more imperious ? If the puritans were such as their enemies
have represented them, the former course was dangerous; if they were such as they represent them-

selves, the latter was tyrannical and cruel. To a party bent on mischief the slightest concession is too great. To zealous allies, sincere although irregular, the greatest concessions are sometimes the truest wisdom, as well as the most ordinary justice.

13. The exercises, or prophecyings, as they were indifferently called, spread through the kingdom with great rapidity. Many of the bishops encouraged them. Grindal, now primate, gave them all the sanction of his venerable name and more venerable office. In ten dioceses the bishops undertook to guide, and in due time stepped forward to defend, them. Their effects both on the laity and clergy were beneficial. In the former they roused a spirit of inquiry; in the latter, of biblical research; in both, of greater knowledge and deeper piety. The exercises were held in general once a month, sometimes once a fortnight. Crowds of the laity attended them, for preaching was rare and the scriptures were in few hands, and the fervent spirit of the reformation had not yet subsided amongst the people. At first laymen were permitted to take a part, but after a while, from some irregularities, this was forbidden and the clergy only ministered. To themselves the advantage was great, for the christian ministry lives and gathers strength in those who exercise it only as it is zealously put forth in fervent and unceasing action. It is a weapon of the highest polish and keenest edge, but rusts when it is laid aside. Ministers and curates were compelled to study in order to take their part in these public discussions.

CHAPTER IV.

ELIZ.

A.D. 1575.

Commentators were read and expositors consulted. The number of able preachers increased rapidly. "I know," says the archbishop to the queen, in a letter which will come before us, "that where there were not three able preachers, there are now thirty fit to preach at St. Paul's cross; and forty or fifty besides able to instruct their own cures." And he ascribes the increase to the introduction of the prophecyings.

14. It was scarcely to be expected that proceedings so novel in the English church should not create opposition. There is always a large class who content themselves with the decent formalities of religion, and condemn its warmth and fervour as so much enthusiasm; there are the stubborn who admit no change, and the timid who, with general longings for improvement, condemn every specific attempt at reformation as ill-timed or injudicious. And even the clerical body has never, in any church, been without its slothful members, who shrink from toil, and condemn the zeal of others chiefly because it reflects upon their own incompetence. Nor were the exercises always free from those real inconveniences which are natural to a new attempt when it assumes the character of a popular movement; for this will ever be the chosen arena of the vainglorious. At some of these meetings, it was said, that confusion and disturbances occurred; some affected to shew their parts, and to confute others who spoke not with equal rhetorical skill. Sometimes heterodox opinions were announced. Ministers who had

been silenced for their non-compliance with the established worship introduced themselves, and spoke against the liturgy and hierarchy. Some indulged in politics, some denounced individual persons. Amongst the people, religion became a matter of debate and argument. Sometimes a layman took upon him to speak, so that the exercises degenerated into factions and cabals; and in consequence a clamour was raised against them, not without some shew of reason. Such are the grave charges alleged by their opponents.

15. Many of these objections, perhaps all of them, were in some measure just. But if so, the question arose whether the good outweighed the evil; seeing that no institution is without its faults; and that the magnitude of the fault is generally in proportion to the greatness of the project. If the puny lichen clings to the bramble, the strangling ivy grapples with the oak. To condemn a new experiment which has promised great results, because the good it does is not unmixed with evil,—nay because the good is not unmixed with some evils hitherto unknown— the new produce of an untried soil—though one of the most common, is amongst the most irrational of human prejudices.

16. The archbishop set himself to redress these irregularities; he drew up a body of rules and orders for the reformation of the alleged abuses; which, if they had been carried into effect, could scarcely have failed to bring the prophecyings

CHAPTER IV.

ELIZ.

A.D. 1575.

into harmony with the church's discipline; and to have retained the good while guarding against any serious evil. In the first place, the exercises were to be held only in such churches and at such times as the bishop of the diocese should, under his hand and seal, appoint. Then, the archdeacon, or some other grave and learned graduate appointed by the bishop, was to preside and moderate. Further, the bishop was to appoint the subjects to be discussed, and give his licence and permission to the speakers. And, *ante omnia* (so runs the document, for this appears to have given most offence,) no lay person was to be suffered to speak in public. If any man speaking in the said exercises should glance openly or covertly against any state or person, public or private, or make any invective against the laws or discipline of the church of England, he was not only to be silenced, but the matter was to be reported to the bishop; nor could the speaker who had so offended take part in any future prophecying until he had confessed his error, and obtained a new admission and approbation from the bishop. And lastly, the bishops were charged that no deprived or suspended minister should be allowed to speak under any circumstances whatever.

17. But it was to no purpose. The prophecyings were already doomed. " For the queen," says the chronicler Strype, " liked not of them;" and the judgment of an archbishop, supported by the experience of his ten suffragans, was of little

weight against the self-will of an imperious sove- CHAPTER
reign and the intrigues of her courtiers. It was ____IV.____
determined they should be suppressed.* ELIZ.

18. The decision deeply affected the archbishop. A.D. 1575.
Almost the last of the reformers, he was, like them,
far before his age ; and had that prophetic wisdom
with which God endows a few great minds. He
saw the whole bearing of the subject ; and marked
the consequences, remote but not the less disastrous, it would involve—the decay of preaching,
the alienation of the laity, the growth of sectaries,
and to crown the whole, the deadening return
to formality, and with it the loss of zeal and
scriptural piety. His high position entitled him,
unasked, to remonstrate. He did not shrink from
the hazardous duty. He addressed a letter to the
queen, which incurred, it is true, her deep displeasure ; but it has entitled him to the reverence
of all posterity.†

19. The letter is prefaced with expressions of Dec. 20,
deep respect and grateful acknowledgments of his 1576.
own personal obligations to her majesty. He then
goes on to remind the queen of the duties of his
office, and that in every age of the church it had
been the privilege of its ministers to speak before
kings in the faithful language of exhortation and
reproof ; "and so," he says, "to come to the
present case, I cannot marvel enough how this
strange opinion should once enter your mind that

* Queen's Letter to the Bishops for suppressing Prophecyings, &c.
Grindal's Remains, P. S. Ed. 467.
† Grindal's Remains, page 375, for the letter to the queen.

it should be good for the church to have few preachers. Alas! madam, is the scripture more plain in any one thing, than that the gospel of Christ should be plentifully preached, and that plenty of labourers should be sent into the Lord's harvest, which, being great and large, standeth in need not of few but many workmen." This expostulation is sustained with various arguments drawn from scripture, and by an appeal to the queen's own knowledge of the good effects of preaching. "If your majesty come to the city of London never so often, what gratulation, what joy, what concourse of people, is there to be seen! Yea, what acclamations and prayers to God, and other manifest significations of inward and unfeigned love, joined with most humble and hearty obedience. Whereof cometh this, madam, but of the continual preaching of God's word in that city, whereby that people hath been plentifully instructed in their duty towards God and your majesty? On the contrary, what bred the rebellion in the north," alluding to a recent outbreak in Yorkshire, "was it not papistry, and ignorance of God's word through want of often preaching? And in the time of that rebellion, were not all men, of all estates, that made profession of the gospel, most ready to offer their lives for your defence? insomuch that one poor parish in Yorkshire, which by continual preaching had been better instructed than the rest (Halifax I mean) was ready to bring three or four thousand able men into the field to serve you against the said

rebels. How can your majesty have a more
lively trial and experience of the contrary effects
of much preaching, and of little or no preaching?
The one working most faithful obedience, and the
other most unnatural disobedience and rebellion."
He then defends his own conduct and that of his
bishops in allowing none to preach but men of
piety, learning, and good judgment. "We admit
no man to the office that either professeth papistry or puritanism;" meaning by the latter term,
no doubt, the extreme principles of Cartwright and
his party. Some wholesome truths follow, which
the queen found it hard to digest. He tells her,
though always in language of the greatest respect,
why preaching was so much decried. Because
the age was light and trifling; many had given
themselves over, he says, to carnal, vain, dissolute,
and lascivious living; and therefore the preaching
of God's word, which to all christian consciences
is sweet and delectable, is to them bitter and
grievous. Some, he tells her majesty, there are,
who dislike the reformation altogether; and, by
silencing the preachers, would subvert the reformation, not in open warfare, but by sapping
underneath, *non aperto marte, sed cuniculis.* So,
said he, the popish bishops in your father's time
would have had the English translation of the
bible called in as evil translated, and the new
translation committed to themselves, which they
never intended to perform; but God forbid, madam,
that you should open your ears to any of these

CHAPTER wicked persuasions, or go about to diminish the
IV.
_____ preaching of Christ's gospel.

ELIZ.   20. "The reading of homilies," continues the
A. D. 1576. archbishop, "hath its use; but is nothing comparable to the office of preaching. The godly preacher is termed in the gospel that faithful and wise servant who can give to each his portion in due season. He can apply his speech according to the diversity of times, places, and hearers, which cannot be done in homilies. Exhortations, reprehensions, and persuasions are uttered with more affection in sermons than in homilies, and move the hearers more; besides homilies were never thought in themselves alone to contain sufficient instruction for the church of England. They were devised by the godly bishops in your brother's time only to supply necessity, and for want of preachers; they are to give place to sermons by the statute whenever they may be had." And he reminds the queen that if sacrilege had not been committed the book of homilies had not been wanted. This was a hard blow, but honesty and truth required it. Sacrilege spoiled the livings—the parochial revenues, which had been set apart in purer ages, and before the dawn of popery, for preaching and teaching. First the abbeys, and then the crown seized upon these appropriations; and now, he says, they are dispersed to private men's possession without hope of restitution." "At this day," he proceeds, "for one church able to support a learned preacher, there are

at least seven churches unable to do so. If every CHAPTER IV. flock might have a preaching pastor, which is rather to be wished than hoped for, then were ELIZ. reading of homilies altogether unnecessary ; but A. D. 1576. to supply the want of preaching of God's word, which is the food of the soul, growing from the necessities aforesaid, both in your brother's time and in your time, certain godly homilies have been devised that the people should not be altogether destitute of instruction : for it is an old and a true proverb, better half a loaf than no bread." He then argues at length in behalf of the prophecy-ings : having fully explained the method in which they were conducted and the pains he had taken to prevent their abuse, he defends them by the precedents of Samuel at Naioth and Elijah at Jericho in the old testament, and the authority of St. Paul in the new. " That exercise of the church in those days St. Paul calls *prophetiam* and the speakers *prophetas*, terms very odious to some in our day, because they are not rightly un-derstood. For indeed *prophetiæ*, in that and like places of St. Paul, doth not, as it doth sometimes, signify prediction of things to come, which gift is not now ordinary in the church of God ; but sig-nifieth there, by consent of the best ancient writers, the interpretation and exposition of the scrip-tures."

21. He concludes in a manner solemn and touching. " I am forced with all humility, and yet plainly, to profess, that I cannot with safe con-science, and without the offence of the majesty of

CHAPTER IV.

ELIZ.

A. D. 1576.

God, give my assent to the suppressing of the said exercises : much less can I send out any injunction for the utter and universal subversion of the same.   I say with St. Paul, ' I have no power to destroy, but only to edify ;' and with the same apostle, ' I can do nothing against the truth, but for the truth.'   If it be your majesty's pleasure, for this or any other cause, to remove me out of this place, (viz. his archbishopric) I will with all humility yield thereto, and render again to your majesty what I received from the same.   I consider with myself ' that it is a fearful thing to fall into the hands of the living God.'   I consider also (quoting from Cyprian) ' that he who acts against his conscience, is building for hell.'   And what should I win if I gained, I will not say a bishopric, but the whole world, and lose mine own soul ?"

22. Finally he implored the queen, in matters ecclesiastical, of doctrine and discipline, to consult the bishops and divines of her realm.   " For these things," said he, (sheltering himself again under the authority of an ancient father) " are to be determined not in a palace, but in a church or a synod, *in ecclesia, seu synodo, non in palatio.*" Her majesty did not disdain to consult the judges on points of law ; he implored her, in matters of religion, to pay the same deference to her bishops. Here again the fathers served him well.   " Ambrose had given the like advice to Theodosius," and to the " good emperor Valentinian," and he quotes his words.   He makes this further request ;

that the queen would be pleased in spiritual things not to pronounce so resolutely and peremptorily, but always to remember that, in the cause of God, the binding decision after all must be the will of God, and not of any earthly prince whatever. " In God's matters all princes ought to bow their sceptres to the Son of God." He bids her to remember that, in her pomp and bravery, she was after all but dust and ashes,—" a mortal creature who must soon appear before the awful judgment-seat of the crucified." " Take heed,"—he concludes, with keen and searching penetration, and in a tone which, if it did not humble the queen before her God, would, he must foresee, be visited in anger on himself, and make him feel how bitter is the revenge which pride, wounded but not subdued, inflicts,—" take heed that you never once think of declining from God, lest that be verified of you that is written of Joash, who continued a prince of good and godly government for many years together ; and afterwards, ' when he was strengthened, his heart was lifted up to his destruction, and he neglected the Lord.' You have done many things well, but except ye endure to the end you cannot be blessed. If you turn away from God, then he will turn away his merciful countenance from you. And what remaineth to be looked for but only a terrible expectation of God's judgments, and heaping up wrath against the day of wrath !"

23. This remonstrance was presented to Elizabeth by the earl of Leicester, who, together with

CHAPTER IV.

ELIZ.

A. D. 1576.

1557.

1581.

the lord treasurer Burghley, was much in favour of the archbishop's views and principles. An ominous silence followed, and eight days after the archbishop wrote to lord Burghley to ask the reason of it, and to give utterance to his anxiety. In short, Grindal was suspended from his office; his archiepiscopal see was placed under sequestration for six months; and the venerable prelate was confined a prisoner to his own house. This occurred in June 1577. In November he was summoned to appear in person before the lords in the star chamber; and to make his humble submission to the queen. The first he was unable to comply with, being laid up with an excruciating internal disease; the second he declined to do, because he had done nothing wrong. His friend lord Burghley drew up and submitted to him a message, urging him to make his submission, and suggesting the proper form, but Grindal refused to make use of it; and the utmost that could be extorted from him were general expressions of dutiful respect, coupled with much sorrow that he lay beneath her majesty's displeasure.* The queen would now have deprived him altogether, but the unpopularity of such a measure prevented its adoption. A convocation was held at St. Paul's in January 1581, when the clergy at first refused to enter upon any business, or so much as grant a subsidy (a power which then pertained to them), until the archbishop was released. It was at last agreed

* Strype's Grindal, page 348, &c.

that doctor Matthew, dean of Christ church, after-
wards archbishop of York, should draw up in Latin
a petition to her majesty, imploring her to restore
the archbishop to the full exercise of his authority.
The bishops of the province of Canterbury addressed a letter to her to the same effect. But he
never regained the favour of Elizabeth; and it is
uncertain whether he was restored to the full exercise of his rights and ecclesiastical jurisdiction.
He was now old and blind, and feeling how little
he was permitted to do for the cause he had at
heart, he was unwilling to retain the name without the office of a bishop. He tendered his resig-
nation, which it is probable Elizabeth would have
received had not a mightier potentate stepped in
and removed him from a world of strife. Grindal
died July 6, 1583.*

24. The name of Grindal was revered by his contemporaries,—those to whom zeal and apostolic
piety were dear. At his death, Spenser embalmed his memory in some of his sweetest verses,
and not only the clergy but the great body of the
people deeply bewailed his loss. Posterity has
done him great injustice. Our popular historians
have passed him over with neglect, or spoken only
to condemn. He is described as a weak man,
whose want of energy laid open the church to the
inroads of schismatics; and these later times, occupied with heroes and idols of their own, have been
contented to receive, and to repeat, the ignorant

CHAPTER IV.

ELIZ.

A. D.

1581—3.

1583.

* Fuller, Ch. Hist., book ix., ch. 10.

slander. Whoever shall search the annals of the church of England, happily not wanting in such materials, for a list of those bishops who have revived the apostolic character, and displayed in their lives the pastoral graces which St. Paul delineates, will not omit the name of Grindal. That his firmness and courage should be called in question must appear strange to those who bear in mind his contest with the court. Of his wisdom let the reverence of his own age bear witness, and the calamities which his neglected counsels brought upon another. Of his freedom from violence and the warping influence of faction, the evidence is this,—that while the courtiers of Elizabeth reviled him as a puritan, the followers of Cartwright reviled him as a persecutor. To his piety, his letters, his sermons, above all his life, bear witness. His love of truth, as in all good men of high example, was greater than his love of victory. The Zurich letters in a single incident explain his character; in confidential intercourse with Foxe, he points out a passage in the martyrology in which a slight injustice had been done to the arguments of the Romish party, and desires to have it removed. For many years he was in possession of a large episcopal revenue. He lived unmarried, but he died poor : for his charities were boundless. But it is enough to say of him, that he was the worthy successor of Cranmer, and that he sustained the part of John the Baptist in the court of queen Elizabeth. He has, it is true, been called the Eli

of the English church, but the likeness exists
only in his old age, his blindness, and his misfortunes.

25. It is evident from the archbishop's letter
to the queen, that he considered the character of
the church of England, as a preaching church, in
danger. It was not for the prophecyings only
that he pertinaciously contended, but for the right
of christian bishops to send forth a free, unfetter-
ed, ministry, "to teach and to preach" in obedience to our Lord's command. The queen and her
courtiers, on the other hand, depreciated the ministry of the word, partly from ignorance of its
value, partly from political apprehensions of dis-
quietude, occasioned by the rashness of a few indiscreet preachers who were ever dabbling in affairs of state, but most of all from that dislike of
earnest and spiritual religion which began deeply
to mark her court. She gained a disastrous triumph. Preaching was discountenanced: it fell
into decay. The puritans assiduously cultivated
an art which their enemies despised. They seized
the rusty weapon, and with it smote their opponents. Both parties suffered; for the extreme
of coldness in the one, produced an artificial fervour in the other, and the sermon undervalued
in the cathedral was doated upon in the meeting
house. But inasmuch as the error arising from
excess was less injurious than that arising from
the contempt of a divine ordinance, the church
party suffered most. The dictum of queen Elizabeth, that one or two preachers were sufficient for

a county, obtained a mischievous currency, and received an almost literal interpretation. Her successor on the throne repeated it in substance, and
discouraged preaching to the utmost of his power.
We became an unpreaching church. Eloquence,
powerful at the senate and the bar, was banished
from the pulpit. Then followed the drowsy audience and the deserted pew, and at length the profound spiritual lethargy of the eighteenth century.
There were great divines, and there were writers of
sermons of high and deserved repute ; but preaching as an art,—as the noblest and most legitimate exercise of eloquence,—had departed from
amongst us ; and an alienation of the hearts of the
common people took place from which we have
never yet recovered. With her usual versatility
Rome began once more to cultivate what she had
formerly denounced. An Englishman still reads
with a blush, and a foreigner with exultation, if not
with incredulity, the irony with which the accomplished abbé Maury contrasts the great preachers
of Lewis XIV. with those of Charles II. But the
pulpit had not then attained its lowest depression.
Towards the middle of the last century the dul-
ness of sermons had become a vulgar proverb ; and
a polite essayist,* himself a clergyman, describes
a good preacher as a kind of antiquated luxury
once in great request ; while a popular teacher†
of rhetoric complains that a minister of the church
of England would not raise his eye or lift his hand

---

* Dr. Vicesimus Knox. Essays.
† Dr. Blair, Lectures on Rhetoric.

to set off the finest composition in the world. The
dread of enthusiasm was the paralysis of the pulpit.
So low had fallen that ordinance of Christ, which
had once overthrown the vast empire of idolatry,
and then shaken the papacy in its strongest holds.
The decay of religion attended the decay of
preaching with equal and melancholy steps ; and
the period in which the pulpit was most despised
was precisely that, in which God was most forgotten. But from any participation in the guilt
of this long series of calamities the sacred memory of Grindal at least is free.

CHAPTER V.

1. ON the death of archbishop Grindal, Whitgift succeeded to the primacy in September 1583.*
He was a man of great learning and of undoubted zeal. But his government was harsh, and his
spirit intolerant ; and his principles led him to
enforce an uniformity the most exact, by measures the most severe. Amiable, it is said, in private life, he used a power that was almost absolute with a severity that was nothing short of
despotism ; and the twenty years during which he
ruled at Lambeth, were years of sorrow to the
puritans.

2. The queen was always ready to urge her prelates to new acts of severity against those who resisted her authority ; and she found in Whitgift a
mind, neither obsequious indeed, nor disposed to
flattery, but naturally, as well as from education,
prone to demand submission as a duty, and to
obtain it by force rather than by forbearance.
Thus the primate was a willing agent to the queen,

* Paul's Life of Whitgift, p. 37.

for their views were similar, and their object was CHAPTER
the same,—namely by the exercise of punishment V.
to produce conformity; and thus too the power ELIZ.
of the crown, as far as it regarded ecclesiastical A. D. 1583.
affairs, was soon vested almost entirely in the
archbishop. Elizabeth's secular advisers had
some reason to complain; and in fact we find
that Burghley and Walsingham were often driven
to remonstrate. They would have checked the
archbishop in his severities; but in ecclesiastical
matters his power was greater than their own,
since he merely carried into effect those principles which the queen espoused not less warmly
than himself.

3. The question of the sovereign's right to interfere in matters of religion had not yet been
decided in England; or, perhaps it would be more
correct to say, it had not yet been called in question. The great problem, in which the rights of
conscience and the rights of law were to adjust
their respective boundaries, was not to be solved
until another century and two revolutions should
have thrown some further light upon it. A nation, like a family, is governed in its infancy by
a power which, with reference to itself, is necessarily arbitrary. The patriarchal form of government is not merely the most ancient, but in
certain stages of society the best. In fact it is in
some cases the only one that is practicable. In
process of time a nation, like a family, approaches
its maturity, and demands a greater freedom. And
this is the crisis of a nation's fate, just as it is of

CHAPTER household happiness. If the parent is unyielding,
V.   and the children undutiful, misery ensues ; and
ELIZ.   the house divided against itself is laid prostrate.
A. D. 1583. In an empire, when wealth has increased and
civilization spread, there is the same consciousness
of power,—the power of self-government,—and
with it the same impatience of restraint. The
crisis has arrived which requires the utmost skill
and wisdom in those who govern, and not less the
forbearance of those who obey. The maxims
which were once useful are now found inapplicable
on both sides. The restraints which were once
necessary have become intolerable. The man
cannot repose in the cradle of his infancy ; and
yet the monarch accustomed to implicit submission cannot brook the rising spirit of independent
familiarity with state affairs ; a spirit, however,
which marks the approaching manhood of his
people. Nothing can be more unjust than to
bring the several actors in the scenes we are de-
scribing to the tribunal of what are now termed
constitutional principles. Of those principles,
they were profoundly ignorant. They arose out
of the collisions which afterwards ensued, or of
which these, in the reign of Elizabeth, were
amongst the very first. To send a puritan to
prison on account of his religion, we should
now consider a flagrant act of tyranny, simply as
an invasion of the rights of conscience ; and we
should condemn it upon this ground alone. But
no puritan thought so in the reign of queen
Elizabeth. The right of magistrates was un-

questioned, to punish false doctrine as we punish
theft, and if necessary to put heretics to death as
we convict for felony. No language can be stronger
than that which Cartwright himself makes use of.
" Magistrates," he says, in his reply* to Whitgift's
defence of the church of England, " ought to enforce the attendance of atheists and papists on the
services of the church ; to punish them if they do
not profit by the preaching they might hear ; to
increase the punishment if they gave signs of contempt ; and if at last they proved utterly impe-
nitent, to cut them off that they might not corrupt
and infect others." Whitgift acted upon the
same principle. The fault laid to his charge, by
his own party, was that he pushed it too far and
had recourse to it too often ; by the puritans, that
he was unjust and a tyrant, not in carrying out
the principle, but simply in applying it to *them*.
The censure which justly belongs to him is that,
occupying a station so exalted, he was only upon
a level with his age ; that he exhibited an ordinary
mind resorting in times of difficulty to ordinary
expedients ; that he learned nothing from the
wise moderation of men like Cecil and Walsingham, and Leicester and Lord Bacon, nothing
from the meek example of his predecessor ; that
he was narrow-minded, severe, and obstinate.
These, it is true, are heavy charges against a name
otherwise venerable and worthy of respect ; but
one of the true uses of history is to display the
infirmities of good men, and to shew how perni-

* Reply &c. p. 51.

cious they may be. For it is with men, as with principles and with institutions—the corruption of the best things produces the worst conse- quences.

4. In Elizabeth the nation placed implicit and unbounded confidence. She was then what in history she still remains, the most popular of English sovereigns. With all her faults, she was the anxious and devoted parent, as well as the lordly mistress, of the commonwealth. Few of either sex ever possessed in an equal, none perhaps in a higher, degree, that attribute of greatness which not only governs the multitude without an effort, but reduces other minds, in some respects greater than itself, to prompt obedience ; making it a post of honour to be submissive. The conse- quence was, that her will was law ; her govern- ment was patriarchal ; the people revered and loved her as a mother ; and she for her own part expressed the honest feelings of her soul, when, being importuned to marry, she replied that she was already married to the state, and her subjects were her children. In her hands the law itself was tractable. She alone personi- fied the state and represented it. She employed martial law when it pleased her, and sometimes on very trivial occasions,—as, for instance, when the streets of London were overrun with vaga- bonds. She uttered a commission, commanding that upon intimation given by the justices of peace in London, or the neighbouring counties, her provost marshal should take the offending

persons, " and according to justice of martial law
execute them upon the gallows or gibbet openly."
" I suppose," says the historian Hume, in relating
this, " it will be difficult to produce another instance of such an act of authority in any place
nearer than Muscovy." The importation of the
pope's bulls was forbidden under the same penalty
of martial law; and more justly, for he had ful-
minated an excommunication upon the queen,
and released her subjects from their allegiance.
But all foreign books and pamphlets were forbidden likewise, and martial law was still the penalty.
Yet it does not appear that the harshness of these
proceedings gave the least dissatisfaction; for
which it will be difficult to assign any other reason
than that which is no doubt the true one,—the
unlimited confidence reposed by the nation in
the judgment and the patriotic intentions of their
sovereign.

5. Such considerations are to be borne in mind,
when we read of Elizabeth's severity to her puritan
subjects. They were not especial objects of persecution, but simply, in her view, delinquents who
set at nought her authority, and ought therefore
to be punished. This, alas, did not mitigate the
depth of their sorrows; nor ought it to abate our
pity and respect. In one point of view it even
adds to our sympathy, for it must have added to
their trials, that they were suffering, not from a
vindictive persecution, but from what their own
countrymen regarded as the operation of an ordinary law.

CHAPTER   6. Before Grindal's death, a terrible earnest had
V.   been given in the burning of two Dutch anabap-
ELIZ.   tists at Smithfield. The venerable Foxe was still
A. D. 1583. living, and wrote to the queen imploring that the
reformation might not be stained with blood : but
his entreaties failed.* Several Romish priests
were executed soon afterwards, not for popery so
much as for their allegiance to a sovereign who
had dethroned Elizabeth, and offered her kingdom
as a lawful prey to catholic princes. A circumstance which occurred in 1573 gave the queen
(whose great infirmity it was to be suspicious) a
handle for severity against the whole body of the
puritans. Birchett, a wild enthusiast if not a
lunatic, persuaded himself that it was lawful to
kill those who opposed the truth of the gospel : he
rushed into the Strand out of the Temple, where
he was a student, and stabbed a person whom he
mistook for Hatton afterwards lord keeper of the
seals, because "he was an enemy of God's word,
and a maintainer of papistry." There was some
discussion on the question how he ought to be
dealt with. Should he be burnt for heresy ; hung
as a felon; or put to death by martial law ? The
last alternative was chosen. But the poor wretch
was now at least insane : he killed his keeper with
one blow, again intending, he said, to have dispatched Hatton; and the next day, after his right
hand had been struck off, he was hanged in the
Strand.† The law in these barbarous times made
little or no allowance for mental aberration : it
regarded the act, while it overlooked the motive.

* Fuller iii. b. ix. 507.   † Neal i. v. 241.

It was cruel to put the law in force against the
person of a madman, but it was a far greater
cruelty to charge a participation in his madness
upon the puritans, and treat them as the in-
stigators of his crime, or his insanity. Several
ministers were soon afterwards deprived. One,
who had been chaplain to Lord Bacon, and
was now the incumbent of St. Clement's in the
Strand, was tried at Westminster for his nonconformity. It was proved he had baptized a child
without using the sign of the cross, and that in
the marriage-service he had omitted the ring.
Refusing to subscribe, he was committed to close
confinement, where he shortly died in poverty
and great distress. A plot was soon got up, as it
afterwards appeared, by one of the servants of
archbishop Parker, in which it was pretended
that the puritans, encouraged by the earl of
Leicester, intended to assassinate both the lord
treasurer and the archbishop. The archbishop
fell into the snare,* and the supposed conspirators
were apprehended, amongst whom were three
eminent puritan divines. But the evidence was
contemptible. They were at once released, and the
circumstance would not have deserved our notice,
except that it tends to shew the extraordinary
panic which prevailed with regard to the motives
and secret practices of the puritan party. Other
ministers were silenced; some for trivial causes,
others for preaching against the hierarchy : some
because they did not wear the surplice ; and others
because they endeavoured to enforce a stricter

* Strype's Parker, p. 466.

discipline in the admission of communicants to the Lord's table. That many of them were men scrupulous, and even absurd, in their tenacity for trifles, is certain. One was confined in the gatehouse prison, for asserting that "keeping the queen's birthday as a holiday, was to make her an idol;" and many of their objections were just as frivolous.

7. It would be painful to recount the numerous cases of hardship and oppression—faithfully registered and transmitted to posterity by the sufferers and their friends—which now followed. The storm which had muttered around the venerable head of Grindal was not likely to spare inferior subjects. His death was the signal for the commencement of a system of intolerance under which puritanism, for a period of twenty years, suffered a persecution which, though neither to be compared with those of pagan nor of papal Rome, was still a disgrace to the reign of Elizabeth, and infamous to the memory of those who shared in it. It consigned to poverty, confiscation, imprisonment, and sometimes death, those who, with a piety the most fervent and a loyalty unimpeached, were guilty, as their greatest crime, of a conscience too scrupulous, or a stubborn selfwill, bristling (often with very harmless menaces) when treated with contempt and cruelty.

8. Whitgift was scarcely seated in the primacy when the queen issued her commands that he should restore the discipline of the church;* which she said was much decayed through the

* Fuller iii. ix. 69; Neal i. vii. 312.

connivance of some prelates, the obstinacy of the puritans, and the power of some noblemen. The archbishop issued forthwith his instructions to the bishops of his province, generally known as the three articles. The first enjoins upon the clergy an acknowledgment of the queen's supremacy in all causes ecclesiastical as well as civil; the second demands conformity to the book of common prayer ; and the third an assent to the thirty-nine articles.* But besides these conditions it was enjoined that all preaching, catechizing, and praying, in any private family where strangers were present, should be " utterly extinguished," and that no minister should preach or teach except he conformed to the whole service and administered the sacrament four times a year ; and that the habits should be worn. Many of the puritans had hitherto satisfied themselves with a partial or occasional conformity, and the bishops had connived at their irregularity. This indulgence then was now withdrawn : and the effect was seen in the immediate suspension or voluntary retirement of some hundreds of the puritan clergy.† Remonstrances and petitions poured in from themselves and their parishioners. The council, the lord treasurer Cecil, the archbishop, and the queen, were by turns importuned. But no redress was granted. On the contrary, the storm increased in its severity. The sufferings of the nonconforming clergy were very great. From several counties, from the cities of London and Norwich,

---

* Neal reckons up 233 in six counties, from MSS. in his possession, "besides great numbers in Peterborough, London, and other counties." i. vii. 215.　　　　　　　　　　　　† Ibid.

the voice of suspended ministers was heard. Their griefs at least were real, whatever judgment we may form as to their scruples in conforming. In touching language they commend " their poor families," " their distressed consciences," and " the cries of their people who were as sheep having no shepherd," to the compassion of the privy council. And they offer terms of conciliation ; namely, to subscribe the doctrinal articles of the church, and the other articles, " so far as they are not repugnant to the word of God." And they promise further, if their subscription be dispensed with, to make no disturbance in the church or separation from it. It was not likely, even if it had been possible, that the ruling party would consent to these conditions. Either the bishops or the puritans must give way. The church must be remodelled, or the dissatisfied must submit; and many of their demands have, to the great majority of their fellow countrymen, both then and ever since, appeared unreasonable. To eject such men in the last resort may have been inevitable : but the severity would have been more wholesome if preceded by some acts of kindness, some earnest and sincere endeavours to promote an accommodation. The persecutions they suffered were such as no obstinacy upon their part can justify ; and which errors such as theirs did not deserve.

10. A petition from the magistrates of Suffolk deserves attention. It is a remarkable document, and painfully instructive.* " The laborious ministers of the word," they say, " are marshalled with

* Strype's Annals, iii. i. 264.

the worst malefactors, presented, indicted, arraigned, and condemned, for matters, as we presume, of very slender moment : some for leaving the holidays unbidden ; some for singing the
psalm, *Nunc dimittis*, (instead of chanting it) ;
some for leaving out the cross in baptism, &c.
Having recited the grievances of their own
party, they proceed thus ;—" by law we proceed against all offenders ; we touch none that
the law spareth, and spare none that the law
toucheth ; we allow not of papists ; of the family of love ; of anabaptists or brownists. No :
we punish all these." " And yet," they add, "we
are christened with the odious name of puritans." The magistrates of Suffolk did not perceive that, in their eagerness to defend themselves, they justified the persecution of which they
complained, by their own example. " The family
of love, anabaptists, brownists, and papists—
we punish all these."* It would be difficult to say
in what respects some of these seceders were
more deserving of punishment than the most
harmless of the church puritans themselves.
When we read such documents we are struck
with the inconsistency and cruelty of each party
in its turn. Our sympathies rest with neither ;
and we are almost disposed to look upon their
mutual strife and alternate sufferings, as the
spectator looks upon the changing fortunes of a
painted battle in a panorama—with curiosity, but
without emotion.

* Strype's Annals iii. i. 264.

11. The family of love, the brownists, and the anabaptists were the first seceders from the church of England at home. About this time they begin to occupy a considerable space in history. Their sufferings, borne with fortitude, and rather coveted than shunned, would alone have made them famous: for upon them the brunt of the puritan persecution fell.

12. The family of love is represented by all parties alike in unfavourable, often in revolting, colours. But the portrait is drawn by their enemies, and with every disposition to exaggerate its faults. We find it exceedingly difficult to account for the real or pretended indignation which their presence everywhere occasioned; except indeed upon the principle that, inasmuch as they were the smallest and weakest of the sectaries, it was a more easy triumph to chase them from the flock: for such is human depravity, that a reputation for courage is sometimes sought by injuring and insulting those who are least able to resist. To the charge of creating a very unnecessary schism they seem fairly exposed. Beyond this their guilt is very questionable. Their views, indeed, of christian doctrine are stated with the obscurity in which enthusiasts love to involve themselves; and it is by no means an easy task to ascertain their real meaning. They were the fathers of that mystic system which Jacob Behmen completed at the beginning of the last century; a system which, to a devout but uninstructed mind, seems to promise much, but is found worthless

upon trial. At first it charms by its apparent
profundity. It bewildered for a time the acute
understanding of John Wesley; a circumstance
which alone would be sufficient to save it from
contempt. Soaring amidst the highest mysteries
it becomes dazzled and confounded: the intellect
is confused; and the reveries of a distempered
imagination pass at length for the suggestions
of the Holy Ghost. The title assumed—the family
of love—afforded a ready topic of abuse. The
quaint yet often generous Fuller cannot forbear
a passing scoff.* Their founder was Henry Nicholas of Amsterdam; and again his name suggests a comparison with the Nicolaitans of old,
(Rev. ii.) who " were hated by God," he says, "for
their *filthiness*." But this grave insinuation is
utterly without support. It has often been revived, (and in general by ignorant persons of careless, if not licentious, minds) whenever a christian
communion has insisted upon the doctrine of
that divine love which God by his spirit diffuses
in the soul, and of that mutual and warm affection which believers owe to one another. " These
familists," he adds, " besides many monstrosities
they maintained about their communion with
God, attenuated all scriptures into allegories ; and
under pretence to turn them into spirit, made
them empty, airy, nothings." The latter part of
the charge does not seem to be ill founded. Their
lives were pure, and yet their creed was mystical

* Ch. Hist. iii. ix.

CHAPTER and their doctrine antinomian,—a strange incon-
V. sistency, yet happily of not unfrequent occur-
ELIZ. rence : for the conscience may be clear while the
A. D. 1583. understanding is perplexed. Nicholas, their leader, defended their morals and their doctrines from the press : and as regards the former with success.

13. The familists did not escape the watchful vigilance of the privy council. They were summoned before it, and commanded to abjure their " detestable heresies :" the result of the interview is unknown. In the year 1580, a proclamation was issued by the queen against them. It would be difficult to find within so small a compass, in any state paper, so much abuse. They are charged with teaching damnable heresies ; they are said to be absurd and fanatical ; they feign to themselves a monstrous new kind of speech ; their books are lewd, heretical, and seditious ; and their sects are dangerous and damnable. Search is to be made for their books ; and those who shall continue to print or distribute them are threatened with imprisonment, and such other bodily punishment as heretics deserve. But the single specific charge is that they hold themselves alone to be elect and saved, and condemn all other churches; and that they refuse to take an oath before the magistrate to their own hurt : " so that by their own confession they cannot be condemned : whereby they are more dangerous in any christian realm."*

* "A proclamation against the sectaries of the family of Love. Given at our mannour of Richmond in the two and twentieth year of our reign," republished in " Liturgical Tracts." Lumley, London, 1848.

They afterwards suffered from time to time under the general pretext of holding private conventicles, until they melted away, and were at length absorbed in the larger communities of the non- conformists.

14. The brownists took their name from Robert Brown, a clergyman of good family, nearly connected with lord Burghley. He was brought up at Cambridge, where his preaching was much admired by the common people ; but his unchastened zeal led his superiors thus early to presage his future mischievous career. After travelling abroad he returned home the inveterate opponent of the church of England, and preached for a time at Norwich amongst the German refugees who formed a large proportion of its inhabitants. Endeavouring to proselyte his own countrymen, he was imprisoned by the bishop. At the instance of Burghley he was at length released, and the lord treasurer's kind offices were used to restore his young kinsman to the affections of a too angry father ; who had resolved to disown his son unless he renounced his schismatic principles. Brown, who appears to have been chiefly remarkable for carrying through life the heat and rashness of untamed childhood, could soon boast that he had been the tenant of two and thirty prisons, in some of which he could not see his hand at noon-day. Fuller, who had often seen him, describes him as of an imperious nature, ready to take offence on trivial occasions if his opinion was not received as an oracle. Nor was

his conduct remarkable for sanctity. Probably through lord Burghley's influence, he retained his preferment (the parish of Achurch, in Northamptonshire) through life; but his reputation seems to have been low. He had in short, says Fuller, a wife with whom for many years he never lived, and a church wherein he never preached. He survived to an extreme old age; and died without honour in the jail of Northampton, to which he had been committed for striking the constable of his parish, in a fit of passion, in the year 1630.*

15. Yet this man was the founder of a sect from which the church of England received, for thirty years, the most determined opposition. His followers shared all his enthusiasm without any of his fickleness. While he professed the utmost abhorrence of episcopacy, he retained a valuable preferment in the church he denounced; and probably became indifferent at length to the cause he had so eagerly espoused. But the brownists, passing by their leader, rushed upon danger and courted persecution. They taught that it was sinful in the highest degree to remain in communion with the church; that it was in truth, no part of the true church of Christ, but the church of antichrist and very synagogue of Satan; that it should be opposed, denounced, and utterly subverted. It was an age in which strong language was seldom far removed from violence of conduct. The moderation was almost unknown that teaches disputants to confide the last issue,

* Fuller iii. ix. 66.

not to the force of arms but to the strength of
arguments. The daring challenge which the
brownists offered, was looked upon by the other
party as tantamount to an act of sedition if not of
treason. Even Cartwright felt compelled, now in
the decline of life, to resume his pen; and while
Fuller taxed his learning to prove that the brownists were but the donatists revived, Cartwright
denounced their presumption in maintaining that
the church of England was not a living member of the true catholic church of Christ. A
singular, and yet in some respects an honourable, task; to combat in old age against the excesses of those opinions which it had been the
business of his life to propagate! The assemblies
of the church of England, he argued, had Christ
for their head and their foundation, though
defective, he still thought, in many points of
discipline. Still they were true members of the
church catholic, and all the foreign churches
gave them the right hand of fellowship. It
was an awful step to excommunicate a single
person; more awful still to excommunicate a
congregation; then, how great the presumption of those who dared to denounce at once
the entire national church of England. A vineyard may have lost its fence, or a city its walls,
and yet the vineyard may be fruitful and the city
may maintain its rights. Thus Cartwright wrote
in his old age; would that he had written thus
in his youth! Barrow, a leader among the brownists, answered, complaining that Cartwright and

CHAPTER
V.

ELIZ.

A.D. 1583.

his friends were setting themselves against their own disciples; that they were afraid of the consequences of their own principles now fully carried out. The consistency of Cartwright is a question to this day unsettled; and one still argued with all the bitterness of party strife. His moderation, in his later years, has never met with its due reward; for it should be remembered that he was himself a sufferer, when he thus took up his pen on behalf of the church from which he was an outcast.*

16. But the anabaptists were the most numerous, and for some time by far the most formidable, opponents of the church. They are said to have existed in England since the early times of the Lollards; but their chief strength was now derived, and their numbers reinforced, from Germany. While Luther was still living this sect had assumed a formidable and dangerous character. Under the guidance of the enthusiastic Munzer and his associates the German anabaptists disclaimed the authority of magistrates and laws, demanded for the saints supremacy on earth, and announced a carnal millennium. They broke out into a ferocious civil war, which was only suppressed after much bloodshed. Among other tenets they held that the baptizing of infants was an invention of the devil; and they received the title of anabaptists because they insisted on *again* baptizing all their converts, although in infancy they had once

* Brooke's Cartwright, 299—307.

submitted to the rite. But even in Germany all anabaptists were not rebels and fanatics. Many, upon the contrary, were men of zeal and piety. In England they attempted no violence, beyond the solitary acts of here and there a madman whose insanity sought importance by assuming their detested name. Yet the anabaptists are spoken of by all the writers of this period with horror. It seems to have been assumed that an anabaptist was of course licentious and a rebel. No pains were taken to ascertain the fact : to doubt the validity of infant baptism was to incur forthwith the penalties which even then belonged rather to treason than to schism. A body of christians among whom the piety of Hughes, the learning and zeal of Marshman, and the eloquence of Robert Hall, found in after ages their congenial home, was then regarded by all men with aversion, by many with indescribable alarm. Their rude tenacity in maintaining the peculiarities of their creed, and their stern contempt of their adversaries; a contempt that often arrayed itself in something of a prophetic garb, while they denounced the vengeance of God upon their opponents, must be allowed their full share of influence in provoking the hostilities of a barbarous and superstitious age. But after every deduction, the sufferings of the anabaptists are a stain upon the annals of Elizabeth and the fame of our forefathers.

17. Some of the puritan writers complain of the indulgence shewn to papists, and contrast it

with their own hard usage. But in truth all the opponents of the queen were treated with horrible and vindictive severity: many Romish priests were executed with a revolting barbarism; greater numbers were exiled and imprisoned. English law, if we do not prostitute the name in applying it to such transactions, knew little but revenge and cruelty. The political trials of this reign, it has been well observed by a great living writer, the historian of the English constitution, are, with scarcely an exception, disgraceful to humanity. And all religious offences were then political. Justice, like a bird of prey, was ever on the wing; and if it stooped or swerved a little from its course, it was to slake its appetite for blood upon some harmless victim as it passed along in quest of greater prey.

18. Whatever may have been Calvin's share of infamy in the burning of Servetus the Socinian, he does not stand alone. In 1584, one John Lewes was burned at Norwich for denying the Godhead of Christ, and other heresies. In the next year John Hilton, a priest, was required to make a solemn abjuration of the same opinions: this he did in the presence of the convocation; and it is probable his office alone saved him from the death of Lewes. He did penance by standing at St. Paul's cross during the sermon, bearing the significant faggot on his shoulder. Coppin and Thacker, two clergymen of Suffolk, were imprisoned five years, and afterwards hanged at Bury St. Edmunds as brownists; Brown's writings being

first burnt in their presence. The persecution
raged for ten years. In 1592 a congregation of
brownists being discovered in London, fifty-six
were imprisoned; where they died, says their indignant historian Neal, like rotten sheep. Their
chief leader and martyr Barrow, a gentleman of
good family, addressed a supplication to parliament, in which he says; " These bloody men" (the
high court of commission) will allow us neither
meat, drink, fire, lodging; nor suffer any whose
heart the Lord would stir up for our relief to have
any access to us. Seventeen or eighteen have
perished within these noisome jails within these
six years ; some of us had not one penny about
us when we were sent to prison, nor anything to
procure a maintenance for ourselves and families
but our labour; not only we ourselves, but our
wives and children, are undone and starved. After
reciting some of their worst oppressions, he concludes with an appeal worthy alike of a patriot
and an Englishman, and in the fearless spirit of
St. Paul himself :—" that which we crave for us
all is the liberty to die openly, or live openly in
the land of our nativity ; if we deserve death let
us not be closely murdered ; yea, starved to death
with hunger and cold, and stifled in loathsome
dungeons."* The latter petition alone was heard.
Barrow and Greenwood, with several others, were
brought before the archbishop of Canterbury and
other members of the court of high commission,

* Neal i. Brooke, art. Barrow and Greenwood.

CHAPTER
V.

ELIZ.

A. D. 1583.

but they refused to take the oath, that is, to convict themselves upon their own extorted testimony. They were then indicted for publishing seditious books and pamphlets, tending to the slander of the queen and government. They denied the charge of disloyalty, shewed no regret and sought no mercy : their quarrel, they said, was not with the queen and her government, but with the hierarchy and the church. They were of course convicted. Ballot, one of the number, confessed his fault, and, with two others who were only accessories, was reprieved and sent back to prison, where two of them died; the third was banished. Barrow and Greenwood were condemned to die. They were brought in a cart to Tyburn, in order that the sight of the gallows might terrify them into submission, and alarm their followers : but they remained unmoved, and were taken back to Newgate. A fortnight afterwards they were carried a second time to Tyburn, and there hanged. With their last words they prayed for the queen, expressed a joyful confidence in God, and triumphed in the cause for which they died. Tyburn itself never witnessed a more wicked execution, or one more senseless and impolitic.

19. These enormities have never been permitted to stand out in English history in all their dark and hideous deformity, and in consequence some lessons of high importance have been lost. Churchwriters tread gently, as if they feared the ground would give way beneath them. The faults of

Whitgift and his party they assume to be the CHAPTER faults of episcopacy and of the church of England; V. at least their cautious dexterity in exculpating ELIZ. the former has had the ill effect of transferring A. D. 1583. the odium of these infamous proceedings to the latter. Were the church of England infallible and unchangeable as that of Rome pretends to be, their conduct would have the justification of necessity; at present it contributes only to the injury of the cause they advocate. The persecutions of Whitgift and his party are only connected with modern episcopacy by that process of sentimental logic which confounds antiquity with authority, and volunteers to take upon itself the vices and the crimes of its forefathers in proof of its own legitimacy. Nonconformists, on the other hand, while protesting, as well they may, with indignant vehemence against these atrocities, have blunted the force of their remonstrance by the facility with which they excuse the guilty violence of the sectaries during the short perio d when they held the reins of power in the next century. For the writer who takes up his pen to extenuate the faults of one party, or dwells exclusively on the provocations of the other, is a pleader and not a judge, a partizan and not an historian; and beyond the limits of his party his voice will not be heard, nor ought it to command respect.

20. While the seceders were thus harassed, the church puritans were not permitted to escape. Conformity was rigidly enforced, and for the detection of delinquents new measures were devised.

CHAPTER VI.

CHAPTER VI. 1. In the month of December, **1583,** the queen issued a new commission at the earnest solicita-

ELIZ. tion of the archbishop.* Forty four commissioners

A. D. 1583. were named, of whom twelve were bishops, and the rest chief officers of state. Three of these had power to act ; whereof the archbishop of Canterbury, or one of the bishops mentioned in the commission, was always to be one. The jurisdiction of the court extended over the whole kingdom, and its power was enormous. During the queen's pleasure the high commissioners were authorized to inquire into all heretical opinions, seditious books, false rumours, or slanderous words; they were to correct, reform, and punish all who wilfully abstained from divine service established by law, all heresies, schisms, et cetera : they were to cite before them, and deprive, such of the clergy as maintained any doctrine contrary to the articles ; and to punish all grievous offences punish-

* Strype's Whitgift, 154. Neale ii. vii. 322.

able by the ecclesiastical laws ; including amongst
graver crimes all outrages, misdemeanours, and
disorders in marriage. So wide the sweep of this
terrible tribunal. Its method of proceeding varied
with the necessities of the case. If the culprit
could not be convicted under " the oath of twelve
good and lawful men," a jury might be dispensed
with, and the court had power to convict by " witnesses alone." If witnesses were wanting, " all
other means and ways you can devise " (such are
the terms of the commission) left room for the
rack, and the oath not less dreaded, *ex officio mero*.
And they had a distinct authority not only " to
examine such persons as they suspected, upon
their corporal oaths," but to punish those " who
refused the oath, by fine or imprisonment, according to their discretion." Under the grinding
pressure of this frightful and ponderous machine,
which was designed to crush the puritans, all the
liberties of England must have perished ere long
had it not been swept away with indignation by
a parliament of Charles the first. The tribunal,
even in the arbitrary times of Elizabeth, was held
to be unconstitutional. The oath *ex officio*, in
particular, was viewed with abhorrence, as contrary not only to the liberties of England, but to
the law of nations and the instincts of nature.
It was a universal maxim, it was argued, that no
man is bound to accuse himself. No canon or
general council of the church, for the first thousand
years of its existence, had resorted to such a measure. Even pagan emperors had disowned and

countermanded it, when it was employed by pro-
consuls and inferior magistrates against the primitive christians. The pope and the inquisition
itself admitted it only in cases of heresy, whereas
it was now levelled against every paltry misdemea-
nour. And lastly, it had been formally repealed
in the reign of Henry the eighth, and again declared unlawful by statute in the first year of
queen Elizabeth. Such were the objections then
made to this ill-omened tribunal ;* and amidst the
deepest disapprobation its proceedings began.

2. As a guide to the commissioners, the archbishop drew up twenty-four articles on which clerical delinquents were to be examined upon oath.
They were framed with an ingenuity from which
no honest puritan could escape ; and, if he refused
to answer them, and declined the oath, he was immediately committed for contempt of the court,
and deprived of his benefice. One article may be
quoted as a specimen of all the rest. " 19. Item.
That within the time aforesaid (that is, for the
space of these three years, two years, one year,
half a year, three, two, or one month last past)
you have advisedly and of set purpose preached,
taught, declared, set down or published by writing,
public or private speech, matter against the said
book of common prayer, or of something therein
contained, as being repugnant to the word of God,
or not convenient to be used in the church ; or
something have written or uttered, tending to the
depraving, despising, or defacing of some things

* Fuller Ch. Hist. iii. ix.

contained in the said book. Declare what, and the
like circumstances thereof, and for what cause or
consideration, you have so done."*

3. A loud and bitter cry was heard from the
distressed puritans. Despairing of relief from the
bishops, they applied to the privy council. Several petitions, addressed to them by the suspended
ministers of Kent, Suffolk, and other counties, were
forwarded to the archbishop by Beal, the clerk of
the council ; a proceeding with which the archbishop was much displeased. He complains to
the lord treasurer that Mr. Beal had used intem-
perate speeches : " He told me, in effect, that I
would be the overthrow of this church, and the
cause of tumult." A prophetic message, even
though delivered intemperately ! The privy council themselves then remonstrated with the primate,
including Aylmer bishop of London in their pointed censure. The remonstrance bears the signature
of eight of the privy council, Burghley, Warwick,
Howard, Hatton, Leicester, Shrewsbury, Croft,
and Walsingham ; some of whom were themselves
members of the court of high commission. They
request both their lordships to stay and temper
their subalterns, in their hasty proceedings against
the ministers. They describe the lamentable state
of the church in Essex : " a great number," they
say, " of zealous and learned preachers are there
suspended from their cures, and their places left
vacant, or filled with persons neither of learning
or good name." On the other hand, " a great num-

† Neal i. vii. 331, for the 24 Articles at large.

ber of persons notoriously unfit, charged or chargeable with great and erroneous faults, drunkenness, filthiness of life, gamesters at cards and such like, are quietly suffered to remain." They inclose with the letter, a catalogue of the names of sundry persons—that is, first, of persons reported to be learned, zealous, and good preachers, who are deprived and suspended; secondly, of unfit persons suffered to continue without reprehension or any other proceeding taken against them; thirdly, of pluralists not resident. "Against all these sorts of lewd, evil, unprofitable, and corrupt members, we hear," say they, "of no inquisition, nor of any kind of proceeding to the reformation of those horrible offences in the church; but of great diligence, yea and extremity, used against those that are known diligent preachers;" and they add, "we do most earnestly desire your lordships to take some charitable consideration of these causes, that the people of the realm may not be deprived of their pastors, being diligent, learned, and zealous; though in some point ceremonial they may seem doubtful, only in conscience not in wilfulness."*

4. The archbishop answered,† in a firm though somewhat subdued manner, that he believed the information of the privy council would prove unfounded and their charges unjust; that of the deprived ministers in Essex, he personally knew but few; that if scandal could be proved against the conforming clergy they should be punished, though

---

* Fuller iii. ix. 36.   † Ib.

few or none of them had been presented, or complained of as evil-doers, by the churchwardens, _____
whose duty it was upon oath to make such pre-
sentments ; and that upon conference with the
bishop of London he would speedily return a more
exact answer. While this affair was pending the
lord treasurer wrote him on the subject of his
twenty-four articles, and in no measured terms.
Burghley had "recommended to his grace's favour,
two ministers, curates of Cambridgeshire, to be fa-
vourably heard." His grace replied, that they were
contentious, seditious, and irregular. Burghley,
on their return to him, " charged them sharply ;"
when they " denied the charges, and asked for a
fair trial and fitting punishment." Upon further
enquiry the lord treasurer discovered that they had
been subjected, not to a fair and open tribunal, but
to the inquisition of twenty-four articles, and that
even of these they were refused a copy. Cecil reminded them that they were " in no danger if they
answered to the truth ;" to which they replied, that
the questions were so many and so different that
they were unwilling to answer them " for fear of
captious interpretation." " Upon this," adds the
indignant lord treasurer, " I sent for the register
who brought me the articles ; which I have read,
and find so curiously penned, so full of branches
and circumstances, that I think the inquisition of
Spain use not so many questions to comprehend
and entrap their preys. I know your canonists
can defend these with all their particles. But
surely, under your grace's correction, this juridi-

cal and canonical siftening of poor ministers is not to edify and reform. And in charity, I think they ought not to answer all these nice points except they were very notorious offenders in papistry or heresy. Now, good my lord, bear with my scribbling; I write with testimony of a good conscience. I desire the peace of the church. I desire concord and unity in the exercise of our religion. I fear no sensual and wilful recusant. But I conclude, that, according to my simple judgment, this kind of proceeding is too much savouring the Romish inquisition, and is rather a device to seek for offenders than to reform any."*

5. It is not to be supposed that a man of Whitgift's character would incur these censures unmoved. He prepared an answer; and those who would do justice to his motives are bound to listen to his apology. Besides, in this his own defence of his own measures all that can be said in behalf of severities under which puritans writhed and from which statesmen recoiled, is summed up with whatever force of argument the case allows.

6. The archbishop's defence is contained in two letters addressed to the lord treasurer. He complains that the accusations brought against him were general; and could only be answered by a bare denial; but that if he or his colleagues were charged with particular acts of an oppressive or an illegal nature, he doubted not but that he could render a reply. His own proceedings against the nonconforming ministers had neither been so ve-

* Fuller iii. ix. 36—55.

hement, nor so general, as some pretended. Great
injury had been done to him in this respect : "if
indeed," he says, "any offence be, it is in bearing
too much with them, in consequence of which
they troubled the church and withstood their
primate." Papists, he said, (in answer to the
treasurer's remark that they rejoiced in these
severities when they saw them exercised by protestants upon each other) were indeed encouraged;
because they saw such persons, who with themselves despised the authorities of the English
church, encouraged in their disorderly conduct.
"Assure yourself," he adds, "the papists are rather
grieved at my proceedings, because they tend to
the taking away of their chief argument, that is,
that we cannot agree amongst ourselves ; and that
we are not of the church because we lack unity."
Touching the twenty-four articles, "he cannot but
greatly marvel at his lordship's vehement speeches
against them. He had caused them to be drawn
up according to law by those best learned in the
laws ; by men who hated alike the Romish doctrine and the Romish inquisition." He had taken
the ordinary course pursued in other courts ; " as,"
he says, " in the star chamber and other places.
And it was the usual one in the court of arches
with which he had the best experience." The
rules of evidence were then ill defined ; and the
civil courts set an example of most oppressive and
horrible tyranny in their conduct towards the accused. In this same year Throgmorton, a gentleman of Cheshire, was charged, on the evidence of
an intercepted letter, with a plot in favour of the

queen of Scots and against the queen's life. While under the torture of the rack he confessed his guilt. The confession he soon retracted, but repeated it on an assurance of the queen's pardon ; was sent to the scaffold, and there declared, what was probably true, that his admission of guilt was a mere fiction for the purpose of escaping a second application of torture. Yet it is not without surprise that we read the following sentence from the pen of one whose penetration was so acute, and whose sincerity so unquestionable, as that of Whitgift : " and without offence be it spoken, I think these articles more tolerable and better agreeing with the rules of justice and charity, and less captious, than those in other courts ; (meaning those in which the accused and the accuser confront each other) ; because there men are often examined at the relation of a private man (that is, on the evidence of an individual) concerning private crimes *et de propriâ turpitudine ;* whereas here, men are only examined of their public actions in the public calling and ministry ; and because the one toucheth life and the other not. And therefore, I see no cause why our judicial and canonical proceedings on this point should be misliked." If the articles were strained, the fault, he added, was in the judge, not in the law ; which hitherto had been administered with moderation. With regard to the ministers suspended, most of them were meanly qualified for their offices, open breakers and impugners of the law, young in years, proud in conceit, contentious in disposition. How could the peace of the church, how could

unity in religion, be restored, if a few young men
should be countenanced against the whole estate
of the clergy, persons of the greatest account for
learning, years, and piety ?   In conclusion, he had
done nothing which he did not think in his conscience and duty he was bound to do; and careless
of the evil tongues of the uncharitable or the displeasure of man, he was resolved to persevere.—
Such was the substance of the archbishop's defence,
which gave little satisfaction to lord Burghley.
" Your grace's proceeding," he replies, " I think
is, I will not say 'rigorous' or 'captious,' (expressions, at which Whitgift had taken offence), but
I think it is scant charitable."   This is the settled
verdict of posterity; whether Whitgift was sustained by the sanctions of the law or not, his
proceedings were " scant charitable;" and all
men now acquiesce in the justice of the remark
with which he concludes the correspondence.
" I have no leisure to write more, and therefore I will end; for writing will but increase
offence; and I mean not to offend your grace.
I am content that your grace and my lord of
London, where I hear Brown is"—one of the two
Cambridge ministers for whom he had interceded
—"use him as your wisdom shall think meet.   If I
had known his fault I might be blamed for writing
for him : but when *by examination only, it is meant
to sift him with twenty-four articles, I have cause
to pity the poor man.*"*

7. Whitgift rejoined without abating anything

* Fuller iii. ix. 55.

CHAPTER of his austerity. He said he had undertaken the
VI. defence, and the rights, of the church of England;
ELIZ. to appease the sects and schisms therein; and to
A. D. 1585. reduce all the ministers thereof to uniformity and
due obedience. "And herein," he adds, "I intend
to be constant, and not to waver with every wind."
Whether obstinacy or resolution dictated the sentence, the crowded prisons and the deserted pulpits
of England, through many a succeeding year of his
primacy, proved that it was at least no empty
threat.

8. Through the influence chiefly of the earl of
Leicester, a conference* was held between the
archbishop, assisted by the bishop of Winchester
on the one part, and the puritans, represented by
Sparke and Travers—afterwards famous in puritan
history—on the other. Leicester, Walsingham,
and lord Grey, were present as assessors. The conference—if it deserve the name—continued two
days, but it produced no important results. The
temper of the primate may be gathered from his
correspondence; that of the puritans may be inferred from an anecdote otherwise not of much importance. The archbishop had no sooner opened
the conference, than Dr. Sparke, after a few in-
troductory words, insisted on beginning the proceedings with prayer, and forthwith "framed
himself to begin to pray." The archbishop interrupted him, declaring that he should not turn

* Neal gives an account of it (from a manuscript in his possession),
i. vii. 341 : and see in Brooke's Lives of the Puritans, art. *Travers :*
who also refers to a MS. register of the proceedings.

the place into a conventicle. We cannot acquit
Sparke of an unbecoming freedom; and Whitgift
probably saw, or suspected, in his conduct, something very different from pure devotion, namely,
an effort to assert his pretensions as a presbyter,
and to place them on a level with those of an archbishop. But a conference thus begun was not
likely to end in any compromise or amicable ad-
justment. The puritans objected to private baptism, and especially against its administration by
women or laymen. This scruple has been often
treated as trivial and captious, but an important
question in theology lies beneath the surface;
viz., "whether children unbaptized perish," and
"whether outward baptism saves the child that
is baptized?" They objected against the use of
sponsors and of the cross in baptism: against
private communion: against the reading of the
apocrypha and the wearing of the surplice; and
lastly, against an ineffective ministry, pluralities,
and consequent non-residence. When the conference closed, each party carried away the opinions or the prejudices they brought with them
to the discussion. Travers was a nonconformist
to his death; and Whitgift was still the enemy of
the puritans. It produced, says an old writer, no
effect on the disputants, little on the auditors, yet
as much on all as any judicious person ever expected. "The probability is," observes sir James
Macintosh upon this occurrence, "that the conference ended leaving the convictions of both
parties as it found them, or rooted more firmly.

CHAPTER
VI.

ELIZ.

A.D. 1585.

1584.

Private meditation may enlighten,—in a public dispute the object is not truth but victory."*

9. A refractory spirit, and much insubordination (to a degree indeed inconsistent with all order and discipline) no doubt existed amongst the clergy. How to reduce it to submission, whether by force or by concession, or by a mild and considerate exercise of power mingled with forbearance, was the question which ought to have been calmly weighed by the rulers of the church. Unhappily the roughest methods were adopted, and apparently with little or no regret. The spirit of Aylmer and Whitgift was the vulgar one to which harsh measures present themselves, not as a last but as a first alternative; and they plunged into them with alacrity. That there were, amongst the puritans, many good and humble men whose conscientious nonconformity was distressing to themselves, they refused to believe. It was evident there were turbulent and factious spirits whom no reasonable concessions would appease,— and no party, struggling for its rights and suffering from oppression, is without them,—but such were not the majority. And the great fault of the primate and his coadjutors was, that they confounded the evil and the good, and practised a degree of severity upon the best of their opponents, which the worst of them scarcely merited. Aylmer, in his visitation this year, suspended, in Essex alone, thirty-eight ministers for refusing to wear the surplice and similar offences. They were men highly esteemed by their parishioners; and

* Hist. of Eng. in loco.

their forced silence was the occasion of deep and
mutual distress. An incredible number were thus
silenced, or even deprived of their parishes, in
various counties.* It is said by puritan writers,
that at one period towards the close of this reign,
no less than a third of the whole beneficed clergy
of England were thus suspended: and to most of
them this was a sentence, which, as its lightest
evil, involved destitution and penury. The sufferings of such a number of ministers, men of
high character and extraordinary zeal and diligence, was alone enough to shew that the dissatisfaction was deep and general. If there
was danger in permitting diversities, was there
none in repressing them? Might not a schism
arise from their secession, which should tear up
the church to its foundations? Were the questions at issue of vital consequence? And was
it not wiser to provide for the effervescence of a
well-meaning zeal, however troublesome, within
the bosom of the church, rather than to cast off
those fiery energies which might, and probably
would, otherwise be arrayed against it? Above
all, ought not christian meekness and moderation
to be shewn, even to the obstinate, much more to
the misguided?

10. But no weight was given to these considerations. The only choice was between strict conformity, and fines, dungeons, and ejectment. One
minister, Mr. Knight, for not wearing the surplice,
suffered six months' imprisonment, and was fined

* Neal i. vi. 287.

CHAPTER a hundred marks.* Another was suspended on
VI. the same account. "His hungry sheep that had
ELIZ. no shepherd,"—for so his parishioners described
A.D. 1585. themselves,—addressed a letter to him entreating
him to conform; but he could not do so, he replied, with a safe conscience, and was deprived.
Amongst a multitude of others scarcely less deplorable, the case of Eusebius Paget, minister of
Kilkhampton,† in the diocese of Exeter, claims
attention. When first presented to the living, he
had expressly informed his patron and the bishop
that he could not use some rites, nor comply with
some directions, in the service book; still he was
inducted. He is described as a learned, peaceable,
and quiet divine, indefatigable in his work, travelling through the neighbouring country, and
preaching in dark places the plain principles of
religion. But he was brought before the high
commission upon several charges; some of which,
if proved, amount to indiscretion, and not one of
them to heresy. He preached, and not without reason, that "the late queen Mary was a wicked woman
and a Jezebel." With more questionable zeal and
equal courtesy, "he called ministers that don't
preach, dumb dogs." Then, he disallowed the use
of organs, and taught that holydays were but the
traditions of men, which we are not obliged to
follow. Another charge was, that he had said
the pope might set up the feast of jubilee as well
as the feasts of easter and pentecost. His false

* Neal i. vii. 342.
† Neal i. vii. 349. Brooke's Lives, art. Paget.

doctrine consisted merely in having taught that
"the sacraments were but dull elements, and did
not avail without the word preached ;" and that
"Christ did not descend into hell both soul and
body." The former of these propositions admits,
if it do not require, a sound interpretation. And
with regard to Christ's descent into hell—meaning
thereby, as no doubt he did, the place of torment,—
no inconsiderable number of the English clergy,
with bishop Pearson as their guide, have always
strongly inclined to the same opinion. His disloyalty was argued from the single fact that he
did not, in his prayers, mention the queen's " supremacy in *both* estates ;" which is at least an admission that he allowed it in one of them ; he
allowed her supremacy as a civil magistrate.—He
pleaded in his defence, that when he undertook
the charge of his parish, he received a promise
from his ordinary that he should not be urged to
a compliance with those ceremonies for neglecting
which he was now accused, " and that although he
had omitted some things mentioned in the book,
he had introduced no novelties of any kind : his
faults were those of omission ; nor did he now
refuse to adopt the common prayer book, hereafter, could his scruples be satisfied. He modestly
asked to be permitted to confer either with his
own bishop, or with other persons to be named
by the commissioners themselves, for the solution
of his doubts ;" which, said he, " I seek not for
any desire I have to keep the said living, but
only for the better resolution and satisfaction of

my own conscience, as God knoweth." This was refused; he was immediately suspended,—and preaching afterwards, deprived. The hardship of the case was thought to be increased by the haste with which the commission proceeded in the first instance; and, further, by the fact that he had obtained from the archbishop a remission, if not a release, from the censure of suspension before he had ventured to resume his ministry. This release he believed to be a sufficient warrant for preaching, the archbishop himself being the chief commissioner. But the court was stern, and his living was declared vacant and disposed of to another. Having a large family, he set up a school. But the relentless court of high commission pounced once more on their mangled victim, requiring him to take out a licence; and, as a previous condition, to subscribe to the articles. This he declined to do, and was at once reduced to beggary. The great naval commander, sir John Hawkins, was his friend. From a letter he addressed to his patron we quote a few sentences: " I was never present at any separate assembly from the church, but abhorred them. I always resorted to my parish church, and received the sacrament according to the book (that is, in a kneeling posture). I thought it my duty not to forsake the church because of some blemishes in it. I am turned out of my living by commandment. I afterwards preached without living or a penny stipend; and when I was forbid I ceased. I then taught a few chil-

dren, to get a little bread for myself and mine
to eat; some disliked this, and wished me to
forbear; which I have done; and am now to go
as an idle rogue and vagabond from door to door
to beg my bread." His sufferings, or at least
his silence, was prolonged through Whitgift's
life. It is some consolation to record, that upon
the primate's death he was reinstated in the ministry, and presented to the living of St. Agnes
in Aldersgate. Kindness accomplished what severity had essayed in vain. A virtuous and
godly minister was restored to usefulness and
honour, and died in conformity with the church
of England.

11. Pages might be filled with similar details :
but the protracted sufferings of Cartwright, still
the great leader of the party, and possessing all
the advantages which superior skill and wisdom
in controversy and the countenance of the great
and wealthy could impart, claim especial notice.
Whether they prove more pertinacity in Cartwright, or severity in Whitgift and his associates,
is now a stale dispute which we shall make no
endeavour to revive. They are events which belong to history ; and the hardships of the master
of puritanism may be taken as a specimen, only
too correct, of the hardships of its meaner disciples. If Cartwright was thus harassed, what
may have been the unknown sorrows of less cautious or less favoured men ?

12. Upon his expulsion from the university,
already noticed, Cartwright retired to the con-

CHAPTER tinent.* For some time he lived at Antwerp, and
VI. presided over the English congregation there;
ELIZ. while the most distinguished scholars of Europe,
A.D. 1585. amongst whom were Beza and Junius, thought
themselves honoured by his friendship. Beza
had indeed long since spoken of him, in one of his
letters, as a young man of the highest promise,
and, for his age, probably the greatest scholar in
the world. After a while he was invited by the
French protestants in Guernsey and Jersey to
their assistance. He drew up a form of discipline for their use, and established their church
on the Genevan model; but he shortly returned
to Antwerp. After an exile of eleven years his
health failed; and his life being in imminent
danger, he wrote to the privy council, requesting
permission to return home. His friends, Leicester and Burghley, not only mentioned his name
with honour in the house of lords, but interceded
with the queen. But their efforts were vain;
the permission to return was not granted; when
Cartwright, on the advice of his physicians,
and resolving to lay his bones at least in his
native land, appeared in England. He had no
sooner reached his native shores, than Aylmer
bishop of London had him apprehended and
imprisoned. Happily for Cartwright, Aylmer, in
the hurry of his zeal, had forgotten to wait for
the queen's permission; and it was not at all of
Elizabeth's temper to suffer these freaks of despotism in her subjects, however much disposed

* Brooke's Life of Cartwright.

to them herself. Cartwright was released; and
Aylmer endeavoured to propitiate the queen in
a letter to lord Burghley. " I leave it to God
and your wisdom," he says, " to consider in what
a dangerous place of service I am. But God
whom I serve, and in whose hands are the hearts
of princes, can and will turn all to the best, and
stir up such honourable friends as you are, to
appease her highness's indignation. In the mean
time, my good lord, I will vow myself to you,
as my chief patron under God and her majesty.
And surely you shall find me neither undutiful
nor unthankful." Were anything wanting to
complete our disgust, it would be the fact that
the man who penned this servility had been
himself a puritan, and had written against the
bishops in a strain of insolent vulgarity* which
Cartwright disdained.—" Come off, you bishops;
away with your superfluities, let your portion
be priest-like, not prince-like;—could the bishops
ruffle in their robes, keep their great horses, and
have their thousands yearly, with all the rest of
their superfluity, if the queen were not their
bulwark, and took not care of them while they
care not for her ?"

13. Whitgift, though severe, was not vindictive;
and he was probably ashamed of Aylmer's cruelty.
It was from the primate Cartwright received his
release, though not until he had been several
months in prison. The interview between the

* In his " Arbour for faithful Subjects," published soon after the
queen's accession.

CHAPTER
VI.

ELIZ.
A. D.
1585—90.

1585.

two great leaders seems to have produced a good impression upon each. Cartwright behaved with respect and modesty, and Whitgift for a time was softened into kindness. The earl of Leicester wrote, as Cartwright's friend and patron, a letter full of gratitude to Whitgift, and even ventured to ask that he might once more be allowed to preach. This request the archbishop declined to grant without longer trial, and until he should be " better persuaded of his conformity." Leicester, however, had founded an asylum, or hospital, at Warwick, and he appointed Cartwright to the first mastership. Here he resided in peace for some years ; and if the friendship and patronage of a majority of the greatest statesmen of an age so rich in statesmanship were a security against persecution, it might have been reasonably concluded that the remainder of his days would have passed in quietness. Among the friends or patrons of this puritan divine, were the earls of Leicester, Warwick, Bedford, and Huntingdon, lord Bacon, lord Burghley, sir Francis Knollys, and sir Francis Walsingham. A man so honoured must have possessed some rare combination of attractive qualities.

14. His leisure was worthily employed. The Romish party, perceiving with dismay the effect produced by the translation of the bible into English, issued a version of their own. It was a translation of the new testament from the Latin vulgate, but was in fact designed to depreciate the English translation, and to insinuate the cor-

ruptions of the church of Rome. It is known to scholars as the Rhemish translation.

15. It was considered among protestants a work of dangerous tendency ; and the rather, on account of the notes and annotations it contained : and the question of Cartwright's high accomplishments, both as a scholar and a divine, is entirely set at rest by the fact that he was solicited to undertake its refutation. One of his biographers asserts that the queen applied to Beza, requesting him to undertake the work ; and that he referred her majesty to Cartwright as a much fitter person. It is certain that the earl of Leicester and secretary Walsingham urged him to this important task, and that the latter sent him the noble present of a hundred pounds towards the purchase of books, with the promise of further assistance were it wanted. The clergy of the city of London and those of Suffolk intreated him to proceed ; above all, the university of Cambridge, or, at least, a number of its principal divines, addressed a letter to him filled with expressions of reverence and regard. " We are earnest," they say, " most reverend Cartwright, that you should set yourself against the unhallowed designs of mischievous men, either by refuting the whole book, or at least some part thereof . . . you see to what an honourable fight we invite you. Christ's business must be undertaken against Satan's champions. We stir you up to fight the battles of the Lord where the victory is certain, and the triumph and applause of angels will ensue. Our

prayers shall never be wanting to you. Christ
without doubt, whose cause is defended, will be
present with you. The Lord Jesus must increase
your courage and strength, and keep you very
long in safety for his church's good. Farewell.
Your loving brethren in Christ." The paper bore
the signature, amongst others, of Dr. Whitaker,
master of St. John's and regius professor, and of
Dr. Fulke, master of Pembroke college, whose
testimony receives a double worth from his profound acquaintance with this particular controversy. In the year 1583 he had published his own
learned " Defence of the English translation of
the holy scriptures, in reply to Gregory Martin's
slanders." Martin was a reader of divinity in the
English college of Rheims, and in the previous
year had published what he called, " A discovery
of the manifold corruptions of the holy scriptures
by the heretics of our days, specially the English
sectaries."

16. With a stretch of power seldom exceeded
in the most arbitrary times, or under governments
the most despotic, Whitgift forbad him to proceed.
It is a curious instance, no less of his resolute
temper than of his unbounded power, whenever the
queen's prejudices coincided with his own. Her
ministers of state at this time were strongly in
favour of the puritans. Walsingham and Leicester
had requested Cartwright to undertake the refutation, and provided him with money for his expenses. Burghley sanctioned it. Yet Whitgift prevailed, and the mightiest statesmen were foiled;

and Walsingham was made to understand that although he was minister of state he was not minister of religion. Whitgift's motives have been
variously construed. He no doubt was apprehen-
sive that puritan notions might be introduced
under the cover of a commentary ; that, professing
to aim at Rome, Cartwright might have struck
at Lambeth. But the same authority which
suppressed the book would have been better
directed, if necessary, in controlling its revisal.
The affair gave rise to much discussion : some
affected to question Cartwright's learning; some
commended the archbishop's care, and some
blamed his jealousy. The time had not yet come
when a sense of justice, forcing its way through all
considerations of policy or convenience, branded
the oppressive act with the stamp of mere tyranny.
Cartwright afterwards resumed the work, but his
death prevented its completion. At length it was
published in an imperfect state in the year 1618.
" A book," says Fuller, " which, notwithstanding
the aforesaid defects, is so complete that the
Rhemists durst never return the least answer
thereunto."

17. But Cartwright's troubles were not over.
His preaching at Warwick provoked the hostility
of the bishop of Worcester, who summoned him in
the consistory court, and charged him with instil-
ling the peculiarities of Genevan churchmanship.
He was permitted, however, to return to Warwick,
where he soon afterwards drew up an able treatise
against the brownists. Meanwhile his patron the

CHAPTER
VI.
─────
ELIZ.
A. D.
1585—90.

earl of Leicester died, and in a short time Cartwright was summoned before the court of high commission. The charges were of the usual complexion. That he had neglected the rubrics; that he had established the discipline of foreign churches; that he had shewn his dislike to the ecclesiastical laws and government; and in particular, that he had written all or some part of "The book of discipline;" and that he knew, or had credibly heard, who were the authors of " Martin Mar-prelate."—The book of discipline was a form or directory of presbyterian worship, published abroad a few years previously, but lately translated into English; and Martin Mar-prelate the title of a series of satirical pamphlets, which caused no little commotion for several years by their ludicrous and malicious scurrility. Whatever Cartwright's share may have been in the former of these productions, his whole character forbids us to suspect him of any connection with the latter; had he not denied, as he uniformly did, all knowledge of the authors, or indeed approbation of the pamphlets.

17. Cartwright nobly refused to take the oath ex officio, which might have compelled him to criminate his friends as well as to become his own accuser. His committal to the Fleet followed of course. He appealed in vain to the archbishop, the lord chancellor, and his tried friend lord Burghley. To add to his sufferings, his devoted flock at Warwick were left untaught; while the agonizing pains of the gout and stone, increased by his confinement, filled up the mea-

sure of his sorrows. After repeated solicitations, CHAPTER
he implored, in a *fourth* petition to lord Burghley, VI.
that he might be imprisoned in the house of ELIZ.
some friend in or near the city, under proper A.D.
securities. One of his children died, and he 1585—90.
asked to return home, giving sufficient bail to
appear when called for. But his petitions were
disregarded. Burghley at length remonstrated
with the queen, and was " bold to tell her majesty that he thought the bishops took a very ill
and unadvised course." Together with other divines, amongst whom were Dr. Whitaker, Travers, Chadderton, and Knewstubs, the heads of
the puritans, he was charged by the commissioners with holding irregular synods, or classes,
in London, Cambridge, and other places, with
the view of promoting the introduction of presbyterianism. The discipline they endeavoured
to introduce was denounced as prejudicial to her
majesty and the realm in several particulars;—
as for instance, that it proposed the abolition of
the rights of patronage, placing in the congregation the election to vacant parishes; and that
in ecclesiastical causes the final appeal was made
not to the queen, but to the church assembled in a general synod. And the prisoners were
accused of wishing to make the prince himself amenable to censure and excommunication.
Still refusing the oath, they were handed over to
the star chamber on Whitgift's motion, and were
from time to time interrogated before one or
other of these tribunals. For it is to be observed,

that the high commission did not lose its grasp, though it called in the star chamber to its assistance. At length public opinion was aroused; magistrates petitioned against the iniquity of punishing without a trial, and of condemning without a hearing; parliament was restless, and the privy council angry; terms were offered to the prisoners, and rejected with disdain. A petition to the queen from Cartwright and his fellow sufferers produced a tardy effect, and at last they were released from prison,—it has been said, at Whitgift's intercession. But even this faint praise appears to be undeserved. A letter from Cartwright, dated 21 May, 1592, and addressed to the lord treasurer, "in dutiful remembrance of so great a benefit," obliges us to confess that to the humanity of the statesman was due an act of justice which the harshness of the prelate had denied.

18. Cartwright was now old and hastening to the grave. He returned to his beloved charge at Warwick, and, still under a bond for his good behaviour, continued to preach. On the Sunday before his death, as if with something of a prophetic forecast, he preached from Ecclesiastes xii. 7, " Then shall the dust return to the earth, and the spirit shall return to God who gave it." His biographer relates that on the Tuesday morning following, he spent two hours prostrate on his knees in humble and importunate prayer; and that, having finished his devotions, he said that " he had found unutterable comfort and happiness,

and that God had given him a glimpse of heaven, before he was called to enter that blessed state." He died within a few hours afterwards, Dec. 27, 1603, aged 68 years. His great antagonist Whitgift expired within three months. They were members and ministers of the same church : upon doctrinal points there was no important difference between them. The one saw the imperfections of the church of England, the other felt the dangers of innovation. They were attached to the same cause, and alike desirous of establishing a national church in England on protestant foundations ; and had conciliation been attempted, there seems little reason to doubt that Cartwright, without forsaking his principles, would have been won over to a more submissive spirit, and to a zealous co-operation with men of real piety—and there were many such among his professed opponents. He attached too much importance to his peculiar opinions of church discipline, and those opinions we conceive were often wrong ; and in the early years of his public life he was not free from the universal vices of his times,—intemperance and personality in controversy. But as age mellowed and persecution broke down his spirit, a noble love of truth, a generous and forgiving temper, a contempt of suffering, and a fervent piety to God, break out with increasing lustre ; and while learning, eloquence, and high talents, associated with exalted religious principles, and these displayed with consistency through a long life of persecution, shall continue to be revered, the name of Cart-

CHAPTER
VI.

ELIZ.

A.D. 1585.

wright will be uttered, by good men of every party, with profound respect.

19. No record of the persecutions which the puritans underwent in the reign of Elizabeth can omit the names of Smith, Penry, and Udal. The former, illustrious for his talents; the other two, for enduring, with the patience of martyrs, the most dreadful sufferings; and all alike for a glowing, though sometimes misdirected, zeal and sincere piety. Henry Smith* was a person of good family and well connected; but having some scruples, he declined preferment, and aspired to nothing higher than the weekly lectureship of St. Clement Danes. On a complaint made by bishop Aylmer, Whitgift suspended him, and silenced for a while probably the most eloquent preacher in Europe. His contemporaries named him the Chrysostom of England. His church was crowded to excess, and amongst his hearers, persons of the highest rank, and those of the most cultivated and fastidious judgment, were content to stand in the throng of citizens. His sermons† and treatises were soon to be found in the hands of every person of taste and piety; they passed through numberless editions ; some of them were carried abroad and translated into Latin. They were still admired and read at the close of nearly a century, when Fuller collected and republished them. Probably the prose writing of this the

* Brooke's Lives, Art. Henry Smith.
† God's arrow against atheists ; Sermons at St. Clement Danes ; Six sermons, with prayers, &c. Printed by John Beale, 1621.

richest period of genuine English literature, contains nothing finer than some of his sermons.
They are free, to an astonishing degree, from the
besetting vices of his age—vulgarity, and quaintness and affected learning; and he was one of the
first English preachers who, without submitting
to the trammels of a pedantic logic, conveyed, in
language nervous, pure, and beautiful, the most
convincing arguments in the most lucid order, and
made them the groundwork of fervent and impassioned addresses to the conscience. The lord treasurer was his friend; and that he was restored to
his lectureship and to the church of England after
a brief suspension, we owe, among many obligations of a similar kind, to the name of Cecil.

20. Udal* was charged with being the author
of a seditious libel, entitled "A demonstration of
discipline," in which the prelates were coarsely
handled, too much in the style of Martin Mar-prelate. The passage fixed upon as the ground of the
indictment, occurs in the preface, and is certainly
unjust and scandalous. "Who can, without blush-
ing, deny you (the bishops) to be the cause of all
ungodliness, &c. You care for nothing but your
dignities, be it to the damnation of your own souls
and infinite millions more." Had the punishment
due to a libeller been awarded to the author, posterity would have confirmed the judgment. But
his fault sinks into insignificance when compared
with his sufferings; we admire his patience, and
forget his libel. He refused to criminate himself

* Fuller iii. ix. 135. Neal i. viii. 399. Udal's Life. Whitgift's do.

before the high commission, and was then tried
for sedition, at the assizes at Croydon, and convicted, though without any sufficient proof that
he was the author of the work in question; it
being generally supposed that he had only contributed the preface. A form of recantation was laid
before him; but neither arguments nor threats
could induce him to subscribe it with his name.
Yet he drew up a qualified submission, acknowledging that as to the book the authorship of
which was imputed to him, though he "could not
disavow the cause and substance of the doctrine
debated in it," yet he "confessed the manner to
be such, in some parts, as might worthily be
blamed;" and he prayed most humbly her majesty's forgiveness. He was respited to the next
assizes, when he was placed at the bar in irons,
with the rest of the felons, and condemned to
death. He delivered a paper, in which he protested against the sentence on several grounds,
any one of which ought to have saved him from
so ignominious a fate. It had not been proved,
he said, that he was the author of the book in
question. The witnesses had not confronted him
in open court. He was condemned on the evidence contained in certain papers and reports of
depositions. The jury had been directed by the
judge to find a verdict only on the fact whether
he was the author of the book; they were cautioned from inquiring into the intent of the
writer; whereas, according to the statute, the
felony consisted in the malicious intent. The

jury too were wrought upon, partly by the promise that the verdict should not endanger the
prisoner, and partly by fear; "as appears from
the grief manifested by some of them ever since."
"And supposing," he adds, "I were the author
of the book; let it be remembered that for substance it contains nothing but what is taught and
believed by the reformed churches in Europe : so
that, in condemning me, you condemn all such
nations and churches as hold the same doctrine.
If the punishment be for the manner of writing,
this may be thought by some, worthy of an admonition, or fine, or some short imprisonment. But
death for an error of such a kind cannot but be
extreme cruelty against one who has endeavoured
to shew himself a dutiful subject and a faithful
minister of the gospel." And he concluded his
address with this solemn premonition; "If all
this prevail not, yet my Redeemer liveth, to whom
I commend myself, and say, as Jeremiah once
said, in a case not much unlike mine, ' Behold, I
am in your hands to do with me whatsoever
seemeth good unto you; but know you this, that
if you put me to death, you shall bring innocent
blood upon your own heads, and upon the land.'
As the blood of Abel so the blood of Udal, will cry
to God with a loud voice, and the righteous Judge
of the land will require it at the hands of all who
shall be found guilty of it."

21. Whether the court were awed by this appeal, or, which is more probable, by the protest
that preceded it, it hesitated to carry the sentence

CHAPTER into immediate effect. Elizabeth herself hesitated;
VI. for Udal was a learned man, of blameless life, re-
ELIZ. markable for his devotion, and an able preacher.
A. D. 1590. A Hebrew grammar, which he composed while in
prison, attests at once his learning and his composure of mind. He had many friends, and multitudes flocked to visit him in prison. James,
king of Scotland, the eager expectant of her
throne, wrote a letter of intercession to Elizabeth
on his behalf, earnestly requesting his pardon as
a personal favour. The merchants of London en-
treated that he might at least be banished; and
offered a chaplaincy in the Mediterranean as an
asylum for him. Meantime, a higher Judge had,
in mercy, reversed the unrighteous sentence, and
while his fate was in suspense, Udal died in the
Marshalsea prison, worn down with sorrow, at the
1592. close of the year 1592. We may believe the historian who tells us, that his friends were glad that
he should die in peace, and that the wisest of his
foes were well contented that he escaped their
vengeance. He was buried at St. George's, Southwark; the ministers of London flocking to the
funeral; and by their presence protesting against
the iniquitous sentence with which a preposterous
tyranny had vainly endeavoured to destroy his
principles, while it cut short his life. It was remarked that his grave was near to that of bishop
Bonner; a few feet of earth separated the bodies
of two men, of principles so far asunder. Time
has long since shewn that might is on the side of
him who suffers, not of him who torments.

22. The fate of Penry was yet more barbarous. CHAPTER
He was a young Welsh clergyman, of ardent zeal, VI.
and possibly but little discretion : and his capacity ELIZ.
was of that ordinary mould which seeks for truth A.D. 1592.
at the antipodes of error. Preaching was depreciated by his opponents ; an error which he cor-
rected by asserting that it was the only means of
salvation ; that a homily was no preaching, and
that mere readers were no ministers. He was
committed to prison, but released after a month's
confinement ; and then fled to Scotland, where he
remained upwards of two years. During his absence, he drew up a petition to the queen, which
might well have provoked,by its rude and offensive
language, a much gentler monarch. It was seized
among his papers, and he was indicted for seditious
language, and was convicted of felony in the court
of king's bench, upon the matter contained in this
petition, although it was but a rough outline, and
certainly had not in any sense been published.
Penry was a brownist, and declaimed upon his
trial with all the vehemence of his party against
" those remains of antichrist " of which he was
anxious, he said, " to have the world cleared ;"
namely, the dignitaries of the church of England.
But after his conviction he did not attempt to defend the petition ; it was confused and unfinished,
he said, containing the sum of certain objections
made by others against her majesty and her government, which he intended at some future period
to examine, but that he had not so much as looked
into them for the last fourteen months.—But he

CHAPTER VI.

ELIZ.

A. D. 1593.

retracted nothing of his principles. " If my blood were an ocean, and every drop were a life to me, I would, by the help of the Lord, give it all in defence of the same."—" Death, I thank God, I fear not. I know that the sting of death is taken away,—life I desire not, if I be guilty of sedition .... but imprisonments, indictments, arraignments, and death are not weapons to convince the conscience that is grounded on God's word." In vain he asked for a conference ; in vain his wife presented a petition to the lord keeper. The warrant for his execution was signed ; and amongst the signatures, the first, be it said with shame, was Whitgift's. The instrument was immediately sent to the sheriff ; and the very same day, while the prisoner was at dinner, he received his summons to the scaffold: that afternoon he was carried in a cart to the gallows and hung, without being allowed, as he desired, to address the assembled crowd, or to profess his faith towards God or his loyalty to the queen. He was but thirty-four years old ; but the zealots of the high court party triumphed in their victory. " By his death," exclaims an old writer, the neck of the fiery nonconformists was broken."* It is more certain that they concealed their grief and nourished their hatred, and that the next generation took, for this and other enormities, a terrible and equally wicked revenge.

* Wood, Athenæ Oxon. i. 229 ; Brooke's Lives ii. 49.

CHAPTER VII.

1. IT belongs to the secular historian to relate how the seeds of English liberty were taking root and gathering strength during the long reign of Elizabeth. The house of commons became the constitutional arena on which the strife of political principles was carried on ; and we begin to perceive the existence of those two great parties, the one inclined to prerogative and the support of ancient usages and institutions, the other to an extension of popular rights, which have survived to our own times unaltered in their essential character ; and upon the equipoise and true balancing of which, our national safety seems, under divine providence, in a great measure to depend. Puritanism naturally found its advocates amongst those who were least inclined to acquiesce in the monarch's high claims to absolute power. Their early connection with the puritans, more perhaps than any other cause, contributed to unite them into a compact body, and to impress

CHAPTER VII.

ELIZ.

A. D. 1595.

them, when thus united, with certain features which have never been erased. To the puritans the country or whig party owes the extraordinary vigour of its youth, and not a few of the principles of its maturer age.

2. The puritans had already laid their griefs before the parliament. We have mentioned that in 1572, Field and Wilcox, eminent men amongst them, assisted by some others, had drawn up and presented a petition, entitled " An admonition to the parliament;" to which, by way of appendix, and to shew how far the foreign churches agreed with them, were added a letter which Beza had lately addressed to the earl of Leicester urging further reformations, and one from Gualter to bishop Parkhurst on the same subject. The attempt was rash: in those days it was thought seditious and revolutionary ; for the admonition petitioned for a church upon the presbyterian model, and the subversion of episcopacy. Elizabeth considered that whatever concerned the royal prerogative was forbidden ground, and under this description she included every thing that related to religion. Field and Wilcox were committed to Newgate, indicted under the statute of uniformity, and sentenced to a year's imprisonment.* The admonition was repressed by royal proclamation, and parliament was forbidden to proceed in the discussion of such questions. On several occasions the queen interfered to controul

* Neal i. v. 224, and Price's History of Non-Conformity, i. 231.

the debates; and at length sent for the speaker,
and charged him sharply "that henceforth no
bills concerning religion should be received into
the house of commons, unless the same should be
first considered and approved of by the clergy,"—
that is, by her council and herself, for the conforming clergy now moved only at her bidding.
Peter Wentworth was one of the most eloquent
members of the house of commons, and he was a
puritan. He took up the cause with the mind of
a statesman; and, rising above the particular
case under discussion, aimed at nothing less than
the establishment of freedom of speech in the
commons house of parliament as the means of
rational liberty in England. "There is nothing,"
he said, " so necessary for the preservation of the
prince and state as free speech; and without this
it is a scorn and mockery to call it a parliament
house, for in truth it is none, but a very school
of flattery and dissimulation, and so a fit place
to serve the devil and his angels in, and not
to glorify God, and benefit the commonwealth."
And with a still more hazardous boldness, asserting the supremacy of the law above the sovereign
himself; "the king," he continued, " ought not
to be under man but under God and the law;
because the law maketh him a king; let the king
therefore attribute that to the law which the law
attributeth to him; that is, dominion and power.
For he is not a king whom will, and not the law,
doth rule; and therefore he ought to be under
the law." The house interrupted him in alarm;

CHAPTER he was committed to the sergeant's custody, and
VII. the next day to prison, " for the violent and
ELIZ. wicked words yesterday pronounced by him touch-
A. D. 1595. ing the queen's majesty." Wentworth was not at
all surprised : he had anticipated the worst; and
was prepared for it. " I have weighed," he said,
" whether, in good conscience and the duty of a
faithful subject, I might keep myself out of prison, and not to warn my prince from walking in
a dangerous course. My conscience said that I
could not be a faithful subject if I did more
respect to avoid my own danger than my prince's
danger. I was made bold and went forward, as
your honours heard." A month's reflection, or
the wiser advice of her ministers, convinced the
queen that her severity was impolitic. Wentworth was released. Constitutional principles
must be regarded as having obtained a great
triumph, and the house of commons a position
which it has never lost. But happily there was
no rupture, nor even a coldness, between the
commons and herself. " Elizabeth," says an able
teacher of modern history, " could always give
way in time to render her concessions a favour.
Unlike other arbitrary princes, and unlike chiefly
in this particular, she did *not* think it a mark of
political wisdom always to persevere when her
authority was resisted. She did not suppose
that her subjects, if she yielded to their petitions or complaints, would conclude that she
did so from fear; she did not conclude, that if

she became more reasonable, they must necessarily become less so."*

3. A few years afterwards, in 1584, the commons themselves undertook the cause of the puritans. They presented an address to the upper
house, containing sixteen particulars. Six were
directed against insufficient ministers, pluralities, and destitute parishes, of which there was
said to be a great number, especially in the
north of England and in Wales. They proceeded
to request that more liberty might be conceded
to the consciences of the clergy; that they might
not be troubled for the omission of some rites or
portions prescribed in the book of common prayer;
that some common exercises and conferences,
such as the suppressed prophecyings, might be
permitted; and that the power of the bishops in
grave matters might not be deputed to commissaries and officials, but executed by themselves
in person : that excommunication should not be
inflicted for small matters, especially upon godly
and learned preachers, who were neither convicted of open crimes nor apparent errors in doctrine : and they prayed that the court of high
commission, except for some notable offence,
should no longer have the power of summoning
and arraigning the clergy beyond the limits of
the diocese in which they dwelt.†

4. These, with a single exception, were reasonable demands. How far the clergy might be in-

* Professor Smyth, Modern Hist. Lect. XIV., where the reader will
also find Wentworth's speech as above.
† Fuller iii. ix.; Neal i. vii.; Strype's Whitgift, 160—190.

CHAPTER dulged in a partial conformity, even supposing
VII. them sincerely attached, upon the whole, to the
ELIZ. communion of the English church, was then, as it
A. D. 1595. still continues to be, an anxious question. The
rude hand of arbitrary power, and the contemptuous spirit of insubordination, feel no difficulty.
Gentler spirits, embued with a deeper love of justice, hesitate and pause. If the enactment must
be rigidly obeyed, it should be framed so as to sit
easily upon a scrupulous conscience,—nay, upon
an independent spirit. Otherwise the energy of the
christian minister is lost, to say nothing of his integrity. Again, since every society, whether secular or ecclesiastical, forced or voluntary, must be
governed by its peculiar laws, which, from the va-
riety of men's minds, will necessarily press with
unequal weight upon its various members, and
which therefore cannot be alike acceptable to
all; it follows that each member must be content
to sacrifice much of his inclination,—nay, it may
be, something of his conscientious principles, of his
abstract ideas of what, in particular instances,
would be the most fitting and the best,—for the
sake of mutual co-operation, and all those other
advantages which result from united as opposed
to solitary action. Each of the contending parties, the prelates on the one hand and the puritans
on the other, admitted the force, not of these joint
considerations, but merely of one or other of them
singly. Neither would admit the truth contained
in what the other party advanced; and of course
while the prelates insisted only on the duty of

submission, and the puritans only on the hardships of canonical obedience, discussion served
but to increase the distance, and aggravate the
quarrel.

5. In the house of lords the discussion turned
chiefly on the question of non-residence; which
archbishop Whitgift defended with an argument
which, had pluralities been limited to the poorer
clergy, would have been triumphant. There were
in England, he said, four thousand five hundred
benefices not valued at more than ten, and most
of them at less than eight, pounds per annum.
How could able pastors, such as the petitioners
required, be provided for such livings? Moreover,
he affirmed, (and the practical wisdom of the assembly in which he spoke would attach its full
importance to the observation) that whatever was
pretended to the contrary, England at that very
time possessed more able ministers than ever;
" yea, that we had more than all christendom
besides." The lord Grey admitted the assertion
as to the number of learned ministers, but he
attributed their increase not to the bishops but to
God. Burghley, the lord treasurer, took a middle
course; and would have allowed pluralities, provided the livings were near each other; " at least
in the same diocese, and not one in Winchester and
another in the north." The archbishop and the
clergy were alarmed, and petitioned the queen to
interfere that the proposed bill against pluralities
might not pass into a law. The certain consequence, they said, of such a measure would be,

the decay of learning, the renewed spoiling of the church, the taking away the set form of prayer in the churches, and in short a return to confusion and barbarism. " Our neighbours' miseries," they add, " might make us fearful." And in truth the confusion then prevailing among the foreign churches was the great argument which induced the moderate and reasonable of all parties to submit to grievous inconvenience, as at least preferable to the hazards of a change. The matter, for the present, went no further.

6. The archbishop and clergy, whether dreading the interference of the house of commons, or being convinced that some reform was wanted, laid before the queen six articles, which fell far short of what the parliament had contemplated, but were probably more suited to the difficulty of their own position, and the necessities of the times. But they were promoted with but languid zeal; nor was it till thirteen years afterwards they were carried into effect. In 1597 they were confirmed in convocation, and afterwards in 1603 introduced among the canons of the church. At the close of the session, the speaker ventured to express a firm hope that her majesty would, by strait commandment to her clergy, insist on the removal of such abuses as had crept in by the negligence of the ministers. The queen's answer is by no means complimentary to the ecclesiastical rulers. After censuring the dissatisfied spirit of those who loved to slander the church, she admits that faults and negligences existed, " all which," she adds, in the

style so peculiarly her own, "if you, my lords of the clergy, do not amend, I mean to depose you. Look you, therefore, well to your charges."

6. Once more the puritans betook themselves to the house of commons. The favour with which it regarded them, and the influence they possessed in it, shew how strongly their principles had taken root amongst the burgesses and citizens of England. For the lower house was now a representative body; and the interests, perplexities, and grievances of its constituents began to find an echo within its walls. Early in 1587, the puritans laid a petition before the house, in which once more they set forth their grievances. They complain of pluralities, non-residence, a slothful clergy, and a non-preaching and tyrannical episcopate. But the same rashness which had hitherto marred their prospects, and brought discredit even on their best intentions, still attended them. In the present temper of parliament, and probably of the queen herself, the redress of real grievances would scarcely have been withheld. We may venture further, and assert that it could not have been denied, if their own conduct had not silenced their best friends, the men of moderate counsels. On the 27th of February, a member presented to the house on their behalf, a bill which prayed that all the ecclesiastical laws in force should be annulled; and that a service book, which he then submitted to the house, should take the place of the book of common prayer. Bishops and archbishops were declared unlawful; the jurisdiction they possessed

CHAPTER
VII.
_____
ELIZ.
A. D. 1587.

was to be vested in an assembly of ministers and elders ; the rights of patronage were abolished ; and, in short, an ecclesiastical revolution was announced.* The puritans crowded around the house of commons, and filled the passages, besieging its members for their votes, and its officials for information. The hopes and expectations of the party seem to have been extravagantly raised. Five hundred clergymen, it is said, approved of the proposed changes, and declared their approbation by signing the petition, or expressing their consent publicly ;—a fact which has been variously interpreted : some writers regarding it as a proof of the lenity of the bishops, notwithstanding the heavy charges brought against them, that men so disaffected were allowed to remain in the bosom of the church ; others, as a proof how needful concession had become, seeing there were so many delinquents who could no longer be awed into submission. It certainly proves the growth of extreme puritanism ; and so far is an evidence that Whitgift's coercive measures had failed. Not uniformity, but a deepening dislike of episcopacy, however modified, was rapidly diffusing itself. Whatever concession might have done ten years before, its day had passed, and it was powerless now. Indeed it was no longer sought : subversion, not concession, became henceforth the cry of the puritans.

7. The queen resented the introduction of the bill : how indeed could she do otherwise ? " It was prejudicial to the religion established, to the

* Neal i. vii. 377.   Strype's Whitgift, i. 490.

crown, to her government, and her subjects;"
above all "it was an invasion of her prerogative;"
and several members of the house, who had supported the bill, were committed to the Tower.
Had it been adopted by the legislature it would
have involved churchmen in the same oppressions
which the puritans found to be intolerable. It
is strange that neither party seems at present to
have conceived the possibility, or indeed to have
understood the meaning, of toleration. Each side
thought it could exist only by the destruction of
the other. The possibility of an establishment
surrounded by dissenting institutions, independent
but not hostile, the peaceful theory of the generous Doddridge and of Dr. Chalmers in later days,
had not yet crossed the mind of man! No such
compromise was sought or offered. It was for
victory they strove on both sides : a victory that
included the extermination of the vanquished.

8. A feeble effort was made once more on behalf of the puritans in 1592.* Two bills were introduced to relieve the consciences of the non-
conforming clergy, and to restrain the violence
of the court of high commission ; especially the
monstrous tyranny which, it seems, it still continued to practise, of depriving those who took
the oath *ex officio* upon their own confessions ;
and of imprisoning those who refused it, as obstinate or contumacious. The bill was supported
by sir Francis Knollys, and by Mr. Morrice. The
latter held an office in the gift of the crown ; the

* Neal i. vi. 425.

former was a statesman of the highest reputation; and both were puritans. But the queen had sufficient power to stop the proceedings : she sent for sir Edward Coke, the speaker, and commanded him on his allegiance not to read the bill should it be laid before the house. Morrice was seized in the house itself; dismissed from his office (he was chancellor of the duchy of Lancaster); disabled from practising in his profession as a common lawyer ; and kept for some years a prisoner in Tutbury castle. Holding a judicial office from the crown, the queen no doubt regarded him strictly as a servant, and punished him as a contumacious one. The house of commons did not resent the double insult offered to them in the person of their speaker, and of one of their leading members. Circumstances had recently occurred which afforded the queen an excuse for the resumption of arbitrary power, and placed the cause of the puritans at the greatest disadvantage. It was but four years since the enthusiasm of the people had been deeply stirred by the appearance of the armada upon the coasts of England. It was now at length evident that the protestant cause and the national independence had been in the greatest jeopardy ; and, besides, the life of the most popular of English sovereigns had been repeatedly threatened by assassins. Popular enthusiasm is always in extremes ; it often passes from one side to another at a single bound. Something of this kind now appears to have taken place. Otherwise it is hardly possible to reconcile the placidity with which the nation looked on, and

saw the house of commons insulted, and a vast
number of its favourite ministers silenced or
imprisoned, with its uneasiness a few years before under circumstances by no means so critical
and alarming. The nation thought, no doubt,
that a season of repose was wanted; that no factious voice, no difference of opinion, ought to be
heard; that a firm united front ought to be opposed to the intrigues of the papacy and the jesuits; and of those foreign powers who regarded
with equal jealousy and wonder the bursting
power and greatness of an empire which they had
hitherto regarded with indifference, often with
disdain.

9. Two other causes must be added, which go
far to explain the reaction that had taken place,
and the want of sympathy now shewn by the
nation at large towards the puritans and their
friends in parliament.

10. One of these was the ill-timed publication
of the Martin Mar-prelate pamphlets. Nothing
could be more abusive than their language, or
more suspicious than the time and mode of their
appearance. The year 1588 was signalized by the
overthrow of the armada, and the execution of
Mary queen of Scots. The object of the former
was undisguised; it was the subjugation of the
realm to popery and to a foreign power. Whatever
may have been the verdict of history with regard
to the latter, it was then universally allowed by
the common people, and by all the puritans, that
Mary suffered a righteous sentence, having com-

CHAPTER passed the death of their own sovereign. Yet Mar-
VII.
tin Mar-prelate seized the inauspicious moment for
ELIZ. the issue of a series of anonymous libels against
A. D. 1588. the queen and bishops, of the most atrocious character. Who or what the writers were, rests, like
the authorship of Junius, in profoundest mystery.
The censorship of the press was in Whitgift's
hands; it is scarcely necessary to add that it was
severely exercised. Yet the Martin Mar-prelate
tracts scoffed at his threats, denounced his office,
and yet escaped his vigilance. Every modern advocate of the puritans condemns them, as most unworthy of their cause; and the great puritan leaders,
when they first appeared, spoke of them, let it in
justice be remembered, with deep dissatisfaction.
But their influence on the common people was
great notwithstanding; and in consequence they
brought down a weight of suspicion and dislike
from the ruling powers, which fell heavily upon
the whole body of the puritans. Martin Mar-
prelate's press was shifted from place to place.
Its secrecy of course added to its importance;
while the vexation of Whitgift and the court, expressed in fruitless denunciations and in vindictive
punishments, increased its mischievous popularity.
A proclamation was issued for the discovery of the
authors, which, from whatever cause, is rather
remarkable for its moderation. The defamatory
libels are described " as drawn up in railing sort,
and beyond the bounds of all good humanity; as
designed to introduce dangerous changes in the
form of doctrine in public service; and with a rash

and malicious purpose to dissolve the state of the CHAPTER
prelacy, being one of three antient estates of this $\frac{\text{VII.}}{}$
realm under her highness." All men are forbidden ELIZ.
to retain the libels in their possession; but if within A. D. 1588.
a month any person who knew their authors or pub-
lishers, should discover the same, he was assured
that for his former concealment he should not
be molested or troubled.* But the libels were
still published with impunity. The press was
tracked from Surrey to more than one parish in
Northamptonshire; thence to Coventry; from
Coventry to Woolston; from Woolston to Man-
chester; where it was seized, in Newton-lane, by
the earl of Derby.† The earliest formal struggle
upon record in our English history, of the press
against the government; and one in every way
instructive! The triumph of the court party was,
after all, equivocal; for what honour could be
gained by the seizure of a printing press? Its
mischievous importance had, in a great measure,
been owing to themselves. Libels of this kind,
if unnoticed, lose half their power: treated with
contempt, they sink into insignificance : and the
mischief was already done; for the libels had
spread far and wide, but the real authors, the
guilty parties, were never discovered.

11. But to those who are engaged in religious controversies, or who contend for the
removal of abuses in the church of Christ, the

---

* A proclamation against certain seditious and schismatical books,
and libels. London : printed by Barker, 1588.
† Fuller iii. ix. 100.

Martin Mar-prelate pamphlets convey a solemn lesson. Their insolent and seditious spirit,—terribly visited at the time upon those they were meant to serve,—has been, however unjustly, charged upon the puritans ever since by most of their opponents. They have never ceased to be spoken of as conveying the real meaning of their party, and honestly confessing to its secret intentions. The vindictive passions they have elicited among high churchmen, are only, if at all, inferior to those to which they once gave expression among ultra puritans. Martin's forty pamphlets were answered by at least an equal number, scarcely less truculent or less contemptuous of the christian virtues of forbearance, truth, and charity. They remain in history, on both sides, a melancholy record of the wickedness and folly of approaching religious controversy in a malignant spirit. Granting that the cause be right, what is it else than to fight the battle of the prince of peace with weapons snatched out of the armouries of hell ?

12. Another circumstance which tended greatly, though most unjustly, to discredit the puritan cause, was the insane attempt of a madman and his two associates to subvert the government. Calmly viewed, and at this distance of time, the affair seems utterly unworthy of a place in history; for history does not record the melancholy aberrations of the insane : she teaches by example, and from such examples nothing can be learned.

William Hacket* had given evidences of insanity
from his youth : he was violent and a fanatic ; he
boasted of his intercourse with heaven by visions
and revelations ; and attested his veracity whenever it was questioned with direful oaths and exe-
crations. He thought himself invulnerable ; and
challenged any one who pleased, to test his Achil-
léan properties, and wound or kill him. As his
disease increased, he successively proclaimed himself the sovereign of Europe, the saviour of the
world, and at length the Deity himself. Had not
the villanies of Joseph Mormon, and the frenzy of
Joanna Southcote, in our own age, taught us
that no pretensions of this nature seem utterly
preposterous to a certain class of minds, it would
have been inexplicable that even *two* converts
should have been gained by such a pleader, and
to such a cause. Edmund Coppinger, a person of
good descent, undertook to be his "prophet of
mercy;" and Henry Arthington, a Yorkshire gentleman, his "prophet of judgment." They proclaimed, from a cart in Cheapside, the advent of
Hacket's reign; which they said was supreme
in all things, both spiritual and temporal. The
crowd was great ; but they gained no converts
amongst the people, who saw them all three committed to Bridewell the next day, with perfect
indifference : though some few even then conceived Bedlam the most proper place for them.
Hacket was tried for high treason and hanged,

* Fuller iii. ix. 114. Conspiracy for a pretended reformation, &c. by
Richd. Cosin, LL.D. published by authority. 1592.

uttering at the last expressions which would indeed have been horribly blasphemous, had there been the slightest reason to suppose that the unhappy wretch was conscious of their meaning. Coppinger died in prison the next day ; having, it was said, starved himself to death. Arthington confessed his folly and was pardoned.

13. It does not appear that the slightest ill-consequences followed this mad outbreak. The people looked on with detestation, or with contempt ; nor was it pretended that the queen's authority had been for an hour impaired, far less imperilled. But Hacket and his associates had been smitten with a love of the Geneva discipline, as it now began to be termed ; and amongst other reformations, they had resolved upon the destruction of the church of England. It was discovered too, or at least asserted, that Cartwright had corresponded with Coppinger. A letter from Coppinger, but one of no consequence, was found in Udal's possession : but Cartwright proved that he had refused to see him (for he was himself a prisoner), and that he had warned his friends from the first to be aware of Coppinger, as a man in a state of mental derangement. One fact alone is sufficient for his justification : no steps were taken to convict him as an accomplice. Dark suspicions were thrown out ; and Dr. Cosin, the dean of arches, and principal official to Whitgift, wrote a treatise, in which he insinuated that the conspiracy was encouraged by the party, and that it was a repetition of the outrages of the German anabap-

tists. Other writers have continued to repeat the slander; "for," as Fuller quaintly observes, "it is the glutinous nature of all assertions to stick where they light." The same historian adds, that the puritans were so hated at court in consequence, that for many months together no favorite durst present a petition to the queen on their behalf. Cosin argues at length against the supposition of the insanity of Hacket and the others, in a strain equally discreditable to his heart and his understanding.

14. While the government was in this temper, an act was passed which was never known to confer the slightest benefit on the church of England, while it has given occasion to its adversaries to load it ever since with the bitterest invectives. It is a mournful instance of panic legislation. Its provisions could not be enforced but at the certain risk of an odium such as no institution could sustain amongst any people who had escaped from a state of barbarism, and were not restrained by martial law or the instant terrors of the Romish inquisition. Resistance was certain; and one would gladly think that the law was intended merely as an empty menace. It enacted* that if any person above the age of sixteen years should obstinately refuse to repair to some church or chapel, to hear divine service and common prayer, he should be, on conviction, committed to prison, without bail or mainprize, until

---

* An act to retain the queen's subjects, &c., 35 Eliz. c. 1. It was directed against the Brownists and Barrowists, &c. Price's Hist. Non. Con. 1. 405.

CHAPTER he should conform and make public confession of
VII. his conformity in terms prescribed by the statute

ELIZ. itself. Refusing to conform, the delinquent was
A. D. 1592. banished for life; and, returning home without
the queen's licence, was liable to suffer death as a
felon. The same penalties were incurred by a
month's absence from church without some lawful cause; by persuading others to deny or im-
pugn her majesty's power and authority in causes
ecclesiastical; or by inducing others to abstain
from church, or to be present at conventicles.
The law was chiefly aimed against the Brownists
and Romanists. Cartwright, and such as he, who
still conformed, were not affected by it. But it
is a dangerous experiment to goad a restive conscience; and the act before us was pregnant with
calamities. It excited opposition in those who
had hitherto yielded at least a formal acquiescence. It placed every man in whom the first
seeds of dissatisfaction had been sown, upon trial
before his own conscience; and pride, if no higher
motive, would compel a verdict against conformity. There was no room for affection beneath
an iron discipline; no merit in love and allegiance
to the church, when the absence of it amounted to
a felony. Thus warmth of feeling, and the enthusiasm that inspires the feeblest cause with life
and makes it triumph at last, passed over to the
puritans. A cold and military discipline, heartless,
exact, and formal, remained with the party who, unhappily for its highest interests, controlled, in this
affair, the destinies of the church of England.

CHAPTER VIII.

1. WHATEVER differences had hitherto separated thepuritansand prelatists, doctrinal questions had no place amongst them.   It was not till near the close of the reign of Elizabeth, that any serious points of doctrine were agitated on which, in fact, there did not exist a perfect harmony between the contending parties.   There are other matters, inferior in interest and importance only to the vital doctrines of revelation, on which an unceasing warfare has long raged among the various bodies of English christians, upon which no note of difference had yet been sounded.   Whether it be accepted in proof of tenderness of conscience, or of mere pertinacity, it is certain that the grounds of the struggle in which the puritans suffered so long, and often so unjustly, were trifling when compared to other grievances which have rent the church of Christ.   Of the questions which have arrayed almost every class of dissenters in hostility against the church of England, or still more unhappily her own members against

CHAPTER each other, those which have since assumed the
VIII.   foreground were yet unknown.   With regard to
_____ the method of salvation, the nature of the sacra-
ELIZ.
A. D. 1592. ments, the character of the christian ministry, and
the national establishment of religion, there was
no dispute.   The controversy, when it had raged
for forty years, was still confined to the ceremonial
of religion, and to the purity not of its doctrines
but of its external fabric.

2. Painful disputes have now for a long time
existed, even amongst orthodox christians, upon
some doctrines the importance of which it is
scarcely possible to overstate.   A discussion of
these points belongs to theology, and not to history ; nor is it possible, without a long induction
of proofs and arguments, to do full justice to the
points raised, and the questions at issue on either
side.   The reader will sufficiently understand the
controversy to which we refer when we say that
it concerns chiefly the method of a sinner's justification in the sight of God.   Whether it is by
faith in Jesus Christ alone, or by faith and good
works conjoined.   The advocates of the former
view charge their opponents with dimming the
lustre of the gospel, and embarrassing the pe-
nitent with conditions which Christ himself
has not imposed.   They maintain that the principles they so unceasingly condemn, tend to
self-righteousness, are subversive of evangelical
obedience, and therefore injurious to man and
dishonourable to God.   On the other hand, it is
asserted that these evangelical principles, if not

inconsistent with a high and pure morality, are at least in no degree conducive to it; that they tend to inflame the imagination rather than to influ- ence the conduct; and, in a word, to make reli- gion more an affair of sentiment than practice. The charge brought by the former party against the latter is, that the truths they teach, though important in their place, are not the gospel of Jesus Christ. The latter reply, in general, with imputing enthusiasm to their opponents. Round these centres other great questions of christian doctrine revolve in their respective orbits. But the points we have mentioned thus briefly are the pivot, in either case, of a system upon which the rest depend. The doctrine of a divine influence with regard to its necessity and extent; and that of the depravity of human nature, whether entire or partial, are closely affected, it must be evident, by the manner in which the doctrine of justification is previously determined. In short, a system of theology, with vast and various consequences, depends, by necessary consequence, upon the determination of this one point;—as Luther perceived when, in words which have become proverbial, he singled out the doctrine of justification by faith only as the token of a living or a sinking church.

3. But these controversies had not yet arisen, nor had the opinions of those who oppose the doctrine of justification by faith only,—the entire depravity of man by nature, and the consequent necessity of a conversion or renewal of the soul

by the Holy Spirit, introducing him into a new state,—in which he enjoys the divine favour, and inherits the promise of eternal life,—at this time found expression either amongst the puritans or their adversaries. Indeed their perfect consent upon every doctrinal point stands out in the most striking contrast with their vehement disputes upon almost every question of church policy. Those of the puritans who carried matters to the greatest length, and even forsook in after times the communion of the church of England, retained her doctrinal peculiarities, and long insisted on subscription to her doctrinal articles as a test of orthodoxy. As they slowly retired, they carried with them, as a treasure of the highest worth, the substance of her forms, and the vital principles which pervaded them. Many of them thought that the vehicle was too gross, the form too cumbrous, for the precious truth enshrined in it; but none of them affected to deny that the doctrines of the church of England were the pure doctrines of the gospel; nor did they charge her with being, in this sense, an unfaithful witness to the truth of God. Rude and fierce was their assault upon " the pope at Lambeth," yet they did not challenge Whitgift himself with unsound doctrine. In their bitterest moments, when they reviled the church of England as the church of antichrist, they applied their censure no further than to what they thought its antichristian practices; they never charged it with antichristian doctrines. If, as may possibly have been the case, a few ex-

pressions drawn from the writings of the most
violent or least scrupulous of the puritans, should
seem to be inconsistent with this assertion, they
produced no impression; and were unheeded by
the great leaders in the controversy. In a summary of the points which went to make up the
quarrel, such charges, if such were made, may
safely be thrown out of the enumeration as the
mere expression of petulance and folly : they made
no impression : the poisoned weapon fell harmless
to the ground.

4. The system of divinity embraced by the
church of England, and indeed by all the reformed churches, was that which has since been
known as moderate calvinism. But the title is
incorrect as regards the church of England;
because, in the first place, her system was not
derived through Calvin, nor based on his authority; and in the second, it differed from the system which he taught in some points of great
importance. Had the founders of the reformed
church of England sought for the sanction of a
name, it is probable that Bullinger, not Calvin,
would have been their leader; and his Decades,
rather than Calvin's Institutes, would have been
made their text book. For Bullinger was better known in England, and his fame was high
for wisdom amongst us, while the name of Calvin
was still obscure. The convocation of 1786 ordered that every minister, under the degree of
B.A. or M.A. and not licensed, should provide
Bullinger's decades in Latin or English, and
every week read at least as much as would

CHAPTER equal one sermon.   In 1785, Aylmer issued the
VIII.   same order to the London clergy ; probably the
ELIZ. most   learned   at   that   period   of   the   clerical
A. D. 1595. body.   The   principles   of   the   reformation   and
its doctrines, were settled, and finally deter-
mined, without reference to Calvin.*   Still it was
improbable that a work of such extraordinary
merit as the " Institutions of the Christian Religion," should not make an impression wherever
it found its way; or that it would not find its
way into every protestant university in Europe.
It was read both at Oxford and Cambridge, with
the sanction of the university ; and from this circumstance sprung up the first dissentions in the
English church upon the doctrines of the christian faith.   The controversy arose at Cambridge,
where the two professors of divinity were opposed
to each other on the doctrines (since then so
often perverted into an occasion of strife and discord), of election and final perseverance.   An inferior member of the university rashly took up the
quarrel in a strain which increased the mischief ;
denouncing from the pulpit of St. Mary's, Beza,
Calvin, and the foreign reformers by name, and
condemning their writings in the mass.   He was
censured by Whitgift ; and quitted the university
in disgust.

5. Whitgift, with the design of appeasing the
disturbance, drew up the famous Lambeth articles,—which have, unhappily, occasioned greater

* Even Heylin, always anxious to exaggerate the evil influences of
Calvinism, repeatedly makes this admission.   Hist. Reformat. i. 134,
&c. and Introd. to Laud. Sect. 4.

and more lasting schisms than they were meant to
heal. They were nine in number; expressed in
Latin, and approved, though with a certain degree of hesitation, by Hutton archbishop of York,
Fletcher bishop of London, Young of Rochester,
by Dr. Whitaker of Cambridge, and some other
divines. They were as follows :*

i. God from eternity has predestinated some persons to life; some he has reprobated to death.

ii. The moving or efficient cause of predestination to life is not the foreseeing of faith, or of perseverance, or of good works, or of anything which may exist in the person predestinated, but the will and pleasure of God alone.

iii. Of the predestinated the number is certain and fore-ordained, it can neither be increased nor diminished.

iv. They who are not predestinated to salvation shall necessarily be condemned for their sins.

v. True, living, and justifying faith, and the Spirit of God justifying, is not extinguished, does not fail, or vanish in the elect, either finally or totally.

vi. A man truly faithful, that is, endued with justifying faith, has the full assurance of faith, of the remission of his sins, and of his eternal salvation by Christ.

vii. Saving grace, by which they might be saved if they would, is not assigned, communicated, or granted to all men.

viii. No one is able to come to Christ unless it

* Fuller iii. c. ix. 147 ; ' Strype's Whitgift, 463.

CHAPTER VIII.

ELIZ.

A. D. 1595.

be given him, and unless the Father draw him, and all men are not drawn by the Father, so that they may come to the Son.

ix. It is not placed within the power or will of every man to be saved.

These articles were transmitted to Cambridge by the archbishop, with an injunction that they should be received by the university, and form the standard of its teaching upon the controverted points. This was done, he said, simply to explain the undoubted meaning of the church of England, and not with any intention of imposing new statutes or interpretations.

6. But the result proved that his measures had been rashly taken. In the first place, divines, even of the school of Calvin, were not prepared to receive with implicit submission the dogmas enunciated in the Lambeth articles. These awful and mysterious questions are treated by the great Genevan with a reverential solemnity which strongly contrasts with the sententious dogmatism of the archbishop. His paper is drawn up in a style of composition much affected by men of clear but narrow minds; and with a hardness in its brief and positive assertions such as, in general, marks a religion wanting in that which is in truth the soul of piety, deep reverence and humility. Charity has lost much by these compendious summaries; in which a decision is given within the compass of a sentence, or the clause of a sentence, upon points on which the wisest and best men are most prone to hesitate; while, in re-

gard to theological truth and accuracy, nothing
whatever has been gained.*   It will always be
found, indeed, that something has been pared
away from the grandeur of divine truth as revealed in scripture before it could be fitted into
the cramped and narrow mould of a human system.   Besides, the Lambeth articles pronounced
with confidence upon several points on which the
church of England had maintained a profound
silence; and these were the most difficult and
painful in the controversy.   To go no further, the
first article asserts a doctrine neither taught nor
implied in the standards of the English church,
the doctrine of reprobation.   The wise caution of
our reformers, in abstaining from dogmatic assertions on this and some other fruitful sources of
unprofitable strife, and confining the national
creed as much as possible to the essentials of
salvation, is alone sufficient to counterbalance all
their faults, and to claim for them the highest

* The following passage from the Rev. E. Bickersteth's Christian
Student is well deserving of attention.   "The leading divines in queen
Elizabeth's reign must be considered as making rather a more distinct
and explicit statement of Calvinistic doctrine than their predecessors.
Calvin's Institutes were read in the schools by order of convocation.
Indeed an ultra-Calvinism, which appears to have been maintained by
some, rather than the scriptural divinity of our first reformers, led, as
might be expected, to opposing statements in doctrine. . . . There
was, however, in the author's view, a serious evil in thus attempting to
fathom the unfathomable mind of Jehovah.   Where angels probably
adore in silent submission, men with too little humility, and with presumptuous curiosity, have either opposed or evaded his plain declaration,
or not stopping in the words of scripture, scrutinized the mind and
character of the only wise God.   How just was bishop Carleton's view
of this!   'In the matter of predestination, I have ever been fearful to
meddle : it is one of the greatest and deepest of God's mysteries.   We
are with reverence to wonder, and with faith and humility to follow that
which God has revealed on this point, and there to stay.' " (Bickersteth,
p. 235.)

CHAPTER place in our regards. But it was well for the
VIII. church, in this instance, that Elizabeth, with her
ELIZ. royal prerogative, interfered. She was much dis-
A. D. 1595. pleased, she said in a letter which Cecil wrote by
her command to the archbishop,* that any permission had been given by his grace and his brethren for such points to be disputed; the matter
being tender and dangerous to weak, ignorant
minds: and she commanded him to suspend his
articles, and to put a stop to the discussion of the
subject from the pulpit. Under all the circumstances, it was a judicious exercise of the power
entrusted to the secular head of the church. But
such is the carelessness of party writers, that the
queen's interference is often represented as the
condemnation by authority of calvinistic tenets:
whereas she wisely abstained from expressing a
judgment upon the truth of the articles, and spoke
only of their difficulty; following in this the moderation of our seventeenth article, on the doctrine of predestination,—and we may add, of Calvin himself, than whom no man has spoken more
strongly upon the danger and folly of approaching
these discussions in an unguarded temper, or without the deepest reverence.†

7. Thus the matter for the present was stifled,
but the embers smouldered, and broke out from
time to time in fierce conflagrations. It happened too, by one of those strange transitions, the
result of obscure and complex movements, which
wear, in the eyes of posterity, an appearance of
absurd and violent inconsistency, that within a

* Neal i. ch. viii. 457.   † Instit. Lib. iii. cap. 21.

few years, Whitgift's ultra calvinism became CHAPTER VIII. the heritage of the ultra-puritans; whose suc-cessors, in the unceasing conflicts they waged ELIZ. with the church of England, learned habitually A. D. 1595. to fall back upon Whitgift's articles, in proof of their own lineal descent from a lofty parentage. And it must certainly be confessed, that if he em-barrassed the puritans while he lived, with his needless severities; he has made them some amends by perplexing the church of England ever since with painful controversies. But to this subject we shall have occasion to revert hereafter.

8. The nature of the sacraments, another fruit-ful source of controversy in later times, had not yet disturbed the church of England. With one accord, it was held that they were signs and seals of grace, and that the reception of the grace conveyed, depended upon their right reception. Between the puritans and the highest of the church party there existed upon these points no difference whatever. The tone and services of the book of common prayer were objected to, it is true; but this was not the ground of objection. Kneel-ing at the eucharist was a grievance, not because the remonstrants were dissatisfied with the teach-ing of the church of England, as to the quali-ties remaining after consecration in the bread and wine; nor because they disputed as to the nature of the blessings connected with the sa-crament; but simply because they thought the posture superstitious, and that it became them to protest against a usage practised in the church of

Rome, and by her perverted to idolatry. So too, they objected to the cross in baptism. The sacrament, they said, was complete without it ; and they denied the right of any church to add to the Saviour's institutions; besides that the sign of the cross was in itself an especial offence to them. They disliked the office, and the name, of of godfathers and godmothers. But it was not because they had any scruples as to the pledges made by the sureties on the child's behalf; but because they thought the parents, or natural guardians of the child, the fittest persons to make them. Seceders from the English church in later times have found their greatest grievances in these offices, and in the doctrines they are supposed to inculcate. But here the puritans, down to the close of queen Elizabeth's reign, had raised no complaints.—Their objections extended no further than to questions of form and manner and church discipline.

9. Indeed the unanimity of the reformed churches throughout Europe, upon the nature of the sacraments, is not a little remarkable. It was one of the great questions of the reformation. It was the hinge of the whole controversy with Rome. Every martyr was examined upon this, many of them on no other, point. The primitive christian in the days of Trajan, might have escaped the sword of the executioner, if he would have scattered a few grains of incense upon the next pagan altar. Our English martyrs would have been spared the horrors of the stake, had they been willing to pay a similar respect to the altars of

the papacy, and adore the real presence in the
consecrated bread. And it is monstrous to suppose that a considerable body of men of sense
and learning, (assuming on their behalf neither
integrity nor holiness) should have squandered
their lives in defence of opinions they had not
investigated ; or that all their powers had not
indeed been fixed, with an energy intense and
deep in proportion to their own peril, upon the
inquiry on the result of which depended, if nothing else, the alternative of a life of honour or a
death of agony and shame. Thus, if there be a
theological subject which can properly be said to
have been exhausted by the researches of former
times,—to have been placed by our forefathers in
such a flood of light that no additional ray has
been seen to gleam upon it,—we are disposed to
place the sacraments, as expounded by the reformers, in that predicament. The obscurity that remains appears to be inherent ; whatever light wisdom and piety and massive learning can shed upon
them, seems to have been imparted.

10. It would not be difficult to shew that all
the foreign churches taught, with scarcely a perceptible shade of difference, the doctrines of our
own. The presbyterian church of Scotland expresses herself in language entirely consonant
with that of the English church, whether in our
office for baptism, our articles, or our catechism ;
and in language of equal strength. " We assuredly
believe that by baptism we are engrafted into
Christ Jesus, to be made partakers of his justice,
by which our sins are covered and remitted : and

that also in the supper, rightly used, Christ Jesus is so joined with us that he becometh the very nourishment and food of our souls. But all this, we say, cometh of true faith, which apprehendeth Christ Jesus, who only maketh his sacraments effectual unto us." Thus she speaks in her confession,* which was first exhibited to, and allowed by, the three estates in parliament, at Edinburgh, in the year 1560; again ratified at the same place, and on the same authority, in 1567; and finally subscribed by the king and his household, at Holyrood house, in 1581. Seventy years afterwards, when the presbyterian divines assembled at Westminster to remodel the church of England, and to carry out the most fervent aspirations of Cartwright in his younger days, the doctrine of the sacraments was still the same. Of baptism they say : " By the right use of this ordinance the grace promised is not only offered, but really exhibited, and conferred by the Holy Ghost, to such, whether of age, or infants, as that grace belongeth unto, according to the counsel of God's own will, in his appointed time."† And of the eucharist to the same effect : "Worthy receivers, outwardly partaking of the visible elements in this sacrament, do also inwardly by faith, really and indeed, yet not carnally and corporeally, but spiritually, receive and feed upon Christ crucified, and all benefits of his death ; the body and blood of Christ being then not corporeally or carnally in, with,

---

* Harmony of Protestant Confessions.
† Westmin. Confession, ch. 28.

or under the bread and wine, yet as really, but
spiritually, present to the faith of believers in
that ordinance, as the elements themselves are to
the outward senses."*

11. These may be received as the views of the
puritans themselves; including that extreme section, who would have overthrown episcopacy, and
established in England a presbyterian or an independent church. For the church of Scotland
naturally felt, and, indeed, formally expressed,
its sympathy with the English puritans : and the
Westminster divines, when the puritans properly
so called had died out, succeeded in their place.
Lord Bacon may be taken as a fair and, all must
admit, a competent representative of the church
party. Though averse to Whitgift's severity, and,
in common with the other courtiers and statesmen of the day, not well pleased to be over-sha-
dowed by the splendours of the hierarchy, still he
was no puritan; he thought their scruples needless, if not schismatical. He has left on record a
confession of his faith which might, for the doctrines it contains, have been written indifferently
by Cartwright or by Whitgift,—by an imprisoned
puritan or by the head of the church of England.
For its singular force and beauty, it well deserves
a place in a religious history of those times. And
it will confirm the position we have endeavoured
to establish, that theological differences on points
of doctrine had no share in the disputes which
then rent the church of England.†

* Westmin. Confession, ch. 29.
† " The sufferings and merits of Christ, as they are sufficient to do

CHAPTER VIII.

ELIZ.

A. D. 1595.

12. The authority of the christian ministry,—the source from whence it is derived, and the channel along which it flows,—has now for a long time been agitated with incessant heat amongst the various classes of religionists in England. It was not, however, one of those points upon which the puritans entertained any peculiar sentiments; or differed from their opponents of the other party. This root of bitterness had not yet sprung up : who were, and who were not, accredited ministers of Jesus Christ, was a point upon which a perfect agreement as yet existed between them. It was in the year 1589 that Bancroft, then chaplain to Whitgift, but afterwards bishop of London and archbishop of Canterbury, preached a sermon at St. Paul's cross which at once opened a new strife.

away the sins of the whole world, so they are *only effectual* to those *which are regenerate by the Holy Ghost ;* who *breatheth where he will of free grace ;* which grace, as a seed incorruptible, *quickeneth* the spirit of man, and conceiveth him *anew a son of God, and a member of Christ :* so that Christ, having man's flesh, and man *having Christ's Spirit,* there is an open passage, and mutual imputation, whereby sin and wrath was conveyed to Christ from man, and merit and life is conveyed to man from Christ : which *seed* of the Holy Ghost first *figureth* in us, the image of Christ slain or crucified, *through a lively faith,* and then reneweth in us the image of God in holiness and charity ; though both imperfectly, and in degrees far differing, *even in God's elect,* as well in regard of the fire of the Spirit, as of the illumination thereof, which is more or less in a large proportion, as namely, in the Church before Christ, which yet, nevertheless, was partaker of one and the same salvation with us, and of one and the same means of salvation with us. The work of the Spirit, though it be *not tied to any means* in heaven or earth, yet it is *ordinarily* dispensed by the preaching of the word, *the administration of the Sacraments,* the covenants of the fathers upon the children, prayer, reading ; the censures of the church, the society of the godly, the cross and afflictions, God's benefits, his judgments upon others, miracles, the contemplation of his creatures ; *all which,* though *some be more principal,* God useth as the *means of vocation* and conversion of *his elect ;* not derogating from his power to call immediately by his grace and at all hours and moments of the day, that is, of man's life, according to his good pleasure."—Works, vol. ii. p. 470. Edit. 1826.

He maintained in his sermon, that bishops were, by the institution of God himself, an order in the christian ministry superior to priests and deacons, and distinct from them; and that they governed the church and the inferior clergy, *jure divino*, by a right inherent to their office, and derived from God alone. The denial of these truths, he said, was heresy.*

13. Episcopalians attach grave importance and high dignity to the office of a bishop. They trace it to the purest ages of the church, and discover, as they conceive, unequivocal tokens of its existence as a separate, and a superior, order in the ministry during the apostolic age itself. And, in general, they believe that our Lord, addressing himself through St. John at Patmos, to the seven angels of the churches that were in Asia, recognized in them the superior claims of the episcopate, and gave to their offices the awful sanction of his own approval. Thus far all episcopalians agree, and all are willing, in the sense here explained, to admit the apostolic institution, and the divine right, of the episcopacy; since the head of the church sanctioned, if he did not expressly found, it; and whatever powers it is intrusted with, are derived from his commission.

14. The subject was viewed in this light at the period of the reformation. The antiquity of the office, its validity and its importance, were questions upon which there was no dispute. Beza and Calvin admit them on behalf of the foreign churches; who dispensed with the episcopate, for

* Strype, Whitgift, 292. Neal i. 389.

CHAPTER VIII.

ELIZ.

A. D. 1595.

the most part, with extreme reluctance, and in submission to a necessity which they could not, or thought they could not, control. And they justified their presbyterian forms of government by the plea, that they did in fact retain the thing, if not the name: that a primitive bishop was but *primus inter pares*, the first among his brethren; endowed with powers which they too virtually possessed as presbyters, but from the exercise of which they voluntarily abstained for the sake of common order and united action. And this view of the episcopate prevailed extensively in England, not only amongst the puritans, but with many of the prelatic party.

15. Others, regarding the office with still deeper reverence, considered the bishop a superior officer, not only in the rank he held, but in the commission he bore; they regarded the tripartite distribution of the christian ministry as that which Christ enjoined, and his disciples set on foot and practised. They thought it necessary to the perfection of a christian church; and consequently regarded the foreign churches, and the church of Scotland, as hastily constructed, and deviating, perhaps rashly, from the ancient practice and the primitive constitution of a church. But this was the extreme length to which they carried their dissatisfaction. They did not hold episcopacy to be one of the essentials of a church; but they held it to be one of the chief ornaments and strongest points of a well constructed one. Their moderation may be seen in the offices of the English church. If there be " a power peculiar unto

bishops," as Hooker speaks, it is unquestionably that of ordaining deacons and presbyters. Yet the church of England associates presbyters with the bishop in the solemn rite of ordaining others by laying on of hands. A signal instance of moderation; because the practice of primitive antiquity did not necessarily require it. It was the custom of some antient churches, not by any means of all of them. We can regard it only as a voluntary concession; a concession that involved, however, no real disparagement of the episcopate. For, as Hooker well remarks, there are no examples in the history of the church of Christ in primitive ages, of ordination performed by presbyters alone, without the presence of a bishop; but there are numerous examples of ordinations by the bishops only, without the assistance of a presbyter. Still Hooker does not hesitate to admit that there may be sometimes " very just and sufficient reasons to allow ordination without a bishop :" there may be " the exigencies of necessity," where " the church must needs have some ordained, and neither has, nor possibly can have, a bishop to ordain them." In such a case the ordinary institution of God, he says, " has often given, and may give, place."* Hooker wrote under the eye of Whitgift, and these moderate sentiments we must suppose were still those of the primate, and of the church of England. But Bancroft's views extended much further. He viewed the episcopate in such a light as to maintain that no church could exist without

* Eccl. Pol. book vii. 14.

CHAPTER
VIII.

ELIZ.

A. D. 1595.

it; no orders were valid which bishops had not conferred: and of course no obedience, no respect
was due to those, however devout or however
gifted, who exercised the functions of the christian
ministry, unless by their authority. This amounted, in fact, to an attack upon the foundations of all
churches that were not episcopal: the inference
was contained within the premises, and the time
came when it was avowed. The cautious policy
of queen Elizabeth was not likely to embrace new
and extreme opinions. Her ministers were too
far-sighted not to perceive at once that the blow
which was meant to stun the puritans would recoil against some of her majesty's best allies
abroad. At first the queen was rather pleased
than otherwise, and checked the zeal of Knollys,
who called her attention to the probable ill consequences of these novel statements; but her
more cautious advisers seem to have prevailed,
and Bancroft's theory of the episcopate was suffered to fall into neglect. Whitgift is said to have
remarked, that he rather wished than believed it
to be true. This would be consistent with his
character: in which, with a severity which was
its greatest blot, were mingled an integrity and
an honesty of purpose that would not stoop to
reach their aims by any means which seemed to
him unworthy of his office and his cause.

16. Hitherto episcopal ordination had not been
considered as of the essence of the ministerial
commission; indeed there are several remarkable
instances in which presbyterian ministers were
not only beneficed in the church of England, but

enjoyed its distinctions and filled some of its highest posts. The case of Whittingham dean of
Durham is well known. He was presented to the
deanery, soon after Elizabeth's accession, in 1563,
having received orders from the reformed church
at Geneva, in the presbyterian manner. It does
not appear that his want of episcopal ordination
would have rendered him obnoxious, had it not
been for the zeal with which he espoused the puritan opinions upon the subject of the vestments.
At length in 1577, Sandys archbishop of York
cited him upon several charges, but the principal was his Genevan ordination. Whittingham however asserted the rights of the church of
Durham, and challenged the archbishop's power
of interference. He then made his appeal to the
queen, who directed a commission to hear and
determine the objections alleged against him.
The president was Hutton dean of York, who is
said to have expressed his preference for presbyterian rather than Romish orders in strong language.* Sandys had sufficient influence to obtain
another commission, and of this the lord president
was a member. When the question of his ordination had been argued, the lord president exclaimed, " I cannot agree to deprive him for that cause
alone : this," he said, "would be ill taken by all
the godly, both at home and abroad ; that we allow
of popish massing priests in our ministry, and
disallow of ministers made in a reformed church."

* Strype's Annals 523. Neal i. vi. 285.

CHAPTER The commission was again adjourned, and here
VIII.   the business dropped; for the next year the dean
ELIZ.   of Durham died.
A. D.   14. The range within which ordination was
1585—90. considered valid in the church of England in
the age succeeding the reformation, is shewn
more strongly in the case of Travers, Hooker's
celebrated coadjutor at the Temple. Whittingham had been ordained by the church of Geneva,
a national institution, the church of a foreign
state with which England was on terms of
amity; Travers may have been ordained deacon
according to the forms of the church of England;
(for he had a divinity degree from Cambridge;)
but he was a member, from the first, of the presbyterian church at Wandsworth, in 1572. Going
abroad, he was ordained a presbyter at Antwerp,
by the presbyterian synod there in 1578.* Yet
we find him associated with Hooker, as preacher
1592. at the Temple, in 1592. During this long interval,
then, his presbyterian orders had been allowed.
He was also private tutor in the family of the
lord treasurer Cecil. When at length silenced
by Whitgift, it was objected to him, first, that
he was not a lawfully ordained minister of
the church of England; secondly, that he had
preached without a licence; thirdly, that he
had violated discipline and decency, by his public refutation of what Hooker, his superior in
the church, had advanced from the same pulpit
upon the same day. Had the first ground been

Fuller, i. book ix. 126—130.

felt by his opponents to have been impregnable, the CHAPTER other charges would probably have been omitted, VIII. and Travers would have been dismissed, no doubt, ELIZ. in a summary way. But it would seem that the A. D. 1592· stress was laid chiefly on the two latter articles ; and indeed Travers was prepared with an answer to the first, and with an answer which he did not fail to use.

15. An act had passed in the thirteenth year of queen Elizabeth, under which he was sheltered. It recognizes the validity of foreign orders; and indeed conveys to us historical evidence that ministers ordained by presbyterian synods were at that time beneficed in the church of England. The anomaly which admits a Romish priest but excludes a presbyter of the Scottish church, did not then exist. It was sufficient that the conforming minister should declare his assent, and subscribe, to the articles of the church of England.* Travers,

* The following is the act at length :—" Anno XIII. Regina Elizabetha. A. D. 1570. Chapter 12.—An act for the ministers of the church to be of sound religion.—That the churches of the queen's majesty's dominions may be served with pastors of sound religion. Be it enacted by the authority of this present parliament, that any person under the degree of a bishop, which doth or shall pretend to be a priest or minister of God's holy word and sacraments, by reason of any other form of institution, consecration, or ordering, than the form set forth by parliament in the time of the late king of most worthy memory, kind Edward the sixth, or now used in the reign of our most gracious sovereign lady, before the feast of the nativity of Christ next following, shall, in the presence of the bishop, or guardian of the spiritualities of some one diocese where he hath or shall have ecclesiastical living, declare his assent, and subscribe to all articles of religion which only concern the confession of the true christian faith, and the doctrine of the sacraments, comprised in a book imprinted, intituled, Articles, whereupon it was agreed by the archbishops and bishops of both provinces, and the whole clergy in the convocation holden at London in the year of our Lord God one thousand five hundred and sixty two, according to the computation of the church

CHAPTER in his petition to the privy council, pleads the force
VIII. of this statute, and declares that many Scottish mi-
ELIZ. nisters were then holding benefices in England
A. D. 1595. beneath its sanction. Attempts, it is true, have
been lately made to shew, that as the church of
England recognized none but episcopal orders, the
act of the thirteenth of Elizabeth cannot possibly
refer to presbyterian ministers. But how far this
assumption is correct, the passage we have cited
from Hooker, and the case of dean Whittingham,
to go no further, will at once enable the reader to
decide.

16. And though silenced at the Temple, Travers was still thought fit for high service in the
church. Doctor Loftus, archbishop of Dublin
and chancellor of Ireland, invited him to Dublin,
and conferred upon him the office of provost of
queen Elizabeth's new and royal foundation.
This Travers accepted, and as head of Trinity
college the world is indebted to him for the
education of the illustrious Usher, archbishop of
Armagh. Civil war, the bane of Ireland, at
length drove the provost from his post; the times
were against him; he grew old and poor. Usher
still reverenced his teacher, visited him in person,

of England, for the avoiding of the diversities of opinions, and for the
establishing of consent touching true religion put forth by the queen's
authority; and shall bring from such bishop or guardian of spiritualities in writing, under his seal authentick, a testimonial of such assent
and subscription; and openly on some Sunday, in the time of the publick
service afore noon, in every church where by reason of any ecclesiastical living he ought to attend, read both the said testimonial, and the
said articles; upon pain that every such person which shall not before
the said feast do as is above appointed, shall be ipso facto deprived,
and all his ecclesiastical promotions shall be void, as if he then were
naturally dead."

and offered him presents of money ; which, it is
said, were thankfully declined.

17. These are the facts of history, on which various reflections will occur. It is enough for our
present purpose to suggest, that, bearing in mind
the narrow and often acrimonious temper of the
puritans, and of Travers himself, upon all, even
the most trivial, matters of church government,
they were treated, in this point at least, with
singular generosity. A minister, of powers such
as those which Travers possessed,—himself ordained by foreigners, and by a church which
owned another discipline,—permitted from year
to year to advocate in the Temple church an
entire change of structure and of polity in the
English branch of the church catholic, and to do
this in contradiction of his superior co-minister,—
that superior no less a man than Hooker,—is
an instance of dignified forbearance to which
few churches can afford a parallel. It is needless to remark, that whatever motives contributed to this gentle treatment, neither fear nor
indifference (which so often put on the cloak of
forbearance) had the slightest share in them.
The friendship of the lord treasurer may have
contributed its influence, however, in behalf of
Travers.

18. Bancroft's sermon was evidently provoked
by the violence of the Mar-prelate libels, and
of the ultra-puritans. It was one of those acts
of retaliation where violence on one side is met
with violence upon the other. But even granting

CHAPTER all that Bancroft asserted as to the divine right of
VIII. episcopacy, the conclusion that the denial of his
ELIZ. position was a heresy, was unsupported by scrip-
A.D. 1595. ture and needlessly offensive. But a time was
approaching when the guarded moderation of the
reformers was no longer to be had in reverence ;
the more extravagant and exclusive the dogma,
the more certain its success.

19. The endowment of religion by the state,
another pregnant source of disagreement in later
times, did not hitherto contribute to alienate the
affections of churchmen and puritans. Upon the
arguments by which this union is defended or opposed it is unnecessary to enlarge; nor would such
a discussion be appropriate. It is sufficient to observe, that at the close of the reign of Elizabeth
the controversy had not yet arisen. It was not
one of the many points upon which puritans and
prelatists contended with each other. Whether
they were right or wrong; whether they were
more enlightened, or more ignorant, than ourselves; whether their political opinions were too
strongly imbued with the theology of the old testament, or ours too careless of the sanctions of the
word of God—still the fact is beyond dispute.
Each party held that it would be monstrous and
sinful in the state not to endow and sustain the
church. That the church should scruple to accept
the succours of the state, does not appear to have
occurred as amongst the possible difficulties of the
most uneasy conscience. And the establishment
that either party had in view was of the most ex-

clusive character. Prelatists excluded puritans, CHAPTER
and puritans prelatists. During Whitgift's reign VIII.
it was accounted necessary to exclude any but a ELIZ.
strict conformist,—it was a duty to repel and A.D. 1595.
punish him. How Whitgift's opponents might
have acted had they been in power, is scarcely a
matter of conjecture. Their children in the next
generation seized the reins and guided the cha-
riot of the state. It then appeared that they were
equally exclusive, equally intolerant with the most
violent of their opponents. The national church
was presbyterian, and the honest episcopalian was
doomed in his turn to suffer all the indignities,
the insults and injustice which, in their most unhappy days, the puritans themselves had borne.
A national church, uncompromising and intolerant, was that for which both parties contended;
and having achieved the victory, each would have
excluded the other from its advantages, and punished them for their contumacy. Toleration, we
must repeat it, was a word unknown. To us of
the present generation, it is, and must ever remain, a problem hard to be resolved, how good
men could carry on so long and fierce a warfare,
while the questions at issue were, by the confession of each party, of secondary, and not of vital
importance. If the controversies between the
different bodies of christians in our own times
are of greater moment, yet they are conducted in
a calmer spirit. And if we cannot pride ourselves
upon a deeper theology, and a profounder reach

of thought than our forefathers, we may at least be grateful for a stronger sense of justice and of human infirmity, and a disposition for mutual charity; humbler virtues, it is true, but not without their recompense!

CHAPTER IX.

1. **THUS** stood the two parties at the close of the long reign of queen Elizabeth. No one doctrine of importance, notwithstanding the vehemence of the long protracted strife, had yet mingled its bitterness with the troubled stream; and it seems as if the quarrel would have worn itself out, and died as it were of mere exhaustion, had not some fresh materials been supplied by which it was at once prolonged and aggravated.

2. A parent's animosities are seldom inherited by his children in their ancient bitterness; and a second generation is unwilling to revive the controversies which otherwise would slumber with the ashes of their forefathers. The restlessness of mankind seeks for new objects even in its hatreds and dislikes. Fame must be won in new fields, and not by simply adhering to a venerable cause : the realities of life press too heavily upon most men, its immediate pursuits are too interesting to all, to allow to an historical quarrel more than a traditionary interest. When the first combatants quit the scene for ever, the survivors are secretly

CHAPTER IX.

ELIZ.

A. D. 1595.

disposed either to compromise their differences, or to re-establish their enmity and renew their conflict upon new and wider grounds.

3. The vestiarian controversy was worn out: for thirty years at least, not a line had been written on either side which placed it in a clearer light, or added anything to the considerations already placed in either scale. If the great men of the reformation had not exhausted the arguments, Whitgift and Cartwright, who followed after, had left nothing to be desired. Hooker, great as he was, could pretend to no originality in his defence of, nor Travers in his assault upon, a point so long and earnestly debated by men in few respects or none inferior to themselves. And the controversy itself had lost its edge. It was only by associating it with other questions,—questions of christian doctrine, and therefore of permanent interest,—that its ephemeral importance could be revived. At the period of the reformation the surplice was associated only with the popish priest and his tawdry superstitions ; at the close of the reign of Elizabeth, and of half a century, a whole generation had arisen and passed away who had never seen a priest or listened to a mass. The surplice was associated in the minds of living men, with the fathers of the reformation. At Salisbury, Jewel the champion of the English church was remembered to have worn it. The saintly Grindal ministered in it at Lambeth ; and had insisted upon its use in the university of Cambridge. In the remoter north, Pilkington at Durham, and Sandys at York,

had not scrupled to appear in it, and to impose
it on their clergy. The hesitation they had felt
was known only to a few learned men and controversialists; their consent to use the vestments
stood in the broad daylight of popular and recent history. The obvious reflection of many
a candid mind would be that such men had
good reasons for their conduct; that when the
alternative lay between a schism and a surplice,
the doubt was instantly resolved ; and that, after
all, the connexion between the habits and the
doctrines of the Romish church was, in part at
least, imaginary not real. Certainly it was not
necessary. For a generation of protestant divines
had worn them, in whom no Rome-ward tendency,
but rather a deepening horror of her crimes, had
displayed itself.

4. That a very large proportion of those who at
first favored the puritan cause had thus gradually
withdrawn from it, admits of no doubt. It was
the case in the queen's council, where, in the early
part of her reign, a decided majority were, to a
greater or less extent, on the side of the puritans ;
but before her death their cause was nearly deserted. Nor was there inconsistency in this.
When new institutions are founded, wise men
will strive with all their might to place them on
a footing of theoretical perfection. But after a
while, perceiving that their aim cannot be achieved ; or that their views of perfection were ideal
rather than practical; or that circumstances which
they cannot bend, refuse to accommodate them-

CHAPTER IX.

ELIZ.
A. D.
1595—97.

selves to the reception of their favorite theory, they will gladly accept a compromise. If the institution *works well*, they will lend it a vigorous support. If the evils they anticipated do not in fact arise, they will be more ready to question their own sagacity than to disturb the harmony of existing institutions.

5. Thus a large body of English churchmen began cheerfully to acquiesce in the established church as then administered; and had it not been for the severities inflicted on the puritans, which produced a natural recoil and a wide-spreading sympathy, their cause would probably (unless some fresh grounds of discontent were introduced) have dwindled in the course of years, and ended in an insignificant secession.

6. Among the causes which contributed to confirm the established church, and with it the episcopate, in the affections of the people, it is impossible to omit so considerable an event as the publication of Hooker's ecclesiastical polity, of which four books were published in the year 1594, and the fifth in 1597: the remaining part was published afterwards. It is one of those rare productions which, like the book of martyrs,* sprung into

1597.

---

* It is stated on page 51, that Foxe's book of martyrs was ordered to be placed in the parish churches. This statement, I fear, is incorrect; though it is certain that the volume was thus chained in many chancels for common use; some copies are still to be found in our old churches. I have seen one at Amport, in Hampshire, a very early, if not the first, English edition. But the Liber Canonorum, issued 1571 by archbishop Parker, commands the churchwardens to provide only a large bible, a book of public prayers, and the homilies. Erasmus's commentary had been already ordered. All archbishops and bishops, however, within the province of Canterbury, are required to place in the

instant popularity; and during a probation of two CHAPTER
hundred and fifty years, has only gathered fresh ^{IX.}
renown. It displays that mighty genius which ELIZ.
is fitted for all ages, which is never antiquated, A. D. 1597.
never out of date. As a defence of the church of
England, its supremacy has never been disturbed.
No serious attempt has since been made by any
master mind to invade Hooker's province or to
supersede his unchallenged reputation. One of
the latest editions of his work has been given to
the world by the adversaries of the church of
England, with notes and comments of their own;
a perfectly fair proceeding, to which churchmen
have nothing to object; and at the same time, a
tribute to Hooker's weight in the field of argument more flattering than any that churchmen
could bestow. A rare and enviable career—to
defend the church of his country against papists,
and to win the admiration of the pope himself;
against sectarians, and yet to claim their reverence; and to accomplish this with so much firmness and so little compromise, that churchmen
of every school gather their arguments from his
profound and thoughtful pages, and are proud to
find a shelter for their opinions under the sanction
of his venerable name !

7. It was not till near the close of this century

halls of their houses or in the great chamber, so that even the guests
and servants of the house may freely peruse it, the whole book of martyrs; plenam illam historiam quæ inscribitur *Monumenta Martyrum.*
Each archdeacon is also instructed, amongst other books, especially to
have in his possession the book of martyrs : et libros alios et nominatim
eos qui inscribuntur *Monumenta Martyrum.* Liber Canonorum, printed
by John Day, London, 1571.

CHAPTER
IX.
_____
ELIZ.
A. D. 1597.

that the literature, the manners, and the habits of the puritans first begin to appear singular, and to wear a sectarian character. Hitherto their language and their literary compositions are untainted with affectation. They wrote and spoke like other men. With regard to purity of language and style, Cartwright and Travers are, at least, equal to Hooker, whose power lies rather in majesty of thought than in felicity of expression. In the pulpit Travers, preaching before the same audience, one of the most accomplished in England, carried away the palm of eloquence from his great opponent by the consent of all parties. Cartwright's eloquence had won the admiration of Cambridge. Henry Smith had preached at St. Clement Danes in rich redundant periods, remarkable alike for force and grace ; the Chrysostom of the age ; whom we are disposed to think no English preacher has since excelled in the proper attributes of pulpit eloquence. The age of pedantry had not yet commenced. The quaintness of the puritans was not assumed, their sentences were not curiously involved, their wit was not elaborate, their sermons were not studiously minced up in tiny fragments, each numbered and duly parcelled beneath its proper head or subdivision, with a view not so much to elucidate the subject as to display the author's dexterity in his only science,—the scholastic logic. All this belonged to a later age.

8. The manners of the puritans were distinguished by their gravity, and among the thought-

less and profane a grave demeanour has ever been
a crime. The presence of virtue is always embarrassing to the wicked, and its indications they
naturally dislike. No doubt the garb of sanctity
is easily assumed. The weak and hypocritical—the
one from nature the other from sheer villany—
readily adopt it; and since keenness in discrimination and a charitable disposition in judging
others, are unhappily but rare endowments, a
sanctimonious hypocrite is in popular estima-
tion the type and standard by which all seriousness is to be measured. We find accordingly
that, as the national mind gradually became less
devout in England, the gravity of the puritans became the frequent subject of a jest. Towards the
conclusion of her reign the example of the court
of Elizabeth was decidedly irreligious, and the
contagion spread rapidly among the common people. A preposterous extravagance in dress and
equipage ; a heathenish delight in jousts and tour-
naments, and public spectacles and plays ; the
prevalence of oaths (freely indulged in by the
queen herself) ; and to crown the whole, the studied desecration of the sabbath, mark too plainly
the hollowness of that religious profession which
even men of fashion were still constrained to make.
All men of real piety lamented the decay of vital
godliness. Hooker, in his preface, deplores it as
feelingly as Travers could have done. But the
cry once raised, a grave exterior and a virtuous
life were regarded as the sure signs of a puritan,
that is, of one disaffected to the state. Men who

CHAPTER had never entered a conventicle, nor had one mis-
IX. giving about the cross in baptism, were wickedly
ELIZ. driven from the church they loved, by cold treat-
A. D. 1597. ment or slanderous imputations; until, to be seen
twice at church on Sunday, and to spend the rest
of the day in reading the scriptures, was enough
to bring upon a whole family the disgrace of puritanism.

9. But at present their manners appear to have
been, in other respects, the manners of the times.
The literature of the age sometimes ridicules
their preciseness, but not their rudeness or vulgarity. The domestic friend and chaplain of
Leicester was not likely to be ill-bred. The
constant associates of Knollys and of sir Walter
Mildmay could hardly have been clowns. The
keen eye of Bacon must have rested upon something more inviting than religious cant and a
visage that affected sanctity, or he would scarcely
have concerned himself with the doctrines of the
puritans. An early puritan comes down to us a
distorted caricature, known only as misrepresented
in the next century by profligate wits or un-
scrupulous enemies. It was not till modesty
and virtue were discountenanced and irreligion
became a fashion, that the manners of the puritans were noticed for their singularity.

10. A great advantage was given to the puritans in a controversy which arose upon the observance of the Lord's-day. Greenham, a pious
1592. and eloquent minister in London, deeply affected
by the prevailing levity, first recalled the nation

to its duties in a book which made a great impression through the whole kingdom, and which Hall,
the pious bishop of Norwich, afterwards embalmed
in a striking epitaph. A few years afterwards,
Dr. Bound published his " book on the Sabbath ;"
in which, perhaps, he pushed the matter too far ;
and opposing one extreme fell into another ; so
as to rest the obligation of the Lord's-day upon
jewish, more than upon christian, principles. Still
he was right upon the whole ; and, when the question was once fairly placed before them, the dullest
congregation of the most stupid rustics could not
but be struck with the monstrous and indecent
inconsistency which every returning Sunday presented ;—the fourth commandment read in the
forenoon with every circumstance calculated to in-
spire the deepest awe and reverence ; the afternoon
devoted to fencing, and shooting, and bowling ; to
May games and morris dances ; the clergyman
himself too often a spectator, if not a sharer, of
the sports. Yet it was thought necessary to suppress Bound's treatise : and the natural consequence ensued ; the book flew through successive
editions, and its principles were diffused through
England. The observance, and the sacred obligation of the Lord's-day, became immediately a
question between the high church party and the
puritans ; and must be especially noticed as the
first disagreement betwixt them upon any point
of doctrine. This sabbatarian question, as it was
called, henceforth entered largely into every con-

CHAPTER troversy ; a rigid or lax observance of the Lord's-
IX.
day was at length the sign by which, above all

ELIZ. others, the two parties were distinguished.

A. D. 1597. 10. It is difficult to account satisfactorily for
the conduct of Whitgift and his party in this
affair. They had no traditionary errors to support ; for a strict observance of the Sunday was
in accordance with the principles and practice of
the great reformers whom they professed to represent.* If the puritan advocates of the Sabbath,

---

* This, I am aware, has been denied ; but I refer the reader to the
following admirable passage in Becon's catechism. Becon was chaplain to archbishop Cranmer. Works, page 500. P. S. Edition.

"What it is to keep holy the Sabbath-day.—To keep holy the Sabbath-day is not to cease from bodily labour, that thou shouldst the more
licentiously give thy mind to the wearing of gallant apparel ; to ban-
queting, to idle talk, to vain pastimes, and such other filthy pleasures of
the flesh ; but that thou, setting aside all worldly businesses, shouldst the
more freely apply thyself to read, hear, and learn the word of God, to
pray in the temple with the congregation, to be thankful to God for his
benefits, to be present at the ministrations of the holy sacraments, to be
partaker of the mysteries of the Lord's body and blood, to give some
good thing to the relief of the poor, to visit and comfort the sick, and
them that are in prison, and casting away the works of the flesh, wholly
to exercise thyself in the fruits of the Spirit."

Coverdale, bishop of Exeter, states with admirable clearness the distinction between the authority of the decalogue under the christian dispensation, and the disannulling of the Mosaic ordinances. " Whoso
now doth well ponder these ten chapters or commandments, and com-
pareth them to the doings and works of the holy patriarchs and old
fathers which had no law in writing, ye shall find that the Lord, now
with this his written law, began no new thing, neither aught that was
not afore in the world."—He instances this in each of the ten commandments. Of the fourth he says, " the Sabbath did not the Lord
here ordain first, but on the seventh day of the creation, Gen. iii. The
same did the fathers keep aright, no doubt. John vii." He sums up
thus ; "wherefore, in these commandments, is nothing written or required, that was not also required of the fathers afore the law, and performed through true faith in Christ. The Lord, therefore, began no
new thing with his people, when he delivered them the tables of the
law. . . . As for all the laws and ordinances which were afterwards
added to these two tables, they were not joined thereunto as principal
laws, but as bye-laws for the declaration and better understanding of

based their conclusions upon false and jewish CHAPTER IX.
premises, still the conclusions themselves were
good, and might have been easily established ELIZ.
upon a more evangelical basis. It is strange, A.D.
too, that they did not reflect upon the certain 1597—1602
and almost self-proving truth, that a religion
which sits easily upon the careless can possess few
charms for the devout; and that the strength of
a religious institution depends not so much upon
the number of its adherents as upon their zeal.
In alienating the strict observers of the Sabbath,
they deprived the church of its most vigorous
supporters, and forced them to transfer their sympathies, if not their allegiance, to the puritans.
Pride and obstinacy, and a resolute determination
to put down their adversaries, whether right or
wrong, may seem unmeasured charges; but the
truth of history suggests none that are less offensive. On the sabbatarian question, Whitgift chose
rather to forsake his own principles than to permit a victory in a righteous cause to be won by
his opponents.

11. Of the relative piety of the puritans and
the prelatic party, at the period of which we
speak, it is, however, by no means easy to form

the ten chapters or commandments. For the perfect sum of all laws,
and the very right rule of godliness, of God's service, of righteousness,
of good and evil conversation, are comprehended or read in the ten
chapters or commandments." "The old faith," page 41. P. S. Edition.
"The old faith," is a translation of Bullinger's "Antiquissima fides
et vera religio." Here, then, we have at once the judgment of two of
the most eminent divines of the reformation as to the perpetual obligation of the Sabbath. Calvin took lower ground, and the pernicious
influence of his views upon the Sabbath still infects the continental
churches. (See Instit. Lib. ii. cap. viii. 34.)

CHAPTER a just opinion. Pure and spiritual religion is
IX. seldom to be accurately measured by any visible
ELIZ. criterion; for while the signs of its absence are
A. D. always painfully decisive, those of its presence
1597—1602. are not to be implicitly relied on. The zeal of
the puritans was repressed; the fervour of the
high church party had visibly begun to wane.
But intermediate between the two, there was no
doubt a large body well affected to the church,
and having little in common with either extreme,
who cherished the principles of the reformation
and the bible, and maintained a consistent life of
piety. The fervour of the puritans was not unmixed with the alloy of a party spirit, and sometimes of a rancorous hatred; nor must it be forgotten that a zeal about religious matters is not
necessarily a zeal for God. The most generous of
the opposite party, Cecil himself for instance,
charged them with a narrow bigotry and a factious temper; and the suggestion is not uncharitable, that a weaker sect, struggling for power
against a well-established rival, must profess,
even if it do not feel, a more fervent zeal, and a
more lofty piety than its adversaries; and to suppose the puritans free from this, perhaps uncon-
scious, insincerity, is to suppose that they were free
from the common infirmities of man.

12. Such abatements must be made. But after
all, the preponderance of real piety lay, we suspect,
at the close of the reign of queen Elizabeth,
amongst those who were roughly classed as puritans. So much constancy in suffering, a zeal as

fervent, domestic habits by the confession of their bitterest enemies so pure and blameless, religious duties piously discharged in the face of scorn and the instant dread of punishment, can in justice be regarded only as the marks of a piety sincere and deeply seated. The gold was not free from dross ; their infirmities, though fewer than their enemies asserted, were greater than they themselves were willing to allow. But their errors lay chiefly with the judgment. The heart was right upon the whole ; and hitherto, when most factious, they still believed—after an earnest scrutiny of the scriptures, which, though often misapplied and misunderstood, were received as their sole guide—that they ought to obey God rather than man : a justification of no value, it is true, when used to the oppression and injury of others, but of unspeakable importance when used to justify the conduct, or to sustain the fainting spirits, of him who suffers for conscience sake.

13. The prospect, on the whole, was gloomy to those who loved the church, and clung to its institutions in the spirit of the reformation. Much of its " first love " had passed away, and pomp and splendour vainly strove to fill up the void. The courage of the reformers too had disappeared. No honest Latimer, mingling reverence to his sovereign with boldness in the cause of God, no Jewel, meek but firm and faithful, now preached to thronging audiences, or rebuked the sins of royalty in the presence of the queen. The spirit of this world had crept in, and quenched the zeal

CHAPTER of those whose principles and doctrines were, how-
IX.   ever, as yet untainted. The piety of the church
ELIZ.   of England received a shock in the affair of Grin-
A.D.   dal from which it had not recovered. Social
1597—1602. meetings for prayer and praise, and for conference
among the clergy, are almost inseparable from a
vigorous piety and an effective ministry ; and
these had been discouraged. They were chiefly
to be met with in the chambers of the puritans. In short, the tendency was already visible, if to fanaticism on the one hand, to a dead
formality on the other ; while on both sides the
catholic spirit of their forefathers had almost
disappeared. Tenacity in imposing and in resist-
ing trifles had in time produced its fruit ; trifles
were looked upon as the very essence of true religion. To comply with a harmless form was regarded as fearful sin amongst the rigid puritans : to
pray extempore and expound the scriptures in private houses was a transgression of equal magnitude in the sight of high prelatic churchmen. In
such a state of things it was impossible that the
power of true piety in men's hearts should not fade
and wither, though it was probable enough their
clamorous zeal would soon break out into shriller
cries, and put on the appearance of a sterner resolution. And this in fact occurred. Moderation
was scouted upon both sides, and the most violent counsels were those alone which now began
to obtain a hearing.

CHAPTER X.

1. QUEEN Elizabeth died in the year 1602, and James hastened from Scotland to occupy the vacant throne. His character has been often drawn, and in it stronger features seems at length to be well understood. There was a strange mixture in it of sagacity and folly; of sagacity that often wore the appearance of consummate wisdom, of folly scarcely to be distinguished from that of an idiot. The sceptre passed from the wisest of women to the most ridiculous of men. But James was shrewd and cunning; he imposed upon the statesmen by whom Elizabeth had consented to be governed, and they stooped, it is evident, to become his willing agents, and were sometimes his dupes. Under a plain exterior, and most unkingly manners, there was a depth of disguise and artifice which, if we must believe them serious, few or none of his courtiers suspected. They speak of him as a paragon of wisdom : posterity have long since spoken of him with contempt. The king-craft in which he gloried has ceased to claim

CHAPTER
X.

JAMES I.

A. D. 1602.

respect; and the virtues which can ennoble kings in the eyes of succeeding generations were wanting to his character.

2. Since the affair of Coppinger and Hackett, and the death of Penry, there had been a truce on both sides. The prelates had ceased to harass, and the puritans to provoke; for each party waited for the turn of affairs upon the accession of the new sovereign; and neither of them was able to calculate with perfect confidence upon the course he would pursue. James had been brought up a protestant, a presbyterian of the straitest sect, the docile pupil of George Buchanan, the patient hearer of the disciples of Knox. Should these early prepossessions last the puritans were safe. They might even hope for the royal countenance in their extreme project of remodelling the church of England after the presbyterian form; at least their presbyterianism would no longer be a crime. But on the other hand, the prepossessions of youth and the impulses of education, cannot always be trusted. It was even possible that the king might not be sincere. The iron hand which held his mother's wrist and compelled her abdication,—the hand of a fierce, feudal oligarchy—had never quite released the son. While he reigned in Scotland there was a power behind the throne far greater than the throne itself; the power of the church and the oligarchs; of Knox and the barons; and they exercised it with little or no disguise. Escaped from this, James might appear in another character; from one extreme he might rush into an-

other; nay, he might avenge upon English puritans the injuries done by Scottish presbyterians to his mother, and the insults to himself. Each party waited eagerly and anxiously for the result.

3. But this uncertainty was of no long continuance. Whitgift dispatched his agents to Scotland to assure the king of the devotion of the prelates, and the puritans met him on his way to London with their famous millenary petition, so called because it professed to represent the wishes of a thousand clergymen, though, in fact, the names actually subscribed were about eight hundred. To the archbishop's envoy James replied in terms which, could his royal word be trusted, were full of satisfaction. He was anxious to follow the steps of his renowned predecessor. He would alter nothing, introduce nothing, without the consent and approbation of the bishops. Yet it was not easy to forget the previous conduct and opinions of this now compliant sovereign. Standing in his place before the general assembly of the kirk of Scotland, with head uncovered and hands uplifted to heaven, he had a few years before protested that their presbyterian church was " the purest in the world," and that as to the neighbouring church of England, "its service was but an evil said mass, in English." Except the adoration of the host, " it wanted nothing of the mass itself." This was in 1590, in a speech to his parliament : eight years afterwards he courteously classed together " the papistical and anglican bishops *." A mind, less acute than Whit-

* Calderwood's Hist. Ch. of Scotland. 256 and 418, Neal ii. 14.

CHAPTER gift's, and a temper less anxious, might then well
X. entertain some misgivings as to the real intentions

JAMES I. of king James.

A. D. 1602. 4. The millenary petition* must be regarded as
the manifesto of the puritans at the opening of
the seventeenth century; and we have no reason
to suppose, that it does not honestly express their
sentiments. James had hitherto appeared as
their friend; he had invited Cartwright to accept
a professorship in Scotland; he had written to
Elizabeth to intercede on his behalf, at a time
when he was in the deepest disgrace, and the
court of high commission in its fullest insolence
of tyranny. He had made obtrusive and uncalled-
for professions of his adherence to the puritan
cause. If then the English puritans had a doubt
as to the course he would pursue, it arose from
their knowledge of the infirmities of his character, not from the indecision of his past conduct,
which was entirely favourable to their cause; and
as the prelates hoped, so the petitioners feared,
that he would lack the energy to intermeddle
with the state of things he found prevailing in
the church of England. If this view be correct,
the millenary petition must be considered to
breathe a moderate tone and spirit. The revolutionary project of remodelling the church of
England after the presbyterian form was now
abandoned. The petition contained no angry
diatribes upon the sinfulness of such officers as
deans, canons, archdeacons, and archbishops. It
did not renew the stale assertion that episcopacy

* Fuller iii. 6. an. 1602—4.

was unscriptural. Those who had framed it, had evidently been learning wisdom where wisdom is learned most easily—in silence, in poverty, in obloquy. They stood in advance of Cartwright, that is, of Cartwright, such as he had been when, in the days of his youthful pride and inexperience, he convulsed the university and the church with wild visions of reform; for Cartwright was now an aged and a temperate man, and on the verge of another world. The petitioners addressed themselves, not any longer to the enforcement of a theory, but to the practical work of achieving a reformation of abuses, or, however, of usages which they considered to be such. It was another crisis in the history of the church of England. Another opportunity of conciliation had unexpectedly returned. Never had the demands of the discontented party been so moderate; never could they have been conceded with so good a grace. Some of them appear to us, it is true, to deserve a place only amongst those trifling quibbles and conceits, (the more trifling in appearance because enunciated with a profound seriousness,) from which puritanism was never free. But with a few exceptions their demands were reasonable. Many of them have since been wrung by a necessity which they could not resist, from churchmen of succeeding days; some, in a far better spirit, have been cheerfully conceded in our own times, by churchmen as well affected, as learned, and as pious, as the most unyielding of their forefathers.

5. The grievances of the puritans were set forth under four heads. First, they objected as of old to the cap and surplice, the cross in baptism, and the ring in marriage. Also they desired that in baptism, the interrogation addressed through the sponsors to the infant, should be done away with, or rendered more simple. Confirmation, as superfluous, they prayed might cease. Divers terms, *priest, absolution,* and some others, ought to be amended ; and the length of the service abridged. Church music required reform. The Lord's day ought to be better kept, and other holydays urged less strictly. The people should not be charged to bow at the name of Jesus ; a uniformity of doctrine ought to be prescribed, and no popish opinions taught. The canonical scriptures only ought to be read in churches,—communicants should be previously examined, and the communion preceded by a sermon. And they prayed that baptism hereafter might not be administered by women.

6. These, upon doctrinal points, comprised the whole of their demands. With one exception, had all they asked been conceded, the church of England would still have remained entire ; she would have made no sacrifice of any one principle which she holds to be important. The rite of confirmation, venerable for its high antiquity in the church, she could by no means forego : it is the correlative of infant baptism. If children be received in infancy into the bosom of the church, it is surely necessary that in riper years they should be solemnly admitted, upon a profession of their faith

made openly by themselves, into full communion:
and that this may be done with due solemnity,
the chief minister of the church receives them
with the laying on of hands, and prayer for the
gift of the holy Spirit. With wise and laborious
preparation on the part of the parochial clergy,
and an intelligent sense of its importance in the
young, the rite of confirmation is a blessing to
the church. Nor can we perceive the superstition
of bowing at the name of Jesus.

7. Secondly, the petitioners asked, that, for the
future, none should be admitted into the ministry
but able and sufficient men. That those already
ordained who could not preach might either be
removed " and some charitable course taken with
them for their relief," or else be compelled to
maintain, according to their incomes, preachers to
supply their lack of service. That non-residence
should cease. That king Edward's statute (which
had been repealed by Mary, and not re-enacted
by Elizabeth,) permitting the clergy to marry,
should be revived; and that no subscription
should be demanded from the clergy but what the
law required.

8. Under the third head the demands of the
petitioners were not quite so moderate. They
required that the bishops should abandon all preferment, save their bishoprics, and that other
" double beneficed men " should not be suffered
to hold, some two, some three, benefices with
cure, and some two, three, or four, dignities besides. But what followed raised an angry storm

CHAPTER from various quarters; for the petitioners requir-
VI. ed "that impropriations annexed to bishoprics
JAMES I. and colleges be demised only to the preachers and
A. D. 1602. incumbents for the old rents, while lay impropriations should be charged with a sixth or seventh
part of the worth to the maintenance of the preaching minister." The lay impropriations (or tithe
and glebe lands,) were then chiefly held by the
descendants of those noble houses amongst whom
Henry VIII. had so profusely squandered the
church's patrimony; and they were very little disposed to make restitution of even so much as a
seventh part of them for the maintenance of a
godly ministry. Thus mere selfishness arrayed
the statesmen and courtiers against the petitioners; and still more bitter, and yet more reasonable, was the displeasure of the universities.
They found themselves much aggrieved that, while
a seventh part of their spoil was all the petitioners
demanded from the laity, colleges and cathedrals
should be more severely punished; being required
to demise to their vicars at the old rents without
fine and without improvement. It is certain that
such a measure would long since have reduced
the universities to penury; so much has the value
of money diminished while that of land has been
constantly increasing. Cambridge immediately
resolved that whoever should promote the petition
or its principles should, ipso facto, be suspended;
and Oxford followed with a public refutation of
the millenary petition.

9. Under the fourth head, the petitioners re-

quested a restoration of church discipline, or at
least that enormities might be redressed. Nothing could be more reasonable than their demands. They protest against the wickedness of excommunication " for twelve-penny matters," for
trifling debts and frivolous offences. They ask
that the oath *ex officio*, whereby men are forced
to accuse themselves, be used more sparingly; and
they subscribe themselves, in conclusion, his "majesty's most humble servants, the ministers of the
gospel, who desire not a disorderly innovation but
a due and godly reformation."

10. Many other petitions were presented to the
king, which were known at the time under the
common name of millenary petitions. Some of
them were of a violent description, and prayed for
the extirpation of bishops and the introduction of
the foreign presbyterianism. These proceeded
chiefly from the brownists, whose numbers had
now considerably increased, and between whom
and the puritans there was as intense a war, as
between the latter and the highest of the prelatic
party.

11. It was resolved to hold a conference, in
which the questions at issue should be discussed
by the representatives of the two great parties,
the prelatists and puritans, in the presence of the
king. Nothing could exceed the wisdom of this
project; nothing but the folly displayed in its
management, and the insipidity of its whole
conclusion. The spectacle would have been
indeed august, and worthy of the brightest

CHAPTER days of christendom, and of the purest annals
X.   of the church;—a wise and christian king, as-
JAMES I. sisted by his counsellors, sitting from day to
A. D. 1603. day, to investigate with calmness and sincerity
the causes of uneasiness which had rankled for
half a century among the brotherhood of Christ,
the ministers of one communion, the devout members of the same reformed church. But, in fact,
the conference widened the breach it should have
healed. Whatever advantages of another kind
resulted from it, it was, as a conference, a mere
pretence. So the puritans affirmed with one voice,
and the verdict of their fellow countrymen has at
length ratified and confirmed their censure. The
history of the Hampton court conference is given[*]
by Dr. Barlow, dean of Chester, who was present:
it was drawn up at the request of Whitgift and
the court : the puritans objected to it at the time,
that justice was not done to the arguments and
speeches of their representatives ; but upon the
whole its general accuracy is admitted. Other
accounts were published by various writers ; and
the importance of the controversy in the eyes of
cotemporaries, may be collected from the fulness
and care with which they have handed down its
most trifling details. The conference was assembled by proclamation at Hampton court, on
the 14th of January, 1603,[†] and the king was

[*] The sum and substance of the conference, &c. at Hampton court :
by William Barlow, D. D. and Dean of Chester. Republished in the
Phœnix, 1707.

[†] The reader will bear in mind, that the year then began on the
25th of March; so that the events of January, February, and March,
belong, according to our reckoning, to the following year. Thus

present with most of the lords of the privy council. On the one side were summoned the archbishop of Canterbury, eight bishops, seven deans
of cathedral churches, and two others. On behalf
of the puritans, to contend with this learned pha-
lanx, four puritan ministers had been summoned
to appear. On the morning of the first day, "all
the deans and doctors attending them, my lords
the bishops went into the presence chamber," so
writes Dr. Barlow, " there we found, sitting on a
form, Dr. Reynolds, Dr. Sparks, Mr. Knewstubs,
and Mr. Chaderton, agents for the millenary
plaintiffs."

12. During the first day the puritans were not
present, being expressly excluded by his majesty's
commands. Yet in their absence the questions
were discussed, and in fact decided, on which they
were most anxious to obtain a hearing. The king
opened the proceedings with a speech, in which he
expressed his satisfaction that he was in the presence of grave, learned, and reverend men ; not
as before, elsewhere, a king without state, without
honor, without order, where beardless boys braved
him to his face. He said he was averse to any
innovation ; at the same time should anything be
found to need redress, he wished it to be done,
though as quietly as possible, and without any
visible alteration ; a remark which he several
times repeated ; and on this account he had called
in the bishops by themselves. He then required

the conference was held, by the present method of computation, in
January, 1604.

CHAPTER their advice upon three points—the first and se-
X.   cond of which, it is evident, could only be discussed
JAMES I. with fairness in the presence of the puritans. He
A. D. 1603. reduced his questions to several heads; the first
having reference to the book of common prayer;
the second to excommunication by ecclesiastical
courts; and the third, relating to the church in
Ireland. Under the first head the questions of
confirmation, of private baptism, and absolution,
were argued and decided; under the second, excommunication was discussed. The day was then
spent, and the assembly broke up. "The king,"
says Barlow, "handled all these points admirably,
both for understanding, speech, and judgment.".
His knowledge of divinity was considerable; nor
was he wanting in dialectic skill. His learning,
too, was prompt and various, if not deep. But
these considerations, it is probable, gave little
satisfaction to the four puritan divines who whiled
away the tedious hours upon the form in the anti-
chamber. Nor would it add to their content
to learn from Dr. Barlow's relation, that his majesty had meanly taken occasion of their absence
to profess his dislike of the puritans ever since he
was ten years old. He had lived among them, he
said, profanely using the words of scripture, but
he was not of them.

13. On Monday, the conference was resumed,
and the four plaintiffs were called into the privy-
chamber, where they found the bishops of London
and Winchester, and all the deans and doctors,
present, as well as Patrick Galloway, a minister

of Perth, who was allowed to be there as a spectator. After a short speech from James, Dr. Reynolds, on behalf of the puritans, presented four
requests: first, that the doctrine of the church
might be preserved in purity according to God's
word; secondly, that good pastors might be plant-
ed in all churches to preach the same; thirdly,
that the church government might be sincerely
ministered according to God's word; fourthly,
that the book of common prayer might be fitted
to more increase of piety.

14. Under the first head, it is well for the peace
of the church that his suggestions met with so
little encouragement. Strange as it may seem,
he urged the introduction of the nine Lambeth
articles into her authoritative formularies. He
would have narrowed the basis of orthodoxy, and
compelled the church of England not only to
speak (for here lay the danger and the injustice
of his proposal), but to speak exclusively, the language of extreme dogmatic calvinism. Whereas
the sixteenth article declares, that " after we have
received the Holy Ghost, we may depart from
grace," he desired to add the words, " yet neither
totally, or finally :" and the Lambeth articles he
prayed to have inserted in that book of common
prayer, in which the church of England compre-
hends her discipline and doctrines. The latter of
these requests he urged a second time upon the
following day. From this dangerous innovation
the church of England was preserved, partly by
the earnest protestations of the bishop of London,

CHAPTER
X.
_____

JAMES I.

A. D. 1603.

who interrupted Dr. Reynolds with a rudeness which the king reproved. However, his remonstrances prevailed, and the doctrine of an eternal decree of reprobation, launched by the God of mercy against individual men yet unborn, was not numbered amongst the doctrines to which a faithful son of the church of England must yield his acquiescence, and every minister subscribe his hand. The moment was critical. The spiritual head of the church of England had himself drawn up, and endeavoured to impose, the Lambeth articles. The leader of the puritans urged the adoption of them. Happily moderate views prevailed above the strife of scholastic theologians. Probably, too, the church owes much to the calmer counsels of the laymen who were present of the privy council. Nor will the reader hesitate to acknowledge the good hand of God. What a host of worthies would have fled dismayed from the church of England, in every age, had this point been carried ; had the church, upon the most awful of all controversies, enunciated, as one of her terms of communion, the most awful of all possible decisions ! And yet, the puritans cannot with justice be charged with the whole impolicy of this narrow project ; the archbishop himself, in his previous conduct, had furnished grounds for the suspicion, that, if he could, he would have incorporated the Lambeth articles with the thirty-nine. How insignificant the scruples of the surplice and the cross, and how trifling the hardships of subscription, compared with the distress which would have spread far and wide, if this decree of eternal reprobation had been once enrolled among the statutes of the church of England! Such, how- ever, were the inconsistencies of men, who smarted beneath oppression, and such their consideration for the consciences of others who differed, if but a hair's breadth, from themselves.

15. Other discussions followed; but the subjects were either of less importance, or had been already determined, in the first day's conference, by the king and prelates. Reynolds objected to confirmation, and to private baptism. As to the first, he was confronted with the testimony of the fathers, and of Fulke and Calvin in later times. Private baptism by women, which had been hitherto allowed, was forbidden; some alterations, chiefly verbal, were promised in the prayer book; and, on the complaint that it was defective, it was agreed that the catechism should be revised, and something added to it on the doctrine of the sacraments. On this point the sense of the reformers was clearly with the puritan divines. It was never supposed that a knowledge of the creed, the Lord's prayer, and the ten commandments, was a sufficient erudition for christian youth. Various catechisms had been set forth in addition; and especially a compendium of Calvin's catechism, by Nowel, dean of St. Paul's. This had the sanction of the convocation of 1562: and schoolmasters were ordered to instruct their pupils in it. Art. 20. It is much to be deplored that

when Nowel's was suffered to fall into disuse, some other catechism, more comprehensive than that we now make use of, and less burdensome to the learner's memory than that of Nowel, was not published by authority. Even with the additions it received at the Hampton court conference, the church catechism is far from affording, without laborious explanations, to which many an anxious parent feels himself incompetent, an outline of all important doctrine. The comments and explanations, constantly published from year to year, and the large demand for other catechisms, still prove the necessity there is for something more simple, and at the same time more comprehensive. To the suggestions of Dr. Reynolds, made this day, the church of England owes that inestimable treasure, the authorized English version of the bible; and to Reynolds himself a debt of gratitude, not only for urging the work, but for the important share he had in its execution. The profanation of the Lord's-day was deplored by the puritans, and a promise (which meant nothing) was given that the evil should be remedied: for henceforth a devout observance of the sabbath was one of the symbols of a puritan, and the court profaned it as if with studied ostentation.

16. The great points of real interest were now to be considered; but it was evident that no concessions were intended. The puritans wished to have some relief in the matter of subscription. Mr. Knewstubs, who had scarcely spoken hitherto, expressed his dislike of the cross

in baptism, and of the interrogatives to the sponsors. He was probably abashed and confused:
Dr. Barlow says his speech was long and perplexed.
It is certain the treatment he received was not
such as to re-assure a timid speaker. " He said
something out of Au'stin, but what it was his
majesty plainly confessed he did not understand,
and asked the lords what they thought he meant."
But when Knewstubs urged, that offence to weak
brethren was given by the use of the cross, " his
majesty," we are told, " answered most acutely,
with a question unanswerable; asking them how
long they would be weak? Whether forty-five
years was not long enough for them to grow
strong? and who they were that pretended this
weakness? for we, saith the king, require not
subscription of laics and idiots, but of preachers
and ministers. Lastly, he said, that some of them
were *strong enough,* if not *head strong;* however,
in this case they pretended weakness." The jeers
and pleasantries of Jeffreys on the judgment-seat,
were scarcely more unfeeling.

17. But his majesty's humour changed when
Dr. Reynolds dared to express the desire, always
universal amongst the puritans, to have the pro-
phesyings revised " as the reverend archbishop
Grindal and other bishops desired of her late majesty;" and that the clergy should be allowed to
meet in provincial constitutions and in synods
with the bishops. " At which speech," says Dr.
Barlow, " his majesty was somewhat stirred, yet,
which was admirable in him, without passion or

CHAPTER show thereof, thinking that they aimed at a Scot-
X. tish presbytery, which, says he, agreeth as well
JAMES I. with a monarchy, as God and the devil. Then
A. D. 1603. Jack and Tom, and Will and Dick shall meet, and
at their pleasures censure me, and my council, and
all our proceedings : then Will shall stand up and
say, it must be thus; then Dick shall reply and
say, nay marry, but we will have it thus: and
here I must once reiterate my former speech, *le
roy s'avisera," &c.*

18. The indecency of this disgraceful scene was
not yet at its height; the king concluded thus.*
" Well, doctor, have you anything else to say ?

Dr. Reynolds. No more, if it please your majesty.

The king. If this be all your party hath to say,
I will make them conform themselves, or else I
will harry them out of the land, or else do worse †."

19. Several modern writers not acquainted with
the force of this expressive Scotticism, have by no
means done justice to his majesty's gracious intentions to his puritan subjects. They have made

* Barlow's Account.
† The bishop of St. Asaph, however, has expressed a very different
opinion upon James's behaviour. " During the whole of the conference
there is nothing more striking than the superiority of the king himself
over both parties : he not only surpassed them in temper and fairness,
but apparently in learning and knowledge of the subject : notwithstanding the insignificance of the objections raised, and in some cases their
senseless futility, he heard them with patience," &c. Dr. Short's Hist.
of the Ch. of England xii. 509. Entertaining the highest respect for
the learning and candour of the right rev. author, I am compelled on
this subject to arrive at a very opposite conclusion. Elsewhere Dr.
Short remarks, (xii. 523), and, I think, more correctly, " James might
perhaps have proved a good king, if his weakness as a man had not
rendered it almost impossible for him to perform the duties of his
station."

him say that he would *hurry* them out of his
kingdom. Those who have heard a pack of *har-*
riers in full cry, will better appreciate the meaning of the royal threat. A threat addressed to
the learned Reynolds, a divine of the highest
rank; and to the wise and eloquent Chadderton, the first master of Emmanuel College;—of
whose eloquence it is recorded that when, having
preached at unusual length to an audience in
Lancashire he expressed an intention of concluding, the whole congregation arose and with one
voice importuned him to proceed *; and of whose
wisdom it may suffice to say, that sir Walter
Mildmay refused to build his college (he was
the noble founder of Emmanuel) unless Chadderton would promise to accept the mastership.
Sparkes and Knewstubs were also eminent divines. The infirmities of such men must surely
have been shaded with some tints of piety and
virtue; and to such men it was, king James
addressed his memorable bravado, " I will harry
them out of the land or else do worse :" this, too,
at a conference in which he had invited or rather
commanded them to sustain a part.

20. The third day's conference began; but by
this time the puritans were disheartened, and
were little more than passive spectators. The
subject of discussion was, the court of high commission, and the oath ex officio by which suspected
persons were compelled to criminate themselves.
Many civilians were present by command, as the

* Fuller's Worthies.

question partly concerned the civil constitution of the state. A nameless lord* had the courage to declare that the proceedings in that court were like the Spanish inquisition ; he was answered by the archbishop and the lord chancellor. And then the king himself defended the court, and especially the oath of conpurgation, with such wondrous wisdom, that all the lords, and the rest of the present auditors, stood amazed at it. The scene that followed is one of the most humiliating upon the page of English history. " The archbishop of Canterbury said, that undoubtedly his majesty spake by the special assistance of God's spirit." "The bishop of London, on his knees, protested that his heart melted within him, as he doubted not did the hearts of the whole company, with joy, and made haste to acknowledge to Almighty God, his singular mercy in giving us such a king, as since Christ's time the like he thought had not been seen."† Nor did the bishop of London mistake the feelings of his audience ; for the lords with one voice did yield a very affectionate acclamation ; and the civilians present confessed, that they could not with many an hour of preparation, have spoken so well and wisely as the king. The years of the primate claim for him the forbearance which is due to decaying faculties, and perhaps a second childishness. The servility of the bishop of London wants this, the only possible, excuse. In the adulation of the courtiers

* Fuller iii. p. 190. † Barlow.

and the facile admiration of civilians, men learned
in the law, we see some at least of the latent
causes of James's infatuation; and, if so, of those
convulsions which brought to the scaffold his
equally infatuated son. Weak, and vain, and insolent as James was, he could scarcely keep pace
with the homage of his courtiers. He was probably the most credulous man then alive; but he
could hardly believe in the nauseous flatteries
with which this memorable conference closed.

21. The result of the conference was received with
various emotions; with triumph by the high prelatic party, by the puritans with disgust and mere
contempt. The part which had been taken in the
management of it by the king, the prelates, and the
puritans, was summed up in one of those pithy sentences into which the result of much observation,
and the comparison of various opinions, is finally
condensed. The king, it was said, was above
himself, the bishop of London appeared even with
himself, and Dr. Reynolds fell much beneath himself. More commodiously expressed, the verdict
of the times is precisely that of posterity. King
James prided himself on his theology, and he had
sought a field on which to display an accomplishment then much in vogue. The prelates (not all
of them, by any means, but those who were extreme against the puritans) had found in the
bishop of London a keen advocate, and an able
expositor. The puritans had been unfairly treated, browbeaten, jeered at, silenced. As will ever
happen in a defeated party, many of the puritans

CHAPTER blamed their advocates. It is true not one of
X. them possessed the resolution of Knox, the fear-
JAMES I. lessness of Latimer, or even the gentle pertinacity
A. D. 1603. of John Foxe. But they had other qualities which
fitted them for their task; deep learning, eloquence, a birth and education which at least entitled them to respect; and above all, the conviction, deep and strong within them, that their cause
was the cause of God, and deeply involved the interests of true religion. But in truth their task
was such as none could have accomplished; namely, to extort concessions from an absolute sovereign, in his own palace, surrounded with courtiers
and counsellors no less determined than himself
that no concessions should be made. It would
have been more politic to have declined the unequal contest, and satisfied themselves with a
written statement of their grievances, and a petition for redress.

22. Within a few weeks of the conference at
Hampton court, Whitgift and Cartwright died;
the two men, the impression of whose character
abides with us still, and will probably never be
effaced from the religious institutions of our land.
The church of England has many features for
which it is indebted to Whitgift. The puritans,
while they continued to exist, then the nonconformists, and now the dissenters, claim Cartwright
as their great founder. Of Whitgift as a man, it
is difficult to speak. Most of what is said of
him by contemporaries appears now extravagant,
whether for good or evil. With a few exceptions,

this was the manner of the times. Biography was a
caricature. But making allowance for this excess,
the character of Whitgift comes down to us as
one blemished indeed, and stained with a severity
which, however meant, was nothing else than
cruelty, but not without the marks of greatness
and of piety ; greatness and piety be it understood,
such as may co-exist with a narrow mind and a
severe temper. His defence of episcopacy, in reply
to Cartwright, assigns him a high place among
controversial writers. The patron of Hooker, and
the prompter from whose suggestions the " Ecclesiastical polity" arose, must have been shrewd in
discerning ability in others, and generous in bringing it to light. Hooker's treatise was meant to
supersede his own ; he foresaw his triumph and
promoted it. Nor was he destitute of kindness.
When Essex was condemned, he pleaded for his
life* with so much earnestness that he lost, for
some time, the favour of the queen, or rather
provoked her passion. As a divine, his powers
have never been questioned ; and those who
were acquainted with him in private life, speak
of him with reverence mingled with affection.
With a gentler spirit, and a lot cast in happier
times, Whitgift might have been one of the bright
ornaments of the English church. Whether, from
the prescience which is sometimes granted to a
wise old age, and seems to be prophetic, or from
that causeless jealousy and fear of coming evil
which is more frequent in decaying years, Whit-

* Paul's Whitgift.

gift, though he had triumphed at Hampton court, dreaded the opening of parliament, and hoped he might not live to see it. He would rather, he said, render an account of his bishopric to God, than continue, among so many troubles, to discharge it upon earth. His last words, twice uttered, were characteristic of the man,—"Pro ecclesia Dei." "For the church of God!"

23. Cartwright was amongst the first, and survived to be almost the last of the early puritans. He was warmly attached to the church of England, and in his later days, at least, no enemy to episcopacy. But another school arose with whom not amendment, but subversion, was the cry. Into this some of the early puritans were absorbed, others submitted to a state of things which they did not approve entirely, rather than incur the perils of change, or even the hazards of resistance. The stream of innovation rushed on, while Cartwright seemed to lag behind. His fate was that which often befals a leader of pure conscience, and defective courage or weak judgment. He had raised a tempest which he could not still. He had taught disciples who lived to scorn their master. He had disseminated principles, so his own pupils told him, which condemned his moderation, and made it seem to be mere cowardice. But whatever his failings as the leader of a party, he was eminent as a private christian. No doubt he felt, as years passed over him, and his mind became more deeply seasoned with spiritual affections, that the church was to be improved, not

by the renovation of its institutions, not by strife CHAPTER
and revolution, but by the grace and spirit of X.
God working in the hearts, and purifying the JAMES I.
lives of professing christians. It was the fault of A. D. 1603.
both parties to attach too much importance to
the mechanism of a church, and to expect from
it results which mechanism could never yield;
and hence arose on both sides a tenacity, which
both sides mistook for zeal in the cause of God.
Cartwright seems to have perceived his error,
without making any formal retractation of the
principles of his early life. His theory of church
government might be still the same; but it no
longer occupied the same place in his affections.
He died in peace, as we have already mentioned, Dec. 27,
in the asylum provided for him at Warwick, by 1603.
his generous patron "the good earl of Leicester."

24. Before Whitgift's death, a writ was issued
to assemble the convocation. Bancroft succeeded
to the primacy, but while it was still vacant he
presided as bishop of London over this great
synod, which was held in the year 1604.*

25. In this famous convocation the constitutions and canons ecclesiastical by which the
church of England is governed were agreed upon.
They are one hundred and forty-one in number,
and were immediately published by the king's
authority under the great seal of England. But
neither then or ever since, have they received the
sanction of parliament, and in consequence they
are not binding on the laity, not binding *proprio*

---

* It is generally called the synod of 1603, because convoked in that
year; but its actual sittings were held during the year 1604.

CHAPTER *vigore*, as Blackstone has observed, but only so
X.
far as they embody other canons which had pre-
JAMES I. viously the authority of laws. They bind the
A. D. 1604. clergy by virtue of their oath of canonical obedi-
ence.

26. Few men of any party will now be found,
to justify the hard and rigourous spirit, which
several of these enactments breathe. They were
no sooner published than some wise and moderate men, (so writes the catholic-minded Fuller,)
expressed their apprehension that they were too
heavy a burden to be long borne; and that it
was enough for the episcopal party to have triumphed over their adversaries without insulting them. If cursing, says a nonconformist
writer,* could have crushed the puritans, we
should have heard of them no more. Excommunication is denounced unsparingly. To deny
the church of England to be a true and apostolic
church; to say that its worship is superstitious
or containeth any thing in it that is repugnant
to the scriptures ; or that the thirty-nine articles
are in any part erroneous ; or that the rights and
ceremonies of the church are superstitous, is to
subject the offender to excommunication, ipso
facto. Such, too, is the punishment of those who
deny the lawful government of archbishops, bishops, deans, &c., and of those who, seceding
from the church, combine themselves into a new
brotherhood, and affirm that their meetings or
congregations are true and lawful churches.†

* Price's Hist. Non-conformists, i. 476.
† Canons agreed on in Convocation, &c. 1603.

These, with some other censures of a similar kind, it is needless to add, were intended to complete the discomfiture of the puritans. The disgrace of these barbarous canons belongs to the convo- cation in which they passed; but prejudice, fomented from time to time by some of her assail. ants, still lays it to the church of England; and it must be allowed that some degree of censure fairly belongs to her for permitting the canons to remain so long without revision. But of the obnoxious canons, some are obsolete, and some illegal. The act of toleration has interposed, to silence the thunder of excommunication. The obnoxious canons, once so formidable, stand, it is true, on the church's statute book; but they stand there antiquated and obsolete; as harmless as the instruments of torture, of the same age, preserved as relics in the Tower. And for nearly two centuries, seceders have been as little in dread of them. The clergy are bound, it is true, to obey their bishops in all things canonical; but the bishops are not superior to the law. No canon can be enforced, even should the rash attempt be made, which the laws of England have superseded and annulled. The oath of canonical obedience must, of necessity, be thus interpreted; the clergy bind themselves to obey the canons, only so far as the canons may be legally obeyed. And with these exceptions, and thus understood, the canons are, upon the whole, a wise and comprehensive code of ecclesiastical discipline, which still suit the circumstances of the church of England,

CHAPTER and are a guide to the consciences of the clergy, and
X. of official laymen charged with spiritual functions,
JAMES I. where the letter of the law is obsolete, or on points
A. D. 1604. upon which it is no where else expressed.

27. But, however harmless these anathemas may be at present, there are few of them which have not done their work of vengeance in their time. They were not passed unanimously. There was, in the convocation of 1603, one man at least, who stood there with christian meekness, and with a firm yet almost pathetic eloquence, to advocate those principles of toleration which in their hearts both prelatists and puritans despised. It was in a discussion upon the cross in baptism, that Rudd, the bishop of St. David's, spoke. His words were the weightier, because he scrupled not the cross himself; "he wished that if the king's highness should insist upon imposing it, all would submit, rather than forego the ministry in that behalf." But he pleaded for concession and forbearance, both upon this and the kindred questions of absolute subscription, the surplice, and the ceremonies. He foresaw the evils of a house divided against itself; and foretold the day, (which came even sooner than he looked for it,) when, "for want of their joint labours, some such doleful complaint might arise as fell out upon an accident of another nature in the book of Judges, where it is said, 'for the divisions of Reuben were great thoughts of heart.'"

28. Who that has sighed over bishop Hall's sufferings, described in his "Hard measure," or

felt a burst of indignation as he thought upon the execution of Laud, will not revert to the con- vocation of 1603, and think too of the prophetic warning of bishop Rudd!—" Consider," he said, " who must be the executioners of their depriva- tion; even we ourselves, the bishops: against whom there will be a great clamour of them and their dependents, and many others well affected to them: whereby our persons shall be in hazard to be brought into great dislike, if not into extreme hatred: whereof what inconveniences may ensue, I leave to your good wisdoms to be considered of."* Yet even Rudd did not foresee the full fury of the storm which in these violent proceed- ings the bishops and their party were contribut- ing to the utmost to excite.

29. The concessions made by the convocation are contained in the canon which explains the nature of the cross in baptism, and justifies its use ; a concession which could not satisfy the pu- ritans, inasmuch as it took for granted the very point against which they protested, namely, the right of a church to add a ceremony to a sacra- ment ; and to decide for them that the addition, though allowed to be superfluous, was not super- stitious. Still it shewed a conciliating spirit ; and was no doubt conceded by the prelatic party not so much to the clamours of the puritans, as to the moderation of men like the bishop of St. David's. Perhaps, too, the array of excommunications with which, to a modern reader, the fortress seems to

* Neal ii. 29.

bristle on every side, wore a somewhat different appearance to an ancient puritan. It would seem that excommunication was not extended, but retrenched. It is not enforced for "twelvepenny matters." It is not deputed to mercenaries; to bishops' officers and laymen, and these too of worthless character, and mean condition. Had the canons been but gently pressed, they might even have afforded some relief to the harassed puritans. Had they superseded the court of high commission, the boon would have been great indeed: but unhappily this was not the case.

1604.   30. A proclamation was issued, commanding strict conformity; and the usual consequences followed. Many of the clergy were silenced; some were imprisoned; their flocks were irritated: the estrangement on both sides was grievously increased; and the lawfulness of separating from the church of England began at length to be generally discussed. The number of suspended ministers rises or falls in the relation of the partial historians of these times with their prejudices. Some say that fifteen hundred or more were ejected; others, scarcely a tenth part of that number. Maunsel, the minister of Yarmouth, and Mr. Ladd, a merchant of that town, are names that have come down to us as those of two of the sufferers in the persecution that ensued. Their case is remarkable. They were summoned before the high commissioners, and Ladd was imprisoned. Maunsel petitioned the house of commons; and for doing so and for refusing the oath,

he was imprisoned without bail. Upon a writ of
habeas corpus, he was brought before the bar of _____
the house; and his counsel, a bencher of Grays
Inn, moved that the prisoners ought to be discharged, on the ground that the high commissioners were not empowered by law to imprison,
or to administer the oath ex officio, or even to
fine any of his majesty's subjects. This was a
bold step; but neither the nation nor even the
house of commons was yet ripe for it. Instead of
serving his clients, Nicholas Fuller, (for his name
deserves to be had in reverence) brought down
ruin on himself. He was imprisoned at the instance of Bancroft, and neither the intercessions
of his friends, nor his own most humble petitions,
could obtain his release till the day of his death.*

31. Arthur Hildersham was a celebrated divine
of high birth and great acquirements. Except in
the matter of his nonconformity, his conduct
won the respect of all, and he was happy in the
veneration and love of his followers. He was descended from the royal house of the Tudors, and
great nephew to cardinal Pole. Elizabeth herself
vouchsafed to greet him as her cousin Hildersham. The history of his sufferings presents no
exaggerated picture of those of multitudes of less
distinguished men. Apart from other considerations, his life has the interest which always belongs to the oppressed.†

32. He was born in 1563. His parents still
clung to the ancient faith, and he was brought up

* Neal ii. 49.　　　† Brooke's Lives of the Puritans, ii. 376.

CHAPTER in the superstitions of popery, and taught to repeat
X.   his prayers in Latin. He was sent to Cambridge,
JAMES I. to Christ's college, and was there converted to
A. D.   the protestant faith. His father was alarmed and
1604—10. angry, and removed him from the university ; resolving to send him to Rome, where he hoped that
the youth would be at once reclaimed and promoted. The son refused to go, and the father
disinherited and cast him off. Such trials must
have frequently occurred when many a house was
divided against itself ; and the father was set
against the son, and the son against the father.
These were the conflicts of the reformation; conflicts more bitter than even the dungeon and the
stake.

33. Young Hildersham left the university in
sorrow and want, and was met by chance in London by a Mr. Ireton, a clergyman of Cambridge,
who inquired the reason of his absence. He told
the story, and what he suffered for conscience
sake. His generous friend was moved, and went
immediately to the earl of Huntingdon, the lord
president of the north, to whom Hildersham was
related. Lord Huntingdon took up his cause,
sent him to the university again, and liberally supported him there. Through the influence of lord
Burghley he obtained a fellowship at Trinity hall ;
but within two years he was deprived of it by the
high commission for having preached before he
was ordained. He appears to have submitted and
confessed his error ; for we find him soon afterwards preaching at Ashby-de-la-Zouch, to which

he had been invited by his constant friend, lord
Huntingdon. In 1590 he married; the same
year found him again before the high commission,
who now suspended him from his ministry, and
exacted a pledge that he would desist from preaching in any part of England, as the price of his
remaining at large. The next year the prohibition was relaxed; he was now forbidden to preach
only on the south of the river Trent. Thus
he was still silenced at Ashby. But owing no
doubt to the influence of his high connexions at
the court, this restraint was soon afterwards removed, and he resumed his ministry. In 1596 he
preached an assize sermon at Leicester, which so
displeased the judge that he required the jury to
indict the preacher; but they refused, and it
was said no Leicestershire jury would have consented to do so. In 1598, the high commission
for the third time attempted to apprehend him;
but whether, says his biographer, he was imprisoned, or concealed himself till the storm was
over, we have not been able to learn. He was at
the conference at Hampton court, and presented
a number of petitions to the king on behalf of
the puritans. Within two years, in 1605, he
was silenced for non-conformity, and remained
for upwards of three years under ecclesiastical
censure. Still he was permitted occasionally,
by the kindness of the bishop of Lichfield and
Coventry, to preach in his diocese; and towards
the close of the year 1608 he was restored to his ministry at Ashby, by the favour of Dr. Barlow, the

new bishop of Lincoln.   Three years had scarcely
passed, and he was again silenced by Neile, bishop
of Lichfield, on a charge which,on the very face of
it, was false and monstrous.   He was accused of
being connected with one Whiteman, who taught
Socianism at Burton-upon-Trent,—an offence for
which he was burnt alive at Lichfield.   It was the
last instance in which this horrible torment was
inflicted on the plea of heresy ; for public opinion
already began to revolt against it.   And yet, after
the lapse of another century, one of the greatest
of English judges hurried an aged female to the
fire on an unproved charge of dealing with foul
spirits.   That judge Hale inflicted this torture on
an old woman on the charge of witchcraft is, perhaps, the most solemn lesson upon record how
prejudice and superstition may darken the purest
reason, and goad it to the most revolting crimes.

34.   Hildersham was of course acquitted ; but
the episcopal censure was not removed.   In 1612
he was once more summoned before the high commission, judicially admonished, and again suspended.   Whether he was restored or not appears
uncertain ; but he probably exercised his ministry
by stealth, as the puritans never ceased to do as
opportunities offered; for in 1615 he was again
before the high commission, and refusing the oath
ex officio, was committed, first to the Fleet, then
to the King's Bench, where he lay some time.
Commissioners were sent down the next year to
Ashby, to examine witnesses against him in his
own parish : he was pronounced refractory and

disobedient, and a ringleader of schismatics. He
was excommunicated, fined two thousand pounds,
degraded from the ministry, ordered to be imprisoned, and to make a public recantation in terms
dictated by the court, and lastly, he was condemned to pay the costs of the judicial suit.
Hildersham, who was now at large, concealed
himself, and petitioned for a mitigation of the
sentence through various channels. At length
the matter was compounded by his payment of a
" great sum of money ;" and he was discharged
from the remainder of the fine. Two years afterwards he was again in trouble; a pursuivant
broke into his study, and carried away his books,
upon what charge does not appear. But in 1625,
he obtained a licence from the archbishop himself, to preach within the dioceses of London,
Lincoln, and Lichfield, and returned to his cure
at Ashby. It must be recorded, that he immediately began a course of lectures on the 51st Psalm,
which were published a few years afterwards ;
they were in number two hundred and fifty-two.
Such was the zeal, and such the ministerial diligence of the puritan leaders.

35. His scruples were not yet removed ; nor
was the wrath of the ruling powers exhausted.
In 1630, he was again silenced for refusing to
make use of the hood and surplice ; but the power
of the high prelatic party had already begun to
wane, and other troubles darkened the horizon.
In 1631, he was finally restored, but his race was
run, and soon afterwards he died in peace; and

when he was no more, men of various parties vied with each other in his praise. He was, says one, a worthy divine, and a just man.* He was, says another, a great and shining light of the puritan party.† He was justly celebrated, says a third, for his singular learning and piety. And Lily, the famous astrologer, who had been a schoolboy at Ashby, closes the many tributes of his eulogists in these words : " He was an excellent textuary, of exemplary life, pleasant in discourse, a strong enemy to the brownists, and dissented not from the church of England in any article of faith, but only about wearing the surplice, baptizing with the cross, and kneeling at the sacrament."

36. Such was the life of a puritan divine in the days of king James the first. While reverence for the good and sympathy for the oppressed continues to be felt among men, the puritans of those times will want neither reverence nor sympathy. As a body they were men of sincere, and sometimes of exalted, piety ; they were yet well affected to the church of England, in spite of their several topics of incessant protest and declamation, and their aversion to some of her usages. Their patriotism was warm, and so too was their loyalty; and it must be confessed both were sorely tried. But it is not inconsistent to add, that their views were often narrow and their objections captious. If it be true that their spirits were sour, this infirmity is the consequence of oppression, which

* Fuller.   † Echard.

maketh even wise men mad, and the disgrace belongs to their opponents as much as to themselves.
But the charge from which it is most difficult
to relieve them, is that of a stubborn perversity.
Their consciences were rather diseased than tender. Admitting even that every grievance was real,
and that all they asked should have been conceded,
their conduct is not entirely justified. For a grievance may be real without amounting to such a
wrong as justifies resistance; and demands may
be reasonably made which, if not conceded, ought
neither to beget ill-will nor obstinacy. Granting
that the rulers of the church were unwise and
intolerant, these are evils which christian men,
much more christian ministers, must bear with
patience. It might be right to protest at first
against the obnoxious ceremonies; could it be right
to embarras the church for half a century with
reiterated and unceasing clamours ? If there was
on the one side a most unreasonable severity, on
the other there was a pertinacity which ill ac-
corded either with the wisdom of the gospel or its
meekness. And meanwhile the common foe was
turning their divisions, with wary zeal and cunning, to his own advantage. It was said that,
under the garb of puritan ministers jesuits introduced themselves and sowed the dragon's teeth
which sprung up into the hydras of rebellion and
apostacy. The puritans complained to the king
that thousands of his subjects had returned to
popery. He answered with a sorry jest, and told
them, by way of reprisals, to go and convert an

equal number of Spaniards and Italians. But it ought to have occurred to them how far the mischief had been owing to themselves : to their obstruction of the episcopal authority and of the just influence of the established church; to the mischievous diversion of the common people from the great and sanctifying doctrines of personal religion, to discussions (which to the multitude must always be unprofitable) upon recondite questions of church government. The faults of the puritans do not strike us, up to this period of their history, as much as those of their adversaries. The intolerance of Whitgift, and the insolent humours of the king, are more palpable and more offensive. And the balance of wrong-doing and of injustice was, beyond a doubt, with the high church, or rather prelatic and court party. But the puritans were not without a full share of blame ; and had they been more kindly used, history would perhaps have summed up their errors with more severity.

CHAPTER XI.

1. THE expectations of the puritans, which had been highly raised on the accession of James, were grievously cast down by the conference at Hampton court, and utterly destroyed by the convocation that followed soon after. One hope alone remained; the hope of the dejected and forlorn. It was embraced with reluctance, and deep misgivings of heart : but once resolved upon, it was carried into effect with such energy as only men exert who are impelled alternately by hope and by despair. A new world had lately been discovered. On shores yet unpolluted by superstition, perhaps untrodden by the foot of man, they might find a peaceful asylum, and, free from the dread of dungeons and courts of high commission, worship God in truth. These were their aspirations; and at the distance of two centuries, none but the most insensible and stupid can read the story of their enterprize, without something of the awe and reverence which great virtue struggling with great adversity, and so achieving

CHAPTER its lasting triumph, never fails, sooner or later, to
XI.   command.*

JAMES I.   2. Such a scheme was not altogether new.
A. D.   The unhappy Huguenots of France had already
1610—23.   sought a refuge in the wilds of North America.
And so great had been their success in colonizing those distant regions, that a patent had been
issued, by their friend and patron, Henry IV.,
giving to De Monts, a calvinist, the sovereignty
of a region which stretches from Philadelphia to
Montreal. His patent secured freedom of religion for the Huguenots, with other privileges. It
even seemed as if a vast empire would be founded
in the west, the protestant colony of France. But
whether from the greater energy of the Saxon
race, or from causes determined solely by a higher
power, and uninfluenced by the conduct of his
creatures, the colony and the institutions of De
Monts have vanished, while the friendless puritans of England laid the first foundation of a great
nation—one of the greatest under heaven : the
representative and offspring of our own. One
third of the European population of the vast
American republic of our times, acknowledges a
puritan origin. Within fifteen years from the
sailing of the first timid bark, freighted with these
anxious emigrants, there had followed four thousand families, consisting of more than twenty-one
thousand souls. Their descendants, twelve years
ago, were numbered at four millions. In the states

---

* For the facts related in this chapter, the authorities are chiefly
Mather's Hist. New England ; Bancroft's Hist. United States of America, (Boston, 1840.) ; Sewell's Hist. of Quakers ; Lives of Robinson,
and others, in Brooke, Neal, &c.

of New York and Ohio, they constitute one half the population. So astonishing the results of the enterprize we are about to relate, and so benevo- lent the purposes of Him who protected their wanderings, and guided their almost desperate adventures.

3. John Robinson, the pastor of a congregation of English brownists at Leyden, first suggested the undertaking which was to lead to such im- portant consequences. In an age when the in- fluence of the christian minister was always great, he had a power of influence and control un- equalled. In days when men aspersed their opponents with bitterness, and reviled each other without shame or restraint, he passed blameless through life, or was blamed only for his noncon- formity. He was one of the first fruits of Im- manuel college ; and churchmen, who cannot but regret the loss of such a name from their glorious calendar of great and good men, will feel, perhaps, that his course through life explains, to some ex- tent, the coldness with which the new puritan foundation was regarded by the rulers of the church. Dr. Chadderton, the master, was a pu- ritan, but moderate, and anxious to conform ; the pupil naturally outwent the teacher, and in a short time resigned his charge in the neighbourhood of Yarmouth, and declared himself a brownist—a dissenter from the church of England. He suf- fered some years of constant hardship ; and at length—though not without extreme difficulty, watched, and threatened—contrived, with his hearers, to escape to Holland. He first attempted

to settle at Amsterdam; but persecution had not yet taught mutual forbearance even to the puritans. There was another congregation of English refugees at Amsterdam, who differed on some points from the brownists. A quarrel and a separation followed; and Robinson, who was a man of peace, retired to Leyden, in 1608. There he and his flock abode for above ten years, and won the confidence and respect of the magistrates and citizens. But they felt it was a life of exile. Neither the manners nor the language of the Germans pleased them. They began to think of migrating in a body across the wide, and as yet almost untried, Atlantic. Robinson gave his influence to the scheme, and under his auspices it was carried into effect.

4. The Greeks of old reverenced with heathenish superstition the ship in which the Argonatus, it was fabled, had once sailed to Colchis. The English at this day regard, with a fondness not to be severely blamed, the vessel in which Nelson died. The children of the puritans, with equal reason, cherish the time-honoured names of the Mayflower and the Speedwell. They were the two ships—if ships they could be termed, the one of sixty tons, the other of one hundred and eighty— in which the exiles of Leyden, *the pilgrim fathers*, embarked upon their voyage.

5. Robinson's congregation exceeded three hundred; and as they were unable to provide at once for the transport of the whole number, it was agreed that their pastor should remain for the present at Leyden, with the remainder of the flock,

whose future steps should be guided by the reports
of the first adventurers. Few events in puritan
history are more touching, or more worthy of
being had in remembrance, than the last parting
(for such it proved) of Robinson, the brownist
minister, and his exiled and heroic band of christian emigrants. Before the day of parting came,
the magistrates bore a voluntary and honourable
testimony to their good conduct. Several of the
Dutch were anxious to go with them, and would
have contributed largely to the expenses of the
enterprise. But the English character was then,
as now, retiring, sensitive, and jealous. They
would have no associates who did not speak the
English tongue, and obey the English monarch ;—
" in a few generations," too, " their own posterity
would become Dutch !" So strong their nation-
ality after all their persecutions.

6. When the ship was ready to sail, the whole
congregation met. There was a solemn fast and
prayer. Robinson then addressed them in a farewell speech, " breathing," says a republican historian, " a freedom of opinion, and an independence of authority, such as then were hardly known
in the world." Happily the speech is on record,
and the exiled pastor of Leyden spoke in a much
wiser and much holier strain. He impressed the lessons of piety, not of a vainglorious self-sufficiency
or a self-willed independence. "I charge you," said
he, " that you follow me no further than you have
seen me follow the Lord Jesus Christ." There
were few men then alive, who could have given

utterance to the sentiment which followed. It bespeaks a wisdom, which few had yet attained. " The Lord has more truth yet to break forth out of his holy word. I cannot sufficiently bewail the condition of the reformed churches, which are come to a period in religion, and will go, at present, no further than the instruments of their reformation.—Luther and Calvin were great and shining lights in their times, yet they penetrated not into the whole counsel of God. The luther-ans cannot be drawn to go beyond what Luther saw : and the calvinists, you see, stick fast where they were left by that great man of God. I beseech you remember it ;—'tis an article of your church covenant,—that you shall be ready to receive whatever truth shall be made known to you from the written word of God." The character of the New England puritans would have come down to us, free from some dark spots, had the audience comprehended the wisdom of their pastor's admo-nition. In conclusion, he advised them to shake off the name of brownists,—in which it seems they took delight,—as " a mere nickname, which made religion odious." A parting feast was given, at the pastor's house, " where," writes Edward Winslow who was one of the guests, " after tears, we refreshed ourselves with singing of psalms, making joyful melody in our hearts, as well as with the voice : indeed, it was the sweetest melody that ever mine ears heard." Overwhelmed as they were with tender emotions they had dauntless spirits and a sure confidence in God. The whole

congregation moved together to Delft Haven,
where the emigrants embarked. Prayer was
again offered by their beloved pastor; tears in
abundance were shed; and they parted in deep
silence, " for the abundance of sorrow." *Cheers,*
and noisy demonstrations, were never much in
vogue among the puritans; but " a volley of small
shot, and three pieces of ordnance," announced to
those on shore the hearty courage and affectionate adieus of those on board :" and so, continues
Winslow, " lifting up our hands to one another,
and our hearts to the Lord, we departed."

7. On the 5th of August, 1620, the two vessels,
freighted with the first New England colonists,
sailed from the Southampton river. Within a few
days, the May-flower was found to need repairs,
and they put back to Dartmouth. Eight days
were lost, and again they sailed. Now the captain of the Speedwell feigned or felt alarm, and
insisted on returning to Plymouth. Here the
Speedwell was dismissed, and some of the company, disheartened, gave up the enterprize, and
went back to London. A hundred souls, men
and wives and infants and children, were crowded
into the little May-flower, and on the 6th of September, 1620, took their last leave of England.
Their feelings, we may believe, were softened towards their native land, and they thought, with
a melancholy pride and thankfulness, of her
glory and her greatness. One who has left a
narrative of a somewhat later voyage of the puritans, has given us their parting ejaculation, as

CHAPTER they lost sight of the land of their fathers. The
XI.
same words, perhaps, escaped the lips, or swelled
JAMES I. unexpressed in the bosoms, of the earlier voyagers
A. D. on board the adventurous May-flower. "They did
1610—23. not say, Farewell Babylon! farewell Rome! But,
FAREWELL DEAR ENGLAND!"*

8. A voyage of sixty-three days brought them
in sight of America. They landed at Cape Cod,
where the two great seaport towns of Plymouth and
of Boston were shortly founded, names which to
this day attest the grateful patriotism no less than
the energy and hope of the pilgrim fathers. Plymouth was so named in remembrance of the christian sympathy they had received from the last
town in which they had sought refuge from
the perils of the sea in England; and Boston
was a memorial of their early home in Lincoln-
shire, before intolerance had forced them into
the swamps of Holland. In front of the town-
hall of Plymouth in New England, there lies a
dark rough mass of granite, which is looked upon
with reverence by every true son of the greatest
republic the world ever saw. On this the pilgrims
landed; upon this stone they stepped; upon this
rock they took possession of an heritage of boundless extent; and here they entered upon a new
career, of which, could they have foreseen the
consequences, it is a question not easily resolved,
whether more of awe and fear, or of gratitude and
exultation, would have taken possession of their
souls. The stone, hallowed by such associations,

* Mather's Hist. b. iii. ch. 1.

has been rolled from its native bed upon the sea-
beach, and placed, a national monument, touching
and appropriate, in the midst of a city, the earliest
that can boast the origin, founded by puritans.

9. The colonists regarded themselves as the
loyal subjects of England. They had obtained a
patent from the company of merchants to whom
king James had entrusted the planting of New
England—for so what are now the northern states
of the American republic were then entitled.—
But their charter proved to be of little value ; and
they seem to have experienced at once the perils
and the relief of perfect liberty. Even in their
little company were some unruly spirits, who, having disdained the yoke of authority at home, were
little disposed to submit themselves abroad to a dic-
tatorship of their own brethren. While they were
yet at sea, the majority found it expedient to draw
up a declaration of their principles of civil government. To this all the men of the party, forty-
one in number, subscribed their hands, and promised all due submission and obedience ; and John
Carver was chosen their president or governor, for
the space of one year. The death of Carver occurred within his year of office ; and a successor
was chosen by general suffrage. In fact, their
civil constitution was a republic, and reminds us of
the democracies of ancient Greece, from its extreme simplicity. Every male inhabitant was a
member of the legislature ; the governor had but
a double vote ; and he was assisted or checked by
a council of seven ; the people were frequently

convened on executive as well as judicial questions. And this state of things continued for
eighteen years; a long period for so loose and yet
so inflammable a system. At length the increase
of population, and the inevitable confusion of a
state in which all by turns obey and govern, and
are submissive and supreme, led to the introduction of the representative system. A committee of delegates was sent from each town
to a general court : the model of the independent
provincial legislatures of the various states of the
great American Union. The change was not
effected without uneasiness; nor were the politics
of these early settlers always free from agitation
and disquiet. But the subject belongs to the secular historian, and we proceed to other matters.

10. The conduct of the new community was at
first well worthy of their cause. They behaved
like men who had forsaken home and kindred,
not for ambition or for gain, but for conscience
and for God. The winter had set in with stern
severity on their arrival; their log huts were not
yet erected, and every hour was important. Yet
the first sabbath-day was observed with deep solemnity. Pestilence and famine came upon them
like an armed man. They arrived in December :
in May one half their number lay in the silent
grave—silent, but not quiet; for the Indians had
heard of the coming of " the pale faced men,"
and began to harass their new settlement. The
graves were ploughed over and sown with corn to
hide them from the desecration of the savages.

Their stores failed; their bread had long since disappeared, or been prudently reserved for seed. For months not a biscuit nor a loaf was seen among them. When they were visited, some time after, by a friendly party of neighbouring colonists, all the hospitality they could offer was a meal of dried shell fish, with "a cup of fair spring water." Yet none repined. When the captain of the May flower, anxious to be gone, spread his sails in the month of May for England, not one of the surviving fifty whom the pestilence had spared, repented of the enterprise and sought permission to return. They formed themselves into a church, of course upon the brownist or independent model, and regulated the conduct of the colony by the principles of scripture. All were compelled to work at first upon a common stock, like the early christians at Jerusalem; not because they adopted the principle of a community of goods, but as a matter of convenience. But after a short trial the system was abandoned, and each family had a plot of ground assigned to it. Crimes were few; but they were severely punished. The governor's journal records the first offence, and its somewhat curious penalty. "The first offence since our arrival is of John Billington, who first came on board at London, and is this month convented before the whole company, for his contempt of the captain's lawful command, with opprobrious speeches, for which he is adjudged to have his neck and heels tied together;" but humbling himself, and craving pardon, the culprit was forgiven. Two men-servants who had carried out, it seems, one of the most preposterous vices of the old world, and introduced it at New Plymouth, were more severely handled. The governor again relates that a duel with sword and dagger took place, in which both parties received a wound. This mutually-inflicted penalty not being thought sufficient, they too "were adjudged by the whole company to have their head and feet tied together, and so to lie for twenty-four hours without meat and drink." The sentence was immediately enforced; but such were the torments of the sufferers, or such the tenderness of the puritans, that within an hour, at their own and their master's humble request, upon promise of better conduct, they were released. What would be the feelings of governor Bradford and the pilgrim fathers, could they know the more than European wickedness with which some of those who boast their puritan ancestry now fight in single combat with the unerring rifle and the murderous bowie-knife?

11. The habits of the New England puritans were devout, and their active virtues worthy of a lasting eulogy. Their sabbaths were solemnly observed; and they could soon boast a school of prophets of their own, "the New England divines;"— a school not easily forgotten, had it included no other names than those of Mather, Cotton, Higginson, and Elliot; by the suffrages of every church and the voice of two centuries, Elliot, the prince of

missionaries and the apostle of North America.
Robinson, their early guide, did not live to accomplish his ardent wishes; poverty and its attending hindrances kept him still in Leyden. But his
pious counsels followed his expatriated flock, and
were received with a due respect. The Indians
were astonished one day, upon a visit to New Plymouth, with the sabbath stillness that prevailed.
Three days they knew had elapsed since the previous Sunday; and yet again all was silent except
the voice of prayer, or the louder tones of fervid
exhortation. It was a fast-day to supplicate for
rain. In a few days the copious rains fell, and a
long and perilous drought was at an end. The Indians began to fear the God of the pale strangers.
Efforts were not wanting for their conversion.
They were visited in their native woods by a de-
putation from the colony, who found them open
to instruction. " We had with them," reports
Winslow, " much profitable conference." The immediate occasion of the discourse of which he
speaks marks the manner of the teachers. The
Indians had observed that their guests " did crave
a blessing on their meat, and afterwards gave
thanks," and asked the meaning of the strange
custom. Their Indian interpreter, Hobbamoc, was
baptized, and in his death " left some good hopes,"
they say, "that his soul went to rest." Hearing
of the sickness of a neighbouring sachem or chief,
medicines and aid were provided; and his tribe
saw with amazement the effect of charms hitherto
unknown to them, in the immediate recovery

of their head. Their benevolence to their own countrymen was, perhaps, more disinterested. Puritans were not the only, nor indeed the first, Englishmen, who explored New England. Sir Walter Raleigh's report of the fabled gold mines of the west had touched the ambition of many an adventurer. They were for the most part idlers, spendthrifts, and men of careless lives, including some gentlemen and goldsmiths, who thought of nothing but sudden wealth, and talked of nothing but how " to dig gold, wash gold, refine gold, and load gold." A Californian hectic in the seventeenth century ! Such neighbours must have been always unwelcome to a colony of puritans. But a more serious inconvenience arose from one of their own friends. Weston, a merchant of London who had assisted them with funds at Leyden and warmly encouraged their enterprise, no sooner 1622. received the first tidings of their success than he resolved to establish a rival colony. He freighted two ships at his own cost, and commissioned the emigrants to colonize for his own exclusive benefit. They were men of another character,—rude adventurers : they had no aim " to do good or plant religion ;" some were openly profane ; others mean and unfit (as may indeed be supposed of those who would undertake such a mission) for " an honest man's company." Yet they were received at Plymouth with gravity no doubt, but with substantial kindness. While hesitating where to settle they lived upon the hospitable puritans, and returned their kindness in acts of daily and nightly

depredation, and in " backbitings and revilings."
Nothing related of the Plymouth puritans, is more
deeply to their honour; nothing affords a more
convincing proof of the wholesome and practical
character of their religion. They saw the graceless
intruders wasting their substance in riot, when
they had scarcely bread to eat, and yet continued
their generosity ; and when, at length, they moved
away to the bay of Massachusetts, they were permitted to leave behind their sick and maimed, under
the care of the surgeon of the colony, who, " by the
help of God, recovered them gratis." But Weston
had once befriended them, and now, with true and
christian forbearance, his kindness was remembered, his subsequent duplicity forgotten.

12. Such were the virtues of the New England
puritans.   Revered beyond the Atlantic, as the
pilgrim fathers, the founders of great cities, and
of states renowned through the wide world, for
wealth, intelligence, and liberty, their memory
is cherished in England, with feelings of silent
respect rather than of unmixed admiration. For
their inconsistencies were almost equal to their virtues ; and here, while we respect their integrity we
are not blinded to their faults.   A persecuted band
themselves, they soon learned bitterly to perse-
cute each other.   The disciples of liberty, they
confined its blessings to themselves.   The loud
champions of the freedom of conscience, they
allowed of no freedom which interfered with their
narrow views.   Professing a mission of gospel
holiness, they fulfilled it but in part.   When

CHAPTER
XI.

JAMES I.

A. D.

1610—23.

opposed, they were revengeful; when irritated, fanatical and cruel. In them, a great experiment was to be tried under conditions the most favourable to their success; and it failed in its most important point. The question to be solved was this. How would the puritans, the hunted, persecuted puritans, behave, were they but once free, once at liberty to carry their principles into full effect? The answer was returned from the shores of another world. It was distinct and unequivocal. And it was this; they were prepared to copy the worst vices of their English persecutors, and, untaught by experience, to imitate their worst mistakes. It is a subject upon which party writers love to expatiate; but to every christian mind it is deeply painful. The severities of Whitgift seemed to be justified, when it was made apparent, on the plains of North America, that they had been inflicted upon men who wanted only the opportunity to inflict them again, and to inflict them on each other.

13. The first occasion upon which the stern unchristian spirit, which at this period disfigured the character of both parties in England, broke out abroad, was within five years of their first arrival. The Indian tribes looked upon them at first with suspicion; then with kindness as they knew them better; after a time, when irritated by some of the marauding settlers, whom they naturally confounded with the puritans, with vexation and hostile sentiments. Not to relate the various aggravations of the quarrel, war was

at last determined on by the whole colony of puritans assembled in open council. The Indians had resolved upon the massacre of the white men; the white men resolved to massacre the Indians. A small party was enough, as the slaughter was to be the work of guile. Nor indeed were the puritans wanting in bravery; so that captain Standish, with eight companions, were judged to be a sufficient force. They affected a friendly bearing towards the chief conspirators, and lured them into an Indian wigwam. On a signal given the door was closed and the butchery began. Standish himself plunged his knife into the heart of one of the chiefs. The whole party returned in triumph unhurt, carrying with them the head of an Indian warrior, which, with a brutality unknown in England—where *traitors*, and not *enemies*, were thus empaled—was fixed upon the fort. The colonists affected to deplore the dreadful necessity. Their pastor still lived at Leyden; and when they looked for his congratulations he wrote thus in mournful accents :—" How happy a thing had it been if you had *converted* some, before you had *killed* any !"

14. A few years passed, and another scene of carnage defiles the history of the pilgrims of America. A settlement had now been made on the banks of the Connecticut. The Indians were alarmed. They saw their fishing grounds invaded, and began, with reason, to dread the white man's supremacy. No part of New England was more thickly covered with aboriginal inhabitants. One tribe, the Pequods, mustered above seven hun-

CHAPTER
XI.
_____

JAMES I.

A. D.
1610—23.

dred warriors; the settlers were less than two; and the Pequods showed a hostile spirit. They entered into an alliance with other tribes, and resolved to sweep the hated intruders from the ancient territories of the Indian family. If there be a justifiable cause of war, it surely must be this, when our country is invaded and our means of existence threatened. That the Indians fell upon their enemies by the most nefarious stratagems, or exposed them, when taken in war, to cruel torments, (though such ferocity is not alleged in this instance,) does not much affect the question. They were savages, and fought white men as they and their forefathers had always fought each other. How then should a community of christian men have dealt with them? Were they to contend as savages or as civilized men?—as civilized men, or rather as men who had forsaken a land of civilization for purer abodes of piety and peace? The Pequod war shows how little their piety could be trusted when their passions were aroused.

15. The staff of office—the marshal's baton—was solemnly delivered to Mason, the leader of the puritans, by Hooker their most venerated minister; and the greater part of the night was spent in prayer offered up, at the soldier's request, by another eminent minister, and they set out upon their march. The sabbath occurred two days afterwards, and the fierce band halted on their way, and observed it rigidly. After a week's

* Bancroft i. 401,

marching, they came, at day-break, on the Indian
wigwam, and immediately assaulted it. The
massacre (so their own chronicler has termed
it) spread from one hut to another; for the Indians were asleep and unarmed. But the work
of slaughter was too slow. "We must burn them,"
exclaimed the fanatic chieftain of the puritans; and
he cast the first firebrand to windward among
their wigwams. In an instant the encampment
was in a blaze. Not a soul escaped. Six hundred
Indians, men women and children, perished by
the steady aim of the marksmen, by the unresisted
broadsword, and by the hideous conflagration.
Of the English only two had fallen. Within an
hour the slaughter was ended ; and when the sun
arose serenely in the east, it was the witness of the
victory of the puritans—and of their endless shame.

16. The work of revenge was not yet accomplished. In a few days a fresh body of troops arrived from Massachusetts, accompanied by their
minister Wilson. The remnants of the proscribed
race were now hunted down in their hiding places.
Every wigwam was burned, every settlement broken up, every corn-field laid waste. There remained, says their exulting historian, not a man
or a woman, not a warrior nor a child, of the Pequod
name. A nation had disappeared from the family
of man.*

17. History records many a deed of blood equal
in ferocity to this. Of aboriginal inhabitants,
driven off and slaughtered for the sole crime of
bravely defending the soil which, by the laws of

* Bancroft i. 402.

CHAPTER nature and of God, was theirs, we may read in
XI.   some dark pages stained with blood, and yet not
JAMES I. extend our search beyond the records of our own
A. D.   times and countrymen. But we shall seek in
1610—23. vain for a parallel to the massacre of the Pequod
Indians. It brought out the worst point in
the puritan character, and displayed it in the
strongest light. When their passions were once
inflamed their religion itself was cruelty. A
dark fanatical spirit of revenge took possession,
not as in other men, by first expelling every
religious and every humane consideration, but
what was infinitely more terrible, by calling to
its aid every stimulant, every motive, that religion jaundiced and perverted could supply. It
is horrible to read, when cities are stormed,
of children thrown into the flames, and shriek-
ing women butchered by infuriated men who have
burst the restraints of discipline. It is a dreadful licence; and true and gallant soldiers, occur
when it may, feel that their profession is disgraced. But this was worse. Here all was delibe-
rately calm; all was sanctioned by religion. It
was no outbreak of mere brutality. The fast
was kept; the sabbath was observed; the staff of
office, as a sacred ensign, was consecrated by one
christian minister, while another attended upon
the marching soldiery, and cheered them in the
murderous design with his presence and his
prayers. Piety was supposed not to abhor, but
to exult in the exploit. This was true fanaticism.
God's word and ordinances were made subservient
to the greatest crimes. They were rudely forced

and violated, and made the ministers of sin. When the assailants, reeking from the slaughter, and blackened with the smoke, returned home, they were every where received with a pious ovation. God was devoutly praised, because the first prin- ciples of justice, nay, the stinted humanities of war, had been outraged, and unresisting savages, with their wives and children, had been ferociously destroyed.

18. The intolerance with which the puritans had been treated at home might at least have taught them a lesson of forbearance to each other. But it had no such effect. It would almost seem as if, true disciples in the school of the high commission and star chamber, their ambition was to excel their former tyrants in the art of persecution. They imitated, with a pertinacious accuracy, the bad example of their worse oppressors; and, with far less to excuse them, repeated in America the self-same crimes from which they and their fathers had suffered so much in England. No political considerations of real importance, no ancient prejudices interwoven with the framework of society, could be pleaded here. Their institutions were new; and their course was hampered by no precedents. Imagination cannot suggest a state of things more favourable to the easy, safe, and sure development of their views. Had they cherished a catholic spirit, there was nothing to prevent the exercise of the most enlarged beneficence. Their choice was made freely; and they decided in favour of intolerance; and

CHAPTER
XI.

JAMES I.

A. D.
1610—23.

1629.

their fault was aggravated by the consideration that the experiment had been tried, and that they themselves were living witnesses to its folly.

19. The colonies of Plymouth and Boston were formed, as we have seen, out of the extreme puritans, the brownists; and it was perhaps to be expected, that in them, as the most persecuted sect, the greatest suspicion of new comers and new opinions should exist. But the mild counsels of their Leyden pastor seem for a few years to have repressed their natural spirit of intolerance; and the persecution began elsewhere.

20. The spirit of enterprise spread rapidly at home as the reports of the prosperity of the first puritan colony were confirmed from time to time. A charter was granted by Charles I. to a new company for colonizing Massachusetts bay. It confirmed upon the settlers the rights of English subjects; but it forbad them to make laws repugnant to the laws of England. Their chief ministers, Cotton, Higginson, and Hooker, were still, when they left home, ministers of the church of England, though puritans. Within a year from the arrival of the colonists, the spirit of persecution had already banished two of their best men.

21. John and Samuel Brown are honourably distinguished as the first professors who suffered for their love to the church of their forefathers.

They were both members of the colonial council; both were reputed to be sincere in their affection for the good of the plantation. In short, they were chief men among the colonists. But

they preferred the service of the book of common
prayer, and resolved to adhere to it. For this
offence they were seized like criminals, banished
the colony, and forced back again with the returning ships to England. The service of the
church of England was now, if possible, a greater
crime in New England, than the conventicles of
the brownists and anabaptists had been at home
in the days of Whitgift and of Barlow. Imprisonment and banishment across the Atlantic for using
the book of common prayer was a device of which
even the court of high commission might have
been justly proud. Cotton was at this time in
Boston; and Cotton was eminent for meekness
and gentleness; yet he saw these vindictive measures without distress, and writes to his friends
in Holland that the order of the churches and the
commonwealth in New England was such that it
brought to his mind the new heavens and the
new earth wherein dwelleth righteousness.

22. Roger Williams, a young and ardent minister, arrived in Massachusetts in 1631. The intolerable oppressions of Laud had forced him from
England, and he fled to the puritans of the new
world for an asylum. The life and sufferings of
Williams throw light upon the puritan character,
as it now began to shew itself, in an aspect altogether new, both at home and abroad.

The character of Williams has been handed
down to us by puritan writers loaded with reproach. He is described by Neal as a rigid
brownist, precise, uncharitable, of most turbulent

CHAPTER and boisterous passions.   But his writings refute
XI.   the first charge, and his conduct, under circum-
JAMES I. stances likely to arouse the gentlest spirit, con-
A. D.   tradicts the second.   His offence was this.   He
1610—23. enunciated, and lived to carry out, the great principle of perfect toleration amongst contending
parties by whom it was equally abhorred.   His
name must be had in everlasting honour, as the first
man in these later ages who taught that the civil
magistrate may not coerce the conscience : that
fines and stripes are not the proper means of
restoring even the worst heretics to the communion of the church, or of the punishing their
contumacy.   As usual with those who announce
some great truth, unknown or bitterly opposed,
he was an enthusiast in defending his principles,
and carried the application of them to an absurd
and mischievous excess.   He not only denied the
right of the magistrate to punish, but he denied
his right to interfere.   He maintained, that as to
civil government, all religions were alike: that is,
he denied the right of a body of christian men to
found a state upon christian principles.   Jews
and Turks, infidels and heretics, were to possess
equal rights ; or in other words, to exercise an
equal share of judicial power and civic influence
with their christian brethren.   Of course, under
such conditions, an established religion was impossible.   He trusted simply to the force of truth
to vindicate her own pretensions.   A plausible
theory, no doubt ; but one, the consideration of
whose merits we may be permitted to postpone,

until a community shall be found composed exclusively of men who are honestly in quest of truth,
and, at the same time, under unerring guidance in
their pursuit of it.

23. The church of England had galled the consciences of the extreme puritans with the canon
which denounced excommunication upon ab-
sentees from public worship. The extreme puritans were no sooner in possession of magisterial
power, than they themselves renewed the same
enactment, and rigorously enforced it. We, said
they, are a colony of christian men : all our
settlers must attend upon the worship of God.
Against this law Williams protested. He was
an ultra-calvinist, and to force men to go through
the forms of worship whose souls were dead in
sin, was, he said, like shifting a dead man into
several changes of apparel. He pleaded the rights
of conscience. The magistrates replied, that no
man's conscience could be pleaded in defence of
sin, and that such principles subverted all good
government. Williams rejoined, that they desired to re-impose "a yoke of soul oppression."
The breach widened, and Williams was, with
much cruelty, banished from the colony. His
chief opponent was Cotton, himself an exile for
conscience sake, and a puritan minister. Williams
suffered the greatest hardships on his journey
through the snow and storms of a New England
winter in search of a secure retreat. For fourteen
weeks he had, he says, neither bread nor bed :
and often in a stormy night, neither food nor fire,

nor a companion to share his sorrow: he wandered without a guide, and found no better shelter than some hollow tree. God opened the heart of a savage chieftain to befriend him: "and the ravens," he relates with gratitude, "fed me in the wilderness." He arrived at length at RHODE ISLAND; and is revered as the founder of a state which still retains the impression of his character and principles in her various institutions.

24. Similar disputes arose with other men of less account than Roger Williams, and the result was in each case the same. The men who had fled from persecution avowed the principles of intolerance; and carried them into terrible effect with fanatical violence.

25. In truth, they began to perceive that the church at home was by no means to be so severely blamed. The principles of Whitgift and his party were not, after all, either tyrannical or unchristian. They had erred, indeed, and their error was one day to produce the most baneful consequences. But it was not an error in the principles they espoused, but in the unreasonable mode in which they were applied, and the excess to which they were carried; and to this the puritans were now awakening. What christian parent would not guide his family into habits of devotion? Who could blame the master of the house if he insisted on a due observance of the Lord's day, and the presence of his children in the house of prayer? But if, as the children grew up to man's estate, they felt, or feigned some scruples in submitting,

it would be preposterous to enforce on men and women the discipline of childhood. The parent may grieve, but he must not punish. He may remonstrate, but he has no longer the right of absolute control. In every case where trust and preference have a lawful place, he may with perfect justice repose his confidence in those who continue to obey him, and whose principles are in accordance with his own. If he be sincere he must do so. If those who have rejected his authority advance opinions subversive of his own, it cannot be denied that he ought to be allowed the right of silencing the objectors; or else of compelling them to withdraw from the society; otherwise his authority depends upon the precarious tenure of mere opinion—the opinion of the dissatisfied and discontented. And further still, as one who is himself accountable to God, it is his duty to repress and silence those opinions which palpably dishonour God's great name. These were the principles of Whitgift, and not less of the New England puritans, and they extended them from families to states. They are still the principles of our own constitution, and we have learned to reconcile them with a perfect toleration. Except for blasphemy, no man suffers punishment. Even members of the church of Rome exercise their worship unharmed, dangerous as some of their tenets are to every civil government which does not own allegiance to the pope. The state has outgrown its infancy. The conditions by which a patriarchal family was governed are no longer

CHAPTER
XI.
───
JAMES I.
A. D.
1610—23. possible. And the alternative now lies, in all free states, not between conformity and toleration, but between toleration and indifference. The state may endow a church, but it can no longer punish dissidents. In the progress of society it has come to this alternative, either to bear with nonconformity, or to make nonconformity impossible by treating all religions and all creeds with equal indifference. In England we adhere to the former choice. The citizens of Rhode Island determined otherwise; but there is nothing in their religious history, for two hundred years, that leads us to retrace our steps and follow their example. The condition of religion in England will at least bear a comparison with that of the most favoured of the New England states.

26. The intolerance of the colonists was the more disgraceful, because in matters purely religious there was scarcely a shade of disagreement between their victim and themselves. Williams was a zealous puritan; and yet he suffered for maintaining that "the doctrine of persecution for causes of conscience is contrary to the doctrine of Jesus Christ." This, like Luther's, protestant theses nailed to the doors of a popish cathedral, spread dismay and indignation. And for this he was an exile from his brethren. His piety was sincere, and it displayed itself in his feelings to those by whom he had been wronged. From his banishment in Rhode Island, he wrote of them in these memorable words. "I did ever, from my soul, honour and love them, even when their judg-

ment led them to afflict me." Such a sentiment
could only proceed from one who, however mistaken upon other points, was a true disciple of
Him who was meek and lowly in heart.

The spirit of persecution, once enflamed, has
too often been quenched in blood. So it was in
New England. Williams had many followers,
who were made to share his fate—Wheelright,
and Aspinwall, and Ann Hutchinson. But the
atrocious cruelties which were inflicted upon the
quakers a few years afterwards, would appear incredible, if not too well authenticated, and throw
into the shade the lighter sorrows of Williams and
his party. It is not without an effort, that even
now the reader can force himself to believe that
the fierce and relentless men who condemned
Mary Dyer to the gallows were the children of
English puritans, and the champions of their fathers' principles.

27. Quakerism was then young, and its
founder, George Fox, was yet alive. It was ardent, and full of enthusiasm; it believed itself
charged with a revelation, spiritual, and immediately from heaven; it despised the restraints,
and sometimes the decorum, of civilized life. Still
its fanaticism, though violent, was harmless and
utterly averse to blood. Its first disciples needed,
perhaps, some restraint, for the sake of public
morals ; but upon the whole, forbearance and compassion would have been more wholesome than
sharper punishments, which, so long as they were
persisted in, served only to inflame the disease.

On some points, the quakers, with all their excesses, had learned a sobriety and wisdom which,
both to high churchmen and puritans, was yet
unknown. Anne Burden, a female quaker, went
all the way from London to North America to
impart the secret to the brownists of Massachusetts; and she had her recompense; "she was
whipped with twenty stripes." Her crime was
unpardonable. She had warned the magistrates
of a New England colony, with the authority of
one who believed herself a prophet sent from God,
of the wickedness of persecution. The punishment,
however, failed; or rather it produced its legitimate
effect. A quaker prophetess, it was discovered,
lost neither caste nor courage in the brutal ordeal
of a public flogging. Other measures must be
tried. Quakers were fined, and maimed, and banished; and quakerism was made a capital offence
in the case of those who, once exiled, returned to
the colony.

28. Mary Dyer, thus expelled from Massachusetts, found an asylum in Roger Williams'
new colony of Rhode Island, where all sects were
tolerated alike. But she believed that she was
urged by the Spirit, who cannot err, to return to
Boston. She "felt a call." Only the flippant and
profane will scoff at the doctrine, or scorn the
words in which it was expressed. It might, for
aught we know, be well worthy of God himself, to
employ this quaker exile to repeat a long forgotten message of christian love at Boston, which
was to rebuke the sour austerity of their religious

pride at once, and to be re-echoed in after ages, to all the ends of the earth, teaching everywhere, as it passed along, the dignity of suffering for conscience and for God, and the infamy of the oppressor. Substantially, Mary Dyer was, with all her errors, a martyr for the gospel's sake; and her persecutors were, in that act at least, the enemies of God.

29. Two friends accompanied her, William Robinson and Marmaduke Stevenson. They had not been many days in Boston before they were seized, imprisoned, arraigned before the governor and magistrates, and in short, sentenced to the gallows. " Give ear, ye magistrates," exclaimed Stevenson, as the sentence was pronounced, " and all ye who are guilty, for this the Lord hath said concerning you, and will perform his word upon you, that the same day ye put his servants to death, shall the day of your visitation pass over you, and ye shall be for ever cursed." Mary Dyer folded her hands together, and meekly exclaimed, " The will of the Lord be done." The bravado of Stevenson the magistrates might disdain ; but for the meekness of Mary Dyer they had no reply. Her calm submission enraged the governor. "Take her away, marshal," he exclaimed harshly. " I return joyfully to my prison," she said. " You may leave me, marshal, I will return alone." " I believe you, Mrs. Dyer," replied the marshal, " but I must do as I am commanded."

30. The prisoners were brought out to the place of execution. Wilson attended the procession : a

circumstance to be recorded not as unusual in itself, but as marking the hearty concurrence of
the New England clergy in these dreadful scenes.
They ascended the scaffold, after affectionately
embracing, and each in turn bore an exulting
testimony to the joy which had taken full possession of their souls. Robinson called upon the
spectators to bear witness, that " he died for tes-
tifying to the light of Christ." Stevenson's last
words were, " This day we shall be at rest with
the Lord." Mary Dyer said, in answer to a cruel
taunt affecting her modesty,—for even this was
not spared in her draught of shame and agony,—
" Are you not ashamed to walk thus hand in hand
with two young men ?" " No, this is to me the
hour of the greatest joy I could have in this world.
No eye can see, nor ear hear, nor tongue utter,
nor heart understand, the sweet incomes and re-
freshings of the Spirit of the Lord, which I now
feel." The execution proceeded, and her companions died. She continued to stand unmoved,
her clothes carefully adjusted, her eyes bandaged,
the rope around her neck, and tied to the beam
above her. At this instant a reprieve arrived, and
she was taken down. She neither shrieked, nor
swooned, nor wept. She stood still, and calmly
told the agitated crowd, that unless the magistrates would annul their wicked law, she would
rather die. She saw, no doubt, that otherwise
the scaffold could one day claim her as its prey,
and had no desire to return to a life of suffering,
nor to die a second death upon the gallows.

31. She was again banished to Rhode Island, attended by a guard; and when the guard left her she returned again to Boston. Once more she was sentenced to be hanged. The trial was short, and not wanting in simplicity. Governor Endicot again presided. He asked her, in the first place—willing, it is said, to afford an opportunity for evasion to the prisoner—whether she were the same Mary Dyer who had been previously before the court ?

" I am the same Mary Dyer."

" Then you own yourself a quaker ?"

" I own myself to be reproachfully called so."

" Then I must repeat the sentence once before pronounced upon you." And he repeated the sentence.

" That is no more than thou saidst before."

" But now it is to be executed; therefore prepare yourself for nine o'clock to-morrow."

32. Her husband—for though young and beautiful, Mary Dyer was a wife and mother—interceded for her life. He had been separated from her while she was in Rhode Island, and was not privy to her return. With the deep pathetic eloquence with which nature alone pleads, he wrote to her iron-hearted judges, and concluded thus—after first acknowledging " her inconsiderate madness"—" I only say this : yourselves are, or have been, or may be, husbands and wives : so am I : yea, to one most dearly beloved. Oh! do not deprive me of her, but I pray give her to me

CHAPTER
XI.

JAMES I.

A. D.
1610—23.

once again. Pity me! I beg it with tears." But his tears flowed in vain.

33. The next day the scaffold was again erected upon Boston common, a mile away from her prison. She was strongly guarded, and before her and behind drums were continually beaten; for the eloquence of the dying is known to be imperishable. When she had ascended the scaffold, Wilson, the fanatic minister, was again at his post. " O Mary Dyer," he cried, " repent, repent." " Nay, man," she answered calmly, in words in which a puritan must have felt a keen rebuke, " I am not *now* to repent." She was again reproached with her pretended visions. She replied, and her peaceful demeanour seemed almost to explain her meaning, " I have been in paradise many days." The executioner performed his office; Mary Dyer was no more; and the crowd dispersed; but the brand of that day's infamy will never disappear from the annals of Massachusetts, nor from the story of the pilgrim fathers.*

34. The execution of Greenwood and Barrow is the darkest stain upon the worst days of Whitgift and his policy ; but it seems to lose something of its atrocity when compared with the execution of Mary Dyer. It almost appears, in short, as if great crimes, like great virtues, were recorded only that they should be imitated, and, if possible, sur-

* For the facts relating to the persecution of the quakers, see Powell's Hist. of the Quakers, Bancroft's Hist. of America (3 Vols. Boston), and article, Mary Dyer, in Nelson's British Library, the writer of which professes to have had access to fresh materials.

passed. Except intolerance, the puritans of New England had learned nothing from the example of their oppressors.

35. There are those who would fain suppress the record of these crimes; as there are those who exult in their recital. The former class is timid, but the latter is malignant. The one fears for the cause of religion; the other triumphs in the exposure of an adversary. Truth has no sympathy with either; and history, the handmaid and minister of truth, ought to shun both alike. The true moral is that which the word of God has long ago supplied : " the heart of man is deceitful above all things, and desperately wicked." Forms of church government have no power to change the heart. Man oppressed is proud, sullen, and vindictive; and when he arrives, as soon or late the oppressed in general arrive, at the power he once dreaded, his nature is unchanged—he is proud andv indictive still. There was nothing in the principles of the high church party of Whitgift and his associates to prevent the exhibition of the grace of God in them, and their attainment of a high degree of christian holiness; and there was nothing in the principles of the extremest puritans which had sufficient power to check in them the risings of the worst passions of which our nature is capable, or to preserve them from its most extravagant excesses. It must be added, that the New England puritans had neither the sanction of English law nor the approbation of the English people. Governor Endicot exceeded his

CHAPTER powers, and, pronouncing sentence of death upon
XI.   the quakers, plunged himself in the double guilt
JAMES I. of treason and of murder. The law of England
A. D.   knew no such punishment for such offences; and
1610—23. yet from that law all his authority was derived;
for he acted under a patent granted by the king
and parliament. Soon after Mary Dyer's execution, Christian, another quaker, was placed before
the same tribunal, and challenged its authority.
"By what law," said he, "will ye put me to
death?" "We have a patent," they answered,
"and may make our own." "But," he rejoined,
"you cannot make laws contrary to those of England. Your heart is as rotten towards the king as
towards God. I demand to be tried by the laws of
England, and there is no law there to hang quakers." From shame or fear the council yielded,
and his life was spared.—But the puritans at home
had, for some time, begun to look with deep concern upon the measures of their New England
brethren, and even to remonstrate against their
bigotry.

36. The unhappy state of affairs during the primacy of Laud, and the last few years of Charles's
power, however disastrous at home, had called a
nation into existence in the western world. In
spite of the efforts, equally tyrannical and impolitic, to prevent their emigration, tens of thousands of the puritans had found their way to their
brethren in the New England colonies. Before
the long parliament had assembled, and the revolution opened, in 1640, the number of emigrants

who had arrived in one hundred and ninety-eight
ships, and with an expenditure of almost a million
of dollars in various enterprises, are numbered at
twenty-one thousand two hundred. In little more
than ten years, fifty towns and villages had been
at least marked out and commenced ; between
thirty and forty churches had been built ; and the
later comers gazed with amazement upon the
unexpected sight of a wilderness reclaimed ; and
devoutly acknowledged the hand of God in this
sudden blaze of prosperity. Already the elements
of wealth and power were within their reach, and
they had learned their value. They had begun to
export furs and timber ; they carried grain to the
West Indies, and cured fish. They had attained
great excellence in ship-building. Before the
year 1643 they had constructed vessels of four
hundred tons ; ships, such as within the memory
of the present generation, ranked in the first class
of merchant vessels.* Four of the newly-erected
states formed themselves into a union,—The
United Colonies of New England. These were
Massachusetts, Plymouth, Newhaven, and Connecticut. But they excluded the plantations of
Providence, and Williams's settlement of Rhode
Island. The people of Rhode Island, a small community, and unable to stand alone, sought the
protection of the mother country ; and Roger
Williams, who was chosen to manage the negocia-
tions on their behalf, arrived in London in 1643,

---

* Bancroft i. 415. He gives numerous authorities for these facts
otherwise almost incredible.

CHAPTER
XI.

JAMES I.

A. D.
1618—23.

when the parliament and the monarchy were already in collision. He was received by the house of commons with great respect; and returned to America with a free and absolute charter of civil government for Plymouth and Rhode Island. He arrived once more at Boston, from whence he had been expelled; secured from harm by letters from the parliament. But as he reached his home a greater triumph was prepared; the water was covered with a fleet of boats; and it seemed as if all the colony had come forth to welcome their benefactor. Thus Providence and Rhode Island were saved. They long retained their affection to the mother country, when the more powerful states had learned to regard it with indifference or dislike.

37. All was now prosperous in New England. The puritan exiles had entered on a boundless career of wealth, and independence, and earthly fame. It has not yet closed : it shews no signs of diminution. But the pilgrim fathers had purer hopes and higher expectations than national prosperity, even the most unbounded, can satisfy. They braved the perils of the sea, not to plant a great republic, but a pure church. What no political visionary, in his wildest moments, ever dreamed, has been accomplished and surpassed. The little May-flower carried that, compared with which Cæsar and his fortunes were insignificant; —the germ of a vast nation, whose past history fills the mind with wonder, whose possible career

hereafter, with awe. But within a few years the religion of the pilgrim fathers seems to have been reduced to the ordinary standard, if not worn out. Twenty years after the foundations were first dug up in either city, we have no reason to suppose that Boston and Plymouth in New England, were more religious than Boston and Plymouth in the mother country. Nor did the puritans lay the groundwork of a religious colony, according to their own views of religion, with success. It is the frequent boast of socinians, that Boston alone contains many thousands of their sect; a greater number, it is said, than are to be found in the three kingdoms of Great Britain. This alone, could they have foreseen it, would have oppressed the soul of the pilgrim fathers, and weighed down their hearts under a sense of the deepest sorrow. Already, while Williams was alive, several towns in his new state were filled with strange men of dangerous principles. There were anabaptists, and antinomians; fanatics, and infidels in crowds. So that whatever were a man's religious opinions, he might have been sure to meet with them in some village in Rhode Island.* From such beginnings, was it possible to infert he growth and prevalence of real piety? While men are prone to evil, and naturally averse to God, the spectacle of other men's indifference, or uncertainty, may distract the attention, but it will scarcely tend to deepen seriousness, or to renovate the heart. Could the pilgrim fathers be

* Bancroft i. 426.

CHAPTER
XI.

JAMES I.

A. D.
1618—23.

summoned from their graves, they would probably tell us that the results of their enterprise had
fallen as much below their hopes in one respect as
they had surpassed them in another. Possibly
they might think America more prosperous, certainly they would not think America more religious, than England in the nineteenth century.
They succeeded as colonists ; but as a band of pious
men, whose chief aim it was to plant the church
of God anew, where it should thrive with a vigour
unknown in England, their attempt has failed.
We see the result of the experiment : and the
feeling of English christians is one, upon the
whole, of disappointment and regret.

CHAPTER XII.

1. TOWARDS the conclusion of the reign of James I. the puritan controversy began to wear a new character. Hitherto, with all its vehe- mence, it had been a quarrel on inferior points, as we have explained already. Now it became vital. So far, it had intermeddled only with ceremonies and forms, with the accidents and externals of religion. Now it descended to the doctrines. The dispute had been, up to this time, how the gospel should be administered. Now it assumed another form, and asked, in what does the gospel consist. We have arrived at the period when the *doctrinal* puritans, so termed by their opponents, first appear in sight; and our attention is called to the strange complication of parties and events which brought them into existence.

2. The decay of piety is often marked by a litigious disposition; for those who are dissatisfied with themselves are prone to be suspicious of all around them. The fervour of the reformation cooled: the men of the next generation succeeded to the offices lately held by martyrs and confes-

sors, but not to their zeal and love : and the third generation, with whom we now begin to mingle, were pupils of another school, and still more unlike the men of the reformation. Those who are unwilling or unable to draw such conclusions from their altered divinity, may trace it in their demeaned intelligence and degraded style. The intense devotion of the reformers communicated itself to all they wrote. They are often coarse, sometimes barbarous, but they are never mean. They are surrounded by an air of majesty and grandeur ; the majesty of a lofty and entire devotion to their cause, the grandeur of a vehement simplicity. We have to this day no finer specimens of popular eloquence than Latimer's sermons ; we have nothing more deeply pathetic than Ridley's last address to the diocese of London. The dialectics of those times afford no specimens of reasoning more acute than the examinations of the martyrs. Contrast with these the theologians of the days of James and Charles, and the degeneracy is striking. There is less of the earnestness and of the composure of men who are contending for vital truths of eternal moment. A fierce conflict there is, with its noise and clamour, but the contest seems to be rather for victory than for truth ; and the combatants are often men of sordid minds, evidently in pursuit of selfish ends. Without hesitation, and without uncharitableness, we infer that their religion is in fault. The piety of the reformers raised them above the level of their age. The worldliness of these men has sunk

them below the level of the reformation. True
religion expands and elevates the mind. The
taste is improved, for the heart is softened : the
intellect is vigorous, for it is employed on lofty
contemplations, which afford it exercise; even
the imagination, while chastened, is brought into
wholesome action by the various subjects of interest which engage the affections. There is something which almost offends our reason in the bare
supposal that a quibbling pedant should be an
eminent christian; that conceits and affectations
should defile the pen, while the heart is free from
vanity and self-conceit.

3. Their literature is heartless, and their divinity
wants real life. This is shewn by endless conceits
in the one, by affectation and litigiousness in the
other ; and in both, by a careful avoidance of what
is great and really important, or an incapacity of
comprehending it. Now feebleness of mind is
not unfrequently accompanied with extraordinary
daring. A daring which is not courage, inasmuch
as it has no perception either of difficulties or consequences ;—as an infant is not brave when with
a smile upon its face it would light up a conflagration. Thus it arose, we conceive, not from the
increase of sound learning, nor the deepening influence of true piety, but from causes the reverse of
these, that questions in divinity the most awful
and difficult, those which require to be treated
with the deepest reverence and to be approached
with the profoundest wisdom, began to take their
place in every-day discussions, and to be submitted

to the most peremptory decisions. These were the points at issue between the calvinists and arminians. The moderation of our reformers, while it has left us in no uncertainty as to their own opinions, has bequeathed to us general and comprehensive statements to which every sincere and enlightened christian may heartily subscribe. And yet moderation is not precisely the word by which their high virtues should be expressed ; for moderation implies that they resisted some temptation which was urging them to extremes. But such temptations either did not present themselves, or were scarcely felt. They were saved from them by minds well balanced, by the practical character of their own piety, by the urgent necessity of the times ; above all, by the grace of God. After a while, religion becoming less practical was more speculative. Baro and others introduced the controversy into England, and Whitgift's injudicious efforts to extinguish it gave vigour to the flames. In a few years nothing was heard of among divines but the calvinistic controversy. The five points— those on which the followers of Arminius and Calvin were opposed—were defended and attacked with a vehemence which nothing could justify except the belief, which indeed was firmly entertained on both sides, that men's salvation hinged exclusively upon them ; and with a bitterness not justified even by this consideration, momentous as it is. Whitgift, the stern opponent of the puritans, had taken the highest ground ; he was, in modern language, an ultra-calvinist. And yet,

within twenty years, by a change not less sudden
than difficult to be accounted for, every trace of
calvinism was banished from the high church
party, while it retained more firmly its congenial
home amongst the puritans; and thus arose the
distinction which divided the puritans themselves
into two great parties, the doctrinal and ceremonial:
the former well affected to episcopacy and the
church of England, but opposed to the new and
fashionable theology ; the latter equally averse to
both.

4. The calvinistic controversy came to its
greatest heat abroad. If England was disturbed,
foreign churches were distracted. In the low-
countries the supreme government, the states-
general, interfered, and in the year 1618 convoked
the first and only synod, bearing something of
the character of a general council, that has been
convened by protestants. It assembled at Dort,
and continued its sittings from November till
May following. Its business was to decide the
questions at issue between the calvinists and
arminians; the latter partly were also termed
remonstrants. James was requested to send over
representatives for the English church, and
chose four divines;—Carlton bishop of Llan-
daff, Hall dean of Worcester, afterwards bishop
successively of Exeter and Norwich, Davenant
afterwards bishop of Salisbury, and Dr. S.
Ward of Cambridge. They were men of learning and moderation, and the choice does honour
to a monarch in whom we find but little to

applaud. First, however, they were commanded to repair to the king, and receive his instructions; and they were commanded to inure themselves to the practice of the Latin tongue, that they might express themselves with greater readiness and facility; a piece of advice which, addressed by the greatest pedant in England to four of its best scholars, provokes a passing smile. With greater reason they were instructed to conduct themselves with moderation, and to look principally to the peace of those distracted churches and to the glory of God, and in discussion to maintain that which was agreeable to the scriptures and to the doctrine of the church of England; and they were especially cautioned to throw their weight into the scale of gentle counsels, and to advise their brethren not to insist from the pulpit upon doctrines which were disputable on both sides, to introduce no innovations, but to adhere to the same doctrines which had been taught for twenty or thirty years past in their own churches; and especially to abide by their own confessions, long since published and known unto the world.* A representative was also present from the church of Scotland.

5. The history of this famous synod is told in various ways. Its decisions were in favour of the doctrines termed calvinistic, and the remonstrants were expelled from Holland: for neither statesmen nor divines had yet learned, it seems, that simple lesson of common sense, that persecution

* Fuller's Church History, book x. 275.

always carries with it a reversal of its own decrees;
that the men who are unreasonably punished
occupy a better position and stand on a loftier
eminence than if they had not been condemned.
The recoil is always greater than the blow; for
here the law of nature is inverted. The majority were even charged by the other party
with having bound themselves by an oath before
they entered upon business, to condemn the remonstrants. The charge was first insinuated by
John Goodwin, the leader of the *evangelical* arminians (an expression we shall have occasion to
explain hereafter) in England. Bishop Hall was
still living when, in 1651, Fuller, the ecclesiastical
historian, laudably anxious to clear up the matter,
wrote to him for an explanation; which, as might
be expected, was forthwith returned in an indignant denial of the charge. But after all, the
accusation of unfairness is not quite disposed of.
Goodwin himself replied to bishop Hall's letter;
and the arminians still maintain that the synod
was unfairly packed. The states-general, it is said,
convened those only who were of one mind,* and,
in accordance with this principle, the Utrecht
deputies, being the only arminians admitted, were
soon excluded; after certain ungracious conditions
had been propounded for their acceptance, which it
was impossible for any honourable men to comply
with.† If so, the majority, however upright, were

* In their Letter to King James, (Fuller, book x. 282), the
states-general say, "Ex omnibus idem sentientibus ecclesiis convoca-
vimus:" but this does not necessarily mean more than that they had
selected their deputies only from protestant churches.
† See the editor's note in Fuller, book x. 286, Nichols's edition.

mere partizans, and the decisions of such a synod could not possess much weight.

6. While these discussions engaged attention abroad, it was scarcely to be supposed that the polemic contagion should not infect the church at home. It is said that the pulpits rang with controversy; and we can believe it; for where the spirit of true piety dies out, that of disputation forthwith comes in. The anti-puritans describe the sermons of their opponents at this period, as consisting of little else than angry invectives and ultra-calvinism. Such statements are always to be received with caution from an opponent; and it is to be borne in mind that the puritans, with not less vehemence, charged the high church party with an utter abandonment, not to say contempt, of evangelical truth and of the doctrines of the reformation. That great faults existed on each side, is but too evident. The puritans had begun too much to confine their views of saving truth to the peculiar dogmas of high calvinism; their opponents, to ritualism and formality. The evil, as regards the puritans, may have been exaggerated; their opponents, in some remarkable writings put forth at this time, answer for themselves. The controversial preaching of the puritans had become 1622. so offensive to the court, that in 1622 directions were issued commanding them to desist; and it is not likely, even in such times as these, that the civil government would have interfered without a strong pretext. These instructions were injudicious, even if well meant; they were ill received;

nor indeed could it have been otherwise. For they
endeavoured to place restraints which it was impossible to enforce, upon consciences which it was
certain must rebel. Preachers were forbidden to
discourse upon matters in divinity not comprehended in the thirty-nine articles or in some of
the homilies. A wide range; for what is the
christian doctrine which an ingenious preacher
could not readily deduce from the articles and
homilies? But the real intention was more fully
displayed in the third article of these instructions,
namely, "that no preacher under a bishop or dean
presume to preach in any popular auditory on the
deep points of predestination, election, and reprobation; or of the universality, efficacy, resistibility
or irresistibility of God's grace." Further, it was
observed with pain that preaching was discouraged.
In the afternoon it was all but forbidden. An exposition of the catechism, the creed, and the ten
commandments was permitted rather than allowed;
and those preachers were to be " most encouraged
and approved of," who confined themselves to the
examination of children in their catechism, which
was affirmed to be " the most ancient and laud-
able custom of the church of England." All parties
were forbidden to question the king's authority,
or meddle with matters of state, or to fall into
bitter invectives or railing speeches against either
papists or puritans. The declaration was no
sooner published than anxiety and consternation
followed. The pious thought it a cruel thing " to
cut off half the preaching in England at one

CHAPTER XII.

JAMES I.

A. D. 1618—23.

blow." The king's authority, instead of being everywhere admitted, was everywhere canvassed. The very declaration which was meant to establish his prerogative in spiritual things, undermined and shook it to its foundations. The command of Christ was to preach the gospel. St. Paul interprets the command "in season and out of season." Shall the king forbid what God enjoins, or has the secular head of the church of England the right to silence licensed preachers of the word, sent forth by Christ himself? And so of predestination and other deep points. By what right could any man presume to interfere, and forbid the preaching of a portion of God's word? It was well indeed, that ignorant ministers of mean parts should be cautioned to speak on this, as on every sacred subject, with reverence and modesty; but it was monstrous that no minister "under the degree of a bishop or a dean at the least," should be allowed to preach upon the questionable points of doctrine. It amounted, in fact, to a prohibition of all doctrinal preaching, and no doubt was entertained but that it was so designed. How could the faithful minister discharge his conscience, or edify his flock, if he might not preach upon the efficacy of God's grace, one of the forbidden topics? Man, said the justly discontented puritans, makes that the forbidden fruit which God makes the tree of life. And the prohibition of all but the dignitaries of the church, to preach on the controverted points, excited the bitter scorn which puts on the air of mirth; as if, said they,

all discretion was confined to cathedral men, and
they preach best who are least accustomed to
preach at all!*

7. In truth, the king had given his pious subjects abundant reasons for distrust. He wished
to promote not moderation but indifference; the
vices of his court were glaring; his own life was
not moral; and the book of sports, just now put
forth, threatened not only the religion, but the
decency and the morality, of England with an
overthrow. We do not pause to waste our indignation upon a document which happily finds no
defenders. The book of sports comes down to us
like some ill-shaped abortion, curious and disgust-
ing, from the dusty shelves on which it has long
reposed. Yet it once portended extensive mischief; and we owe it to the firmness of the
archbishop that the immediate consequences were
not more disastrous. The king in 1618 paid a
visit to his Scottish dominions, and Laud was his
attendant: a significant fact, as will be seen hereafter.† In passing through Lancashire the king
observed, that the reformation had but imperfectly
made its way: numbers of the common people,
and many of the higher gentry, still adhered to
the ancient faith. This is yet the case in Lancashire. Considerable districts may be found in its
remoter parts, where the gentry and their tenants
still cling to the Romish superstition. James

---

* Fuller iii. book x. 320.
† Laud, however, did not return with the king through Lancashire,
nor did he draw up the Book of Sports. Heylyn's Laud. i. 48.

CHAPTER persuaded himself that he had penetrated into the
XII. causes of their non-conformity, and proceeded
JAMES I. forthwith to accomplish the reformation of Lan-
A. D. cashire. The magistrates, he found, were too pre-
1618—23. cise, and the ministers were too puritanical; so
that the people were hindered from Sunday recreations, and the papists were persuaded that no
honest mirth or recreation was tolerated in our
religion. Full of his project, the king returned to
Greenwich, and there, upon the 14th of May, set
forth a declaration to this effect :—his pleasure
was, that after the end of divine service his good
people should not be discouraged from any lawful recreations. These are carefully recited. They
are such as dancing, either of men or women;
archery for men, leaping, vaulting, or any such
harmless recreations; nor from having may-games,
whitsun-ales, or morris-dances, and setting up of
maypoles, or other sports used therewith : provided all were done without impediment to divine
service. The women, too, had leave to carry
rushes* to the church, for its decoration according
to their old custom. Unlawful games were prohibited : such were bear and bull-baiting, interludes,
and bowling. This was the book of sports. The
clergy were commanded to publish it in their

* This practice lately prevailed, and probably still prevails, in Lancashire. The rush bearing is a parochial festival, observed, in general,
on the day of the saint to whom the parish church is dedicated. Up
to this period our forefathers sat with their hats on at church, lifting
them only (according to the "Instructions" of queen Elizabeth, 1559) at
the name of Jesus. For the sake of warmth and cleanliness the church
was strewed with straw; or, in the northern counties, where straw was
scarce, with rushes. The rush-bearing might be an innocent custom;
but why should it take place on Sunday?

parish churches. Some had resolved to decline submission, and risk the consequences. Others would
have read it with aching hearts, as an act of obedience to the sovereign whom God had set over them.
A third party determined, with more questionable
honesty, first to read the declaration, and then to
preach against it ; hoping thus to avoid the danger
of disobedience on the one hand, and of profaneness
on the other. But the firmness of Abbott, now
archbishop of Canterbury, saved for awhile the
church and country from profanation and disgrace.
He was at his country seat at Croydon, and there
he forbad it to be read. His courage awed the
king and his foolish advisers, and an order from the
court appeared excusing the clergy from compliance. Fifteen years afterwards the book of sports
was re-enforced by Charles, under Laud's advice,
and the consequences were fatal.

8. The decay of piety towards the close of the
reign of James I., that is, when his pernicious
example and worthless character had wrought
their full effect upon the nation, is an afflicting
topic. The lewdness of his court was such, that
those who drew the sword against his son, and
brought him to the scaffold, do not hesitate to
contrast the many virtues of king Charles, and
the decorum of his courtiers, with the low and
infamous debaucheries of the court of James.[*]
Under the name of puritanism, zeal and earnestness in religion were everywhere treated with
contempt. Pious churchmen, who had never con-

* Mrs. Hutchinson's Memoirs of Colonel Hutchinson, p. 84.

cerned themselves with the surplice controversy, and were perfectly indifferent as to the cross in baptism and the ring in marriage, found themselves compelled, in self-defence, to associate with the only party by whom they were not insulted. Lucy, the wife of Colonel Hutchinson, and the eloquent historian of her husband's virtues, was then a child. She relates, with a becoming indignation, how fiercely the storm of insult and reproach fell upon her father's household, and upon others who, like him, were men of rank and loyalty, yet dared to be nobly singular, and to fear God. However loyal these men were, if they disputed such impositions as the book of sports, they were held to be seditious, and soon found that they were marked out for evil. Did a country gentleman discountenance vice, he was a puritan, however exactly he conformed. Did he shew favour to men of piety, relieve their wants, or protect them against oppression, he was a puritan. If, in the county in which he lived, he promoted public virtue or public interests, and discouraged popery, he was a puritan. Above all, if he had some zeal for God's glory, and could endure a sermon, and permitted serious conversation at his table; neither swearing, nor scoffing, nor sabbath-breaking, nor indulging in ribald conversation, he was a puritan; and if a puritan, then an enemy to the king and to his government, seditious, factious, and, in short, a hypocrite. It was well if some neighbouring pulpit did not hold him up to popular scorn, or if, as he passed along the

village, the drunkards did not make their songs at
him. For every stage, every table, every puppet-
play scoffed at the puritans; and fiddlers and mi-
mics learned to abuse them, " as finding it the most
gainful way of fooling."* We may admit, for so does
Mrs. Hutchinson herself, that amongst the puritans
there were wolves in sheep's clothing; the un-
principled and ambitious, who sought the importance they were denied elsewhere, and seduced
their indiscreet hearers into acts of violence in
order to betray them, or out of some private
malice and revenge. Others, mere hypocrites,
enriched themselves by preying upon the simplicity of the unsuspecting. Great sums of
money, it is said, were thus pillaged from the
puritans on pretence of charitable alms, and
appropriated to their use by various impostors.
Their own piety too was now waning. They had
not faith enough—these are still the sentiments of
our eloquent historian—to disown all who adhered
to them for worldly interests. In their low condition they gladly accepted all who would come
over. Discipline of course decayed, and confusion
followed.†—Richard Baxter, so famous afterwards
in nonconformist story, was also in his boyhood
at this period, and his youthful recollections are
in painful unison with those of Mrs. Hutchinson.
His parents were virtuous and respectable, and
lived in strict conformity. Their son Richard had
grown to manhood before he knew what "pres-

* Memoirs of Colonel Hutchinson, p. 82.　† Ibid. p. 83.

bytery or independency was, or ever spoke with a man who seemed to know it." The inhabitants of the village danced round a may-pole on the Lord's day; and his parents, with three or four other families who were shocked with such a profanation, and spent the day in acts of devotion, were reviled as puritans. Of the non-conforming puritans of Cartwright's school few remained; and of those few scarcely any could be found who troubled themselves with the discussions, once so fiercely agitated, as to the presbyterian or independent forms of government. The puritans whom Baxter knew, with scarcely an exception, rigidly conformed. But they read the scriptures and books of piety and remembered to keep holy the sabbath day. They prayed in their families, and they prayed alone; some with the aid of a book, and some without one. They would not swear, nor curse, nor take God's name lightly: but in some few places, where they were in sufficient numbers, they met after divine service on the Sunday to repeat the sermon with each other, to sing a psalm, and to join in prayer. And when there was no sermon at home, (or probably none from which they derived instruction), they wandered to other parishes where they could listen to a more efficient minister. This was the extent of their irregularity; and for this they were prosecuted in the ecclesiastical courts, fined and censured, if not excommunicated, and severely harassed. The arguments of Cartwright and the brownists had failed to make any lasting impression. The old presbyterians were dead, and very few succeeded them : there were but one or two in a county : but these violent proceedings accom- plished all that the most inveterate brownist could have wished. In the course of a few years the spiritual courts in which the puritans were thus cruelly treated, were only thought of with ab- horrence, and the bishops were only spoken of as the enemies of real godliness. The sacred office was made to bear the indignation due to the misconduct of the men who dishonoured it ; and a bitter storm of invective and reproach was directed, not merely against a few tyrannical bishops, but unhappily against the episcopate itself. Some of the bishops (for in these evil days there were many bright exceptions) thought by severity to stop the growing disaffection ; and thus they confirmed the opinion, daily gaining strength, that they were the determined foes of all serious and earnest piety—"the captains of the profane."* Such is Baxter's account of the state of parties in his youth ; it was written many years afterwards, when his judgment was mature, and his prejudices had cooled ; and its general truth cannot be denied.

9. The puritans affirm that at this period all true piety was discountenanced ; and if by true piety be meant the religion of the reformers and the reformation, the allegation cannot be easily disproved. But another school was rising : that which assumed, and has ever since retained, the

* Baxter's True History of Councils, &c., pp. 91—93. in Orme's Life of Baxter, p. 31.

title of high churchmen. Amongst its founders were men whose piety was both deep and earnest; but it was not, we conceive, the piety of the reformation; which from this time began to be represented by those whom their opponents styled the doctrinal puritans. This body never seceded from the church, and are now represented by that section of the church of England termed evangelical. These, however, are points, let the reader be forewarned, upon which great diversity of opinion still exists; and the subject is to be considered calmly. Certain it is, that the fears of a great number of those whom we must consider as amongst the wisest and best of their age, were painfully aroused. Were their apprehensions needless, were their alarms unfounded? Amongst the causes of their deep misgivings of heart, they reckoned up the following as the chief: the increase of popery; the growth of arminianism; and the introduction of ritualistic worship, and the undue importance attached to it. In each of these they saw a dreaded foe; in the triad an appalling monster. By one party their apprehensions were regarded as prophetic; by another their vaticinations were treated with contempt. And in the great chancery court of free opinion, the question lies yet, to some extent, unsettled; for each turn of our modern church politics presents the subject in some new light: and our ecclesiastical affairs are still, to a vast extent, beneath the influence of those impulses which they received in the days of James the first.

10. (i.) It was the mean ambition of the king to ally his son in marriage, not with the protestant princes of Germany, but with the more noble blood of the French or Spanish Bourbons. The later days of his reign were occupied with ma- nœuvres to effect a match with the infanta of Spain; an affair in which his conduct appeared to the whole of England contemptible and degrading. Charles, the future king, travelled with his tutor Buckingham, on this inauspicious errand, to Madrid; the match was broken off; but no wonder that Charles, upon his return, should have lost for ever the confidence of every puritan. The concessions which his father and himself were willing to have made, showed, if not a secret wish to restore the papacy in England, at least a profound indifference to the reformed religion. One of the public articles of the intended marriage provided that the infanta should choose nurses for her children, and bring them up in her own religion till they were ten years old. The term was afterwards extended to twelve years, and in the match which actually took place with Henrietta Maria, to thirteen years; nor would the children lose their right of succession to the crown, although they became Roman catholics. There were also secret articles sworn to by the king and the prince of Wales; and the latter, by his oath, engaged himself, if indeed the relation is not incredible, " that as often as the infanta should desire it, he would give ear to divines and others, whom her highness might be pleased to employ, in matters of the Roman

catholic religion; that he would hear them willingly without all difficulties, and laying aside all excuses!" In short, no facilities should be wanting on his part, for nothing less could be the meaning of these concessions, to facilitate the restoration of popery into England.* The articles, indeed, were secret; but the elation, not to say the insolence, of the papists about the court, was sufficient to create alarm. Abbott, his faithful archbishop, addressed a solemn remonstrance to the king, reminding him that he himself had written against those heresies, of which he now seemed to be the patron. With a freedom becoming his high office he besought his majesty to consider how hateful his conduct must be to God, and how grievous to his subjects; and above all, he implored him to reflect lest he drew upon the kingdom in general, and himself in particular, God's wrath and indignation.† The parliament likewise remonstrated, and petitioned, among other requests, that all papists might be removed from the court. The king, with exquisite duplicity, replied, protesting before God that his heart bled when he heard of the increase of popery. "What religion I am of my books declare. I wish it may be written on marble, and remain to posterity as a mark upon me, when I swerve from my religion."‡ Yet he told

* Rushworth, Vol. i. 86—89.   Rapin's Hist. 543; or in Neal, Vol. ii. ch. ii. 223.   It was afterwards alleged that these articles were inserted to deceive the Pope, and without any intention of observing them. Hume remarks, that the children of Henrietta Maria were actually educated under protestant tutors.   To an honest mind, however, the apology is as offensive as the secret article itself.   See note in Hume, Vol. v. ch. 5, p. 104. 4to ed.
    † Fuller iii. x.   ‡ Rushworth, i. 143.

his courtiers in private that what he had written
against the pope was not meant " concludingly ;"
that when he heaped upon his holiness every contemptuous and hateful epithet, and proved him
antichrist, the man of sin, the babylonish harlot,
it was but a scholastic exercise : he had meant no
more than to show the papists what an ingenious
and learned writer like himself could plausibly
advance against them in the way of retaliation !
The effort to make it seem that the differences
between the church of England and the church of
Rome had been exaggerated, was made without
the least disguise. That Rome was Babylon, that
the pope was antichrist, " that man of sin, the son
of perdition," was no longer to be maintained.
The unanimity of all our reformers, and of every reformed church, in thus expounding prophecy, could
not, it is true, be questioned; nor did the new school
of divines refute their interpretations. Little was
published, by them, on prophecy, and that little
was never held in much esteem. They satisfied
themselves with intimating that these expressions
were chiefly found in the private writings of the
reformers, and were of course only private men's
opinions ; though it was found more difficult to
explain away some hard expressions in the book of
homilies. The tendency of all they wrote upon
the subject, was to prove rather how much truth
Rome still retained, than with how much deadly
error she was leavened: their labours were directed
to shew in how many points we still agreed, rather
than in how many fundamental ones we differed.
The controversy was not conducted honestly. Ad-

vantage was taken of the imperfect statements made in the time of Henry VIII. and of Edward VI., while the reformation was advancing. These formed the standard of doctrine with the Laudian school; and to these were forced to bend those later statements made in the reign of queen Elizabeth when the reformation was complete. In this manner they attempted to prove that the holy table was an altar, the supper of the Lord a sacrifice, and the presence of Christ in the sacrament a real presence, the nature of which the church had not determined; concealing the fact that it had determined at least that it was not the presence of Christ's natural body; and that the martyrs of our church, with scarcely an exception, died in defence of a distinction which every pains was taken now to represent as trivial. But in truth the memory of the martyrs had ceased to be had in reverence. The Laudian party held their coroner's inquest on their death (we adopt the language of a contemporary divine*), and found them little better than felons dying in their own blood for a mere for. mality: for a question, *de modo*, a metaphysical quibble of the manner of the presence, and of a sacrifice in the sacrament. " Within the narrow scantling of my experimental remembrance," he mournfully complains, " I have observed strange alteration in the world's valuing of those learned men;" he speaks of Ridley, Cranmer, Latimer, and Hooper, and in short the martyrs and reformers of our church. The growth of this indifference deeply distressed all those who refused to attach them-

* Fuller, Holy and Profane State Book, iv. ch. 11.

selves to the now dominant party, of which Laud was becoming the acknowledged head. In justice to Laud himself, it should be noticed, that on some important points he never appears to have embraced all the extreme opinions of his party. It is impossible to read candidly his controversy with Fisher the Jesuit, without perceiving that he had in his own mind a clear view of some strong line of demarcation between the churches of Rome and England; and that he felt their differences to be such as to admit of no compromise on our side. On the great doctrine of justification too, his views appear to have been more scriptural than those of his party. His dying prayer upon the scaffold might have been uttered, under the same circumstances, by Ridley in the former generation, or by Richard Baxter in the next. But thus it often is in the race of error; the pupils outrun the master and the guide. In the search of truth, religious truth at least, such precocious alacrity is rare.

11. James's interference with the affairs of the church in Scotland, increased the general anxiety. It is said that he had long projected the restoration of episcopacy. In the conference of Hampton court, he took no pains to conceal, or rather he peevishly intruded, his detestation of the presbyterian kirk; of which, while king of Scotland, he had been himself a member, and which he had sworn to cherish and protect. He nominated bishops to the thirteen Scotch bishoprics which he had formerly abolished, and in the year

CHAPTER
XII.

JAMES I.
A. D.
1618—23.

Oct. 31,
1610

1606 obtained an act from the Scottish parliament to restore their temporalities, and with these their dignities as lords of parliament. The general assembly of the high court of the kirk of Scotland protested ; and much discussion followed of importance, which it does not fall within our province to relate. But in effect the king prevailed. Three Scotch divines were consecrated bishops in London, under a commission addressed to the bishops of London, Ely, Bath, and Rochester; these, upon their return to Scotland, consecrated other bishops. It is said, and subsequent events do not permit us to question it, that they found themselves hated both by ministers and people. Those indeed who most revere episcopacy will most deplore the obloquy and degradations to which it was exposed in Scotland by the king's misconduct. The whole proceeding was rash and illegal, and moderate men in England interpreted it as an ill omen. The puritans, who had always been on terms of warm friendship with the kirk, were filled with apprehension. And those who loved episcopacy, were unwilling to see its claims advanced at the cost of the presbyterian church by law established.

12. (ii.) The growth of arminianism was another cause of anxiety to the puritans. They were now rigid calvinists ; many of their leaders insisted with peremptory dogmatism upon points on which the reformers had spoken, if not with reserve, with caution and humility. A reaction of necessity took place ; of necessity, we say, because one

extreme in these matters has invariably been the
parent of another. We begin to find arminianism, in the fears of the puritans, curiously entwin-
ed with popery ; and in fact the house of commons,
a few years afterwards, vehemently denounced
the two, as the growing evil which threatened to
overwhelm both liberty and religion. Yet popery
has no necessary connection with arminianism,
nor the puritan cause with ultra-calvinism. The
church of Rome, embarrassed by the opinions of the
greatest of the fathers, has long been in the dilem-
ma of accepting calvinism or rejecting St. Augus-
tine. The puritans, boasting a perfect emancipa-
tion from human systems, and relying only on
the scriptures, could not reasonably censure those
of their own party who might think fit to appeal
from Bullinger* or Calvin to the purer fountain of
the written word. Thus among themselves doctrinal arminianism forced its way. Its apostle in
England was John Goodwin, in all other points
an ultra-puritan ; one who was persecuted by
Laud, became a presbyterian, and so passed on in
due time to the ranks of the independents. Of
English divines he is still the master mind
amongst evangelical arminians. John Wesley in
the last century espoused his opinions, and republished his works ; which, in force and perspicuity,
and freedom from the cumbrous verbiage of the

* I seize the opportunity, while this sheet is passing through the
press (7th May, 1850), of saying that my views of Bullinger's influence
on our reformation have been entirely the result of my own reading and
reflexions ; and especially that every passage in which his name occurs
was written before the present controversy arose, in which the name of
Bullinger is once more rendered famous in the church of England.

CHAPTER times, are remarkable. Candid auditors at the synod
XII. of Dort could not refrain from some regret that two
JAMES I. parties, who often differed scarce a hair's breadth
A. D. from each other on doctrines essential to salvation,
1620—23. should contend so bitterly on points of metaphysical divinity. On many of those points, on which
Goodwin wrote, and was assailed, with bitterness, the same reflection will arise. Not only the
devout reader, but even the acute theologian, is
often at a loss to perceive wherein the difference
lies about which the angry conflict rages. And
when he discovers it, he is apt to think, that after
all it is but a strife of words. Goodwin maintains
the great doctrine of justification by faith only,
with the emphasis of Luther, and with Hooker's
scholastic accuracy; and yet, upon a question
nearly connected with it, he contrived to establish
a distinction so subtle as not to be easily explained
(in any words, at least, except his own), and yet of
such seeming or real importance, that thousands
of even illiterate men have contended, and would
now contend, for it, should the controversy be
revived, as if for the whole substance of salvation.
Hooker, echoing the voice of the reformation,
and we conceive of holy writ, had spoken of the
imputation of the righteousness of Christ as one
of the blessed consequences of our justification.
Goodwin, too, maintained that nothing is required
of any man for his justification but faith in Christ;
and he admits, to use his own words,—" that this
faith shall be as available for his justification, as
a perfect righteousness should have been under the

first covenant." And yet he denies Hooker's
assertion that the righteousness of Christ is imputed to the believer. Although he admits that
a justified person may be said to be clothed with
Christ's righteousness in a sense such as that in
which Paul's necessities were said to be supplied
by his own hands. " These hands, says he (quoting
the apostle's words) have ministered to my necessities. Yet Paul neither ate his fingers, nor spun the
flesh of his hands into clothing ; and yet, was both
fed and clothed with them. So may a believer be
said to be clothed with the righteousness of Christ,
and yet the righteousness of Christ itself not be
his clothing, but only that which procured his
clothing to him."* Perhaps the reader, if unac-
quainted with the niceties of theological expression, will scarcely perceive a shade of difference
between Hooker and Goodwin ; perhaps he may
suspect that if the parties had been obliged
to give their meaning in other words, they
would have found that they taught the same
doctrine : the one maintaining that the sinner is
accounted righteous before God, by virtue of the
Saviour's righteousness imputed to him; the other,
that the sinner is accounted righteous before God
by virtue of the faith he has in the Saviour's righteousness ; this faith, however, being the gift of
God himself, and not in any sense a meritorious
work of man's. Both views are held extensively
in the church of England, and among other de-
nominations of evangelical christians. The Wes-
leyan body adhere exclusively to the views of

* Jackson's Life of Goodwin, 44.

CHAPTER XII.

JAMES I.

A. D.
1620—23.

Goodwin, and attach considerable importance to the distinction. On other points Goodwin has claims upon our gratitude of a less questionable kind. The cheering doctrine of scripture, and of the church of England,* that Christ died a sacrifice for all men, without exception, was falling into oblivion; by many of the puritans it was resolutely denied. Goodwin may be said to have spent his life in combating the rising error : he several times disputed in public with its advocates in the presence of some thousands of people, and at length published the substance of his speeches; and, some years afterwards, he assailed the entire system of calvinism in a larger work, which, in the alliterative taste of his age, he entitled, Redemption Redeemed.

13. It does not appear, however, notwithstanding all the advocate's eloquence and popularity, that his opinions extended far among the puritans ; nor was he sanctioned by Laud and the high church party. The bishop of London cited Goodwin and his opponents, and charged them on both sides to desist from further discussion in the pulpit. And, in a letter to the king, Laud mentions some distractions as having arisen, both among the ministers, and the people, in the city of London, " occasioned at first by some over nice curiosities, preached by one Mr. Goodwin, vicar of St. Stephen's, Coleman street, concerning the imputation

* Nothing can be more explicit than the church catechism ; drawn up, the reader will remember, early in the reign of Elizabeth. " I believe in God the Son, *who redeemed me and all mankind*, and in God the Holy Ghost, who *sanctifieth me, and all the elect people of God.*" Redemption extends *to all ;* the sanctifying influence of the Spirit, to *all the elect.*

of Christ's righteousness in the justification of a sinner." The evil, he adds, had been prevented by convening the parties.* Thus Goodwin was assailed on both sides; and such appears to have been his fate through life.

14. But the arminianism of Laud, and of the great party which he led, was of another kind. They did not hold, as Goodwin held, the doctrine of justification by faith alone, but of justification by faith and works conjoined, or which is virtually the same, by a faith to which good works are prevenient and accessary. It was the other extreme—the rebound from ultra-calvinism : that verged on fatalism : this on the pelagian error that man can restore himself by good works to the favour of God. The one led to antinomianism, teaching men to continue in sin that grace might abound; the other, to a withering neglect, and in many instances to an absolute contempt, of the doctrines of the gospel; that is, of the atonement, and of the work of the Holy Spirit on the soul. The great error of this party was, and has ever been, that it does not distinguish clearly between faith as the ground of our acceptance, and faith as the source and parent of good works. They argued, and with great truth, that faith without good works and a holy life was a mere fiction ; they inferred, which was perfectly erroneous, that these good works were a part of faith itself, and therefore necessary, in the same sense as that in

* Goodwin's Life, 30.

CHAPTER
XII.

CHAS. I.

A. D. 1624.

which faith itself is necessary, to salvation. Whereas the doctrine of the church of England is unquestionably this, that until through faith we are restored to the divine favour, in other words are justified, good works cannot be performed; but afterwards they follow as the necessary results of a true and lively faith. On the doctrine of the sacraments this new party began to speak a language long unknown in England. The Lord's supper, they affirmed, was not only a sacrament, but a sacrifice. They carefully insisted that the communion table should be called an altar; and having obtained this point, they proceeded to make it the foundation of another: we have the wood, said they, and the altar, but where is the lamb for the burnt offering? Thus they inferred the doctrine of the real presence—the real presence of the natural body of Christ.[*] With regard to baptism, they taught, in opposition to the reformers both at home and abroad, that it conferred the grace of regeneration upon all who received it alike; that is, they affirmed that all baptized persons were introduced in baptism into a state of grace and of acceptance; and if they lived in habitual sin, this was a proof, not that they were unconverted, but that they were relapsed.

15. Here then was a new system of theology; new at least in England, and to the churches of the

---

[*] I quote the arguments, and often the very words, of Heylyn in his Introduction to the Life of Laud; to which I refer the reader who may not be disposed for more laborious investigation, for a clear and able synopsis of the Laudian school of theology drawn up by one of themselves.

reformation.* Divines of the school of the refor- CHAPTER
mation rejected the new doctrines with alarm, XII.
and denounced them from the pulpit; and hence CHAS. I.
arose another division in the church. Laud's A. D. 1624.
party were in the ascendant, and they fastened
on their opponents the charge of doctrinal puritanism; and thus they succeeded in stigmatizing
those who were attached to that true and genuine
doctrine of the church of England, which, says a
learned and competent author, they laboured to
eradicate. One of the first who used these scoffing words, was bishop Montague, in controversy
with bishop Carlton, to whom the latter meekly
answers : " this is the first time that ever I heard
of a puritan doctrine in points dogmatical, and I
have lived longer in the church than he hath done.
I thought that puritans were only such as were
factious against the bishops in the point of pretended discipline; and so I am sure it hath been
understood hitherto in our church."† Even our
modern historian Hume, little unhappily as he
knew of christian doctrine, had the sagacity to
perceive that, " the doctrinal puritans rigidly
defended the speculative system of the first reformers."‡ It is a significant fact, that the controversy which has ever since existed among us,
now for the first time made its appearance.
The construction forced upon the baptismal

---

* For the proof of this assertion, I refer the reader to the Rev. W.
Goode's Doctrine of the Church of England as to the Effects of Baptism,
&c., where he will find an array of evidence which sets the question
at rest.
† Goode, &c. 337.   ‡ Hist. of Eng. vii. 272.

offices, rendered its phraseology the object of suspicion and dislike. Hitherto, as we have had occasion to remark, the puritans themselves had uttered no complaints on this head. Scrupulous as they were, and prone to clamour, the doctrines of our baptismal service had given rise to no scruple and to no remonstrance; a proof that no construction had hitherto been put upon them differing in any degree from the received doctrine in other reformed churches, more especially those of Scotland and Geneva; for upon these the puritans were ever anxious to fall back, and by them to test the purity of the church of England.

16. (iii.) While pious and thoughtful men were distressed by these novelties in doctrine, certain external signs gave significant intimation to the least observant that some great change was contemplated. All at once an extraordinary zeal broke out for the practices which the reformation had, seventy years before, condemned. Ridley and Parker had not been more anxious in their day to root out superstitions, than the Laudian school was upon restoring them; and the ingenuity displayed in reconciling its practices with the known injunctions of the church might, in a better cause, have raised a smile; it was the perfection of scholastic quibbling. It was admitted that articles had been issued, for instance, in the first year of Elizabeth, which were still in force; that they were directed against the superstitious decorations which popery had introduced into churches and

private houses. It would seem, we think, to a CHAPTER XII.
candid mind impossible to devise terms more comprehensive than those employed in queen Eliza- CHAS. I.
beth's injunction. The clergy and others were A. D. 1624.
commanded " to take away, utterly extinct, and
destroy, all shrines, coverings of shrines, all tables,
candlesticks, trindals, and rolls of wax, pictures,
paintings, and all other monuments of feigned
miracles, pilgrimages, idolatry, and superstition,
so that there remains no memory of the same in
walls, glass windows, or elsewhere within their
churches or houses."* There are several articles
to the same effect ; in one the clergy are instructed
to declare in public the abuse of images, relics, or
miracles ; in another, to set forth the great threat-
enings and maledictions of God against works
devised by man's fantasies, besides what is enjoined
in scripture ; as things tending to idolatry, and
superstition, which of all other offences God doth
most detest and abhor.† In short, if there be an
honest, simple-hearted document in existence, and
one which shews the intentions of the reformers,
the injunctions of the first year of queen Elizabeth
deserve that character. And so thought the puritans,—the church puritans, such men as bishops
Hall and Carlton. But their objections, if stated in
general terms, were treated with contempt ; and if
they objected in the words of the " injunctions,"
the Laudians made answer, that they carried their
own refutation with them. It was quite mani-

* Injunctions, &c. published in 1559, Art. 23.
† Arts. 2, 3.

fest, they said, from the words themselves, that
it was never the meaning of the queen and her
counsellors really to condemn, abolish, and deface
all images, but only to remove such pictures of
false and feigned miracles as were destitute of
truth.   Images of Christ himself, and of the prophets, apostles, martyrs, confessors, and other
godly fathers, were not included; the abuse of
these was only to be reformed. It would have been
well to have shewn, in order to make good the argument, that no idolatrous worship had ever been
paid to true apostles and real martyrs, but only
to fictitious ones; or that the reformation allowed   one   kind   of   superstition,   and   merely
denounced   another.   The homilies, it is true,
were still commanded to be read in churches,
in obedience to these very injunctions; and
that " against peril of idolatry " declared, that
images, without any exception, are but " great
puppets and babies for old fools;"* and in language, and with an illustration, which the greater
refinement (would that we could say, the greater
purity, of modern days) forbids us to repeat,
scorns the contemptible conceit that men   can
gaze upon these incentives to spiritual lewdness
without spiritual defilement. With regard, however,
to images of Christ and his saints, one passage may
be quoted : " no image," says the homily, "can be
made of Christ but a lying image ; for Christ is God
and man.   Seeing therefore that, of the Godhead,
which is the most excellent part, no image can be

* Hom. xiv. pt. 3.

made, it is falsely called the image of Christ; where- CHAPTER XII.
fore images of Christ be not only defects, but also
lies: which reason serveth also for images of saints, CHAS. I.
whose souls, the most excellent part of them, can by A. D. 1624.
no images be represented or expressed. Wherefore,
seeing that religion ought to be founded upon
truth, images which cannot be without lies, ought
not to be made or put to any use in religion, or
to be placed in churches or temples, peculiarly
appointed to true religion, and the service of God."
In this passage the voice of the reformation is
very clear. The churchmen who adhered to the
doctrines of the reformation (doctrinal puritans
we must henceforth term them) were at once
indignant and dismayed to find themselves betrayed by those who were the highest dignitaries of
the church, and who ought to have been the guardians of its purity, and the expositors, not the
corrupters, of its doctrine. The homilies themselves are cited by Heylyn as admitting that images
are not forbidden by the new testament; from
which he infers that no offence is committed
against the gospel by restoring them to the
churches, if they be used only for history, example,
and pure devotion; and he calls in the sanction
of pope Gregory, who terms them, "not unfitly,"
the laymen's books. The homily had anticipated
him,—"either they be no books, or if they be,
they be false and lying books, the teachers of all
errors."

17. These opinions were not suffered to lie inert.

CHAPTER XII.

CHAS. I.

A. D. 1624.

Everywhere, so far as the influence of the new party extended, churches were restored and decorated after a fashion long unknown. The communion table was transformed into an altar, or was placed "altar-wise," if carved in wood. It was decorated with costly hangings, and bore its load of massive plate and the two symbolic candlesticks; and it was again surmounted, as of old, with paintings and stained glass, descriptive of sacred persons or events in ecclesiastical tradition or church history. It had been the goodly custom of the church to bow at the name of Jesus : now the worshipper was required to make due and lowly reverence when he entered into the church ; the place on which he stood being, by consecration, made holy ground. It was true, for this neither rule nor rubric could be shewn ; but, in the absence of all authority, catholic antiquity was a formula in the hands of the Laudian school, which justified every innovation, and silenced every objector. Bowing towards the east was introduced and defended by this sole argument. It was alleged to be the ancient custom. And, in short, whatever rites were practised in the church of Rome, and not expressly abolished at the reformation,[†] nor disclaimed by any doctrine, law, or canon, were held to be consistent with, if not binding upon, the church of England. As if a thousand canons could, or ought to have been, framed to enumerate and denounce as many superstitious practices ; or

* Heylyn's Laud, Introd. p. 11.   † Ibid. p. 12.

as if the tone, the general purport and intention of a statute, were to be studiously concealed when its application and its uses were considered !

18. And as if it were not enough that the scruples of the old church party should be treated with contempt, their zeal (if they dared to shew it) on behalf of the reformation, was met with insolence and cruelty. The biographer and panegyrist of Laud relates with satisfaction the vengeance he inflicted soon aftewards on Sherfield, recorder of Sarum. In one of the windows of his parish church was the story of the creation, expressed in painted glass, in which was a representation of the Deity, " in the shape of an old man." This was one of the abominations expressly forbidden and denounced : it was, so the reformation taught, idolatrous and impious. Sherfield, anxious for its removal, laid the matter before the parish vestry ; and the parish vestry removed the superstitious relic, and " set up another window of plain white glass in the place thereof." Such was Sherfield's crime, as reported by his enemies, and they admit that he believed that he was acting lawfully. The only outrage, if such it was, being, that Sherfield broke the idolatrous effigy in pieces with his staff But we are at a loss to perceive in what points either Sherfield or the vestry deserve the slightest blame. They obeyed the injunctions of Elizabeth, and they obeyed not with tumult and violence, but in a legal manner. They did not, it is true, consult the archdeacon or the bishop. This might have been courteous, but it was not necessary :

CHAPTER for the law of the church was plain; and the parish
XII. wardens were competent to enforce it. Their
CHAS. I. conduct would have been highly meritorious under
A. D. 1625. the primacy of Parker, and no law had passed to
make it otherwise under the primacy of Laud.
But every expression of protestantism was now a
crime; and even parish vestries were looked upon
with suspicion in high places. " They were but
bastard elderships." The elders of the vestry had
superseded, so cried the Laudian party, the elders
of the conventicle. It was resolved to inflict a
punishment which should put a stop to such
proceedings; and certainly, could punishments
have done it, no more windows, however superstitious, had been broken. Sherfield was summoned before the star chamber, and there Laud*
" did not only aggravate the crime as much as
he could, in reference to the dangerous consequences which might follow," but shewed too,
with a dangerous casuistry, " how far the use of
painted images might be retained in churches."
In brief, under the pretext that an affront had
been done to the bishop of the diocese; and because, says honest Heylyn, it was looked upon as
a great discouragement to the moderate papists—
and, he adds, to some moderate protestants also,
Sherfield was deprived of his recordership, fined a
thousand pounds, bound to his good behaviour
for the time to come; and compelled to make a
public acknowledgment of his offence, both in the
parish church, and in the cathedral.

* Heylyn's Laud, Book iii. 146.

19. It is not necessary to load the memory of Laud and his disciples with reproaches; nor are we disposed to do so. They displayed, no doubt, sincerity, great earnestness, and, according to their own views, even piety. But their influence was calamitous; and these were the darkest days of the church of England: for while her enemies thundered at the gate, her own chieftain betrayed the citadel. The theological system of Laud, whatever place it held with the fathers of the western church, was unknown till his time, in the reformed church of England. The most able and the most honest of his followers in our day, declare that he was the founder of a school which had no existence in England; none, however, since the reformation. He was himself, they say, the true reformer of the English church. The discussion is foreign to our purpose. The fact thus broadly asserted is capable of abundant proof. Whether for good or evil, Laud was the founder of a new theology. If it were true, its truths had been overlooked or discarded by the divines of the reformation; if false, it was, so far, a return to those errors against which they contended even unto death. The violent spirit in which he enforced his principles, and their consequences, in creating new discontents, and in giving new life to the worn out and exhausted puritans,—these are the points to which our attention must now be called.

CHAPTER XIII.

CHAPTER XIII. 1. THE influence of Laud was considerable during the later years of James I., but it rose to a much CHAS. I. greater height during the first years of Charles. A. D. 1624. His party was now formed; it had acquired solidity and force; its aims were clear and well defined; and its means were resolved upon. The church was to be re-established upon another basis; the papists (this household word was now discountenanced) were to be conciliated; and puritanism, at whatever cost, was to be destroyed and for ever rooted out. A party had suddenly arisen, which had the entire confidence of the court and of the aristocracy, sufficiently powerful to resist and overawe the two archbishops, a majority of the bishops, a vast number of the clergy, almost all the middle classes, and the common people. They declared themselves the church, the true church of England; and they succeeded in fastening on their opponents every term of ecclesiastical reproach: they were schismatics, genevans, calvin-

ists,—worse than all, they were puritans; a term CHAPTER
the meaning of which, by this new application of XIII.
it, was rendered more than ever vague. But words CHAS. 1.
adroitly used are, with designing men, the instru- A. D. 1624.
ments of the sleight of hand they practise. They
divert attention from themselves, and silence those
they cannot answer. Thus, church, or doctrinal,
puritan was a convenient phrase for conveying
the idea of disaffection to the church, or to the
state, or to both at once.

2. A change so great, and at the same time so
sudden, has seldom occurred. Whenever it takes
place it must be traced, if not immediately to some
remarkable interposition from on High, to previous
causes, which have passed unnoticed, or of which
the tendency was not understood till their issues
were determined. Upon a sudden, new men, and
with them new doctrines, or at least new construc-
tions of doctrine, had appeared. Montague and
Laud were the founders of this school, and they
lived to see it in its full maturity. That their
principles should so soon have prevailed in England,—have superseded and denounced the principles of Davenant and Hall,—would, in the last year
of Elizabeth, or sixteen years after when the synod
of Dort was held, have seemed incredible. And
yet the causes were at work which would probably,
perhaps necessarily, produce, at no distant period,
a Laudian or an infidel school, and invest it with
a transient popularity. For the latter the nation
was not prepared. It is the vice of the flippant
or of the coldly speculative; and the English cha-

racter stands at opposite, and perhaps at equal, extremes from each. The choice then was a relapse into religious pageantry and form ; and this we conceive was the natural consequence—natural, because, in accordance with the laws which God has impressed upon us—of the state of feeling which already shewed itself amongst the people, as well as of the character which the theology of the age had assumed. For, in the first place, the piety and earnestness of the two previous generations had passed away. During forty-four years, the reign of Elizabeth had been one of unclouded and increasing splendour. She found England poor, and, in the scale of nations, insignificant, and left it great and powerful. The increase of wealth in her time had been astonishing. And with wealth luxury had diffused its charms. Every class of society down to the meanest, had shared in the general prosperity. The farmer and the yeoman had succeeded to the comforts of the ancient gentleman, and, in many an instance, to the feudal hall, deserted by its owner for a more modern and magnificent residence. The London tradesman was on a footing with the London merchant of his youth : the cottager, whose father had been little better than a slave, living in a mud hut, which had provided neither for light nor fire, was possessed of most of the conveniences, and perhaps lived in the same tenement now possessed by his descendants. But they know little of mankind, and of the true church of Christ, who need to be informed, that long seasons of worldly prosperity are unfavourable to the soul. It is amidst the tempests of persecution, and in the dark days of trial, that the church gathers strength. Beneath unclouded sunshine it languishes and faints. The increase of profession is no conclusive proof that piety increases. A religious age is not necessarily an age of religion. Professions, indeed, are of themselves of little value; they are often assumed to conceal the absence of piety—as knavish men are most forward to proclaim their own integrity. In one sense the reign of James is the most religious part of our history; for religion was then fashionable. The forms of state, the king's speeches, the debates in parliament, and the current literature, were filled with quotations from scripture, and quaint allusions to sacred things; but underneath this promising exterior the current of real piety was shallow, we suspect. It wanted earnestness, depth, sincerity. The king was eminently a religious man (in the sense in which the term was then applied), but he was an habitual swearer, a drunkard, and a liar. Yet he was committed to the grave with most unmeasured eulogies. The bishop of Lincoln, in his funeral sermon, compared him with king Solomon, and shewed that he was his equal in every point, his superior in not a few : and he assured his audience, in conclusion, that their departed monarch was " now reigning gloriously with God in heaven." Bishop Hall followed in a strain of adulation scarcely less offensive. If the best men could stoop to this, we leave the reader to infer the

CHAPTER
XIII.

CHAS. I.

A. D. 1624.

average standard of morality in England; and how far, in the general practice, virtue and religion were divorced from each other: the one banished with disdain; the other, or rather the phantom which had assumed its form, retained, and pampered, and caressed.

3. The divinity of the times, as we have already said, partook largely of the same heartless character: it was at once artificial and, to a great degree, misdirected. Admiration seemed to be the preacher's highest aim; and if the structure of words and sentences, elaborately complicated, deserves applause, it is pre-eminently due to these divines. But it is difficult to believe that such things ever reached the heart; it is difficult to believe that they were seriously meant to reach it. They strike us as being merely college exercises, delivered at unseasonable times and places; and the preacher who could not display his scholastic niceties in the schools of Cambridge or Oxford, seems to have appeased his vanity by a recitation in the parish church. No man who is much in earnest delivers himself in quibbles and conceits; but in the strong impassioned words of nature, and in them alone. Tastes, it is true, may vary; but human nature in all ages appears to be very much the same.—Theology, too, had taken a most unhappy direction. The endless discussion of the five points of the calvinistic and arminian controversy was certain " to minister strife rather than godly edifying." Far be it from us to encourage the vulgar levity which would speak of

these points, or of any one of them, without the deepest reverence. They are truly amongst the deep things of God. Nor do we for a moment doubt that minds, deeply imbued with the spirit of true religion, and these too of the highest order, have dwelt upon them with intense study, and often with intense delight. Indeed, it is from such men that we expect a hearty concurrence in the assertion that a ministry that turns incessantly upon the discussion of these questions is misdirected and abused; and that its effects will be seen ere long in training up hearers " heady and high-minded." Yet when the Laudian party first appeared, such discussions appear to have taken almost exclusive possession of our pulpits. It was the natural consequence of the general heartlessness in religion. Under the same circumstances the phenomenon constantly re-appears. While the minister and his congregation are in a state of healthy piety, such stimulants are not required. When luxury, and sloth, and spiritual indifference, appear, speculative questions, which amuse but do not disturb, are the refuge of those who still endeavour to persuade themselves that all is right. But such a state of things cannot last : it is indeed one of the symptoms of decay. And if, at such a juncture, men of fearless minds, self-confident and resolute, assault the existing opinions, they find an easy triumph and are astonished at the facility with which the victory is won, over opponents who seemed to be invincible.

CHAPTER   4. Thus the way was prepared for a new party,
  XIII.   and its leaders soon appeared. Their accession to
CHAS. I.   power was rendered more easy by political cir-
A. D. 1628. cumstances, for which the reader will naturally
           seek elsewhere. Laud was placed in the see of
           London; Montagu succeeded his opponent, bishop
           Carlton, at Chichester; and the Laudian party
  1628.   was now consolidated. Its temper was soon ap-
           parent; it was persecuting, angry, and exclusive.
           It meant to brook no rivals, and to suffer no
           opponents to exist. This was the short, unhappy
           period during which the king's prerogative was
           violently strained, and made the plea for every
           outrage. The Laudian party availed themselves
           of it, if indeed they did not direct it; and they
           proceeded at once, thus sheltered, to denounce
           the puritanical bishops, and to assail the spiritual
           heads of the church themselves. Dr. Toby Mat-
           thew was still archbishop of York: he died about
  1628.   this time, old and full of years, one of the last of
           the reformers; connected, by marriage with his
           daughter, with bishop Barlow, a confessor in the
           Marian persecution. He was the speaker of the
           convocation in the memorable year when it re-
           monstrated with queen Elizabeth upon her se-
           verity to archbishop Grindal; he drew up the
           protest on its behalf; and his principles had never
           changed.

           5. Archbishop Abbott had succeeded Bancroft in
           the primacy. He was a man of blameless life,
           learned, vigilant, of exemplary piety, an unwearied
           student, an able statesman. Such are the admis-

sions of both parties. His admirers add that he was an excellent divine, an able preacher, and a prelate of primitive sanctity. Yet, like his great predecessor Grindal, he fell into deep disgrace. Upon a visit to a nobleman with whom he had long held "a dear and entire friendship," in order to revive his spirits (from which we infer that he was unwell in health) he was invited to witness a chase, and a cross-bow was put into his hand to shoot one of the deer.* Unhappily it swerved, and his arrow killed the keeper on the spot. His grief was overwhelming. He retired to Guildford, his native place, and took up his abode in the hospital which he himself had founded. James, who with all his faults was not in general un- just, silenced the scruples of those who reminded him that the primate was now a man of blood, and therefore incapable of the primacy, at once, by extending to him his royal pardon, and a full dispensation. The archbishop resumed his functions, but never forgot his griefs. Through the remainder of his life he kept a weekly fast on the day of his calamity. And he maintained the widow with a very liberal pension. The unfortu- nate occurrence ought to have been forgotten. Good men might have been expected to feel a deeper reverence for one thus constantly oppressed with unavailing sorrow. But Abbott was the friend of those who were now decried as puritans, and it was necessary to accomplish his disgrace. A commission was issued to five bishops, (of whom

* Heylyn's Laud, B. ii. 56.

CHAPTER XIII.

CHAS. I.

A. D. 1628.

Laud, at this time bishop of Bath and Wells, was one) to whom his jurisdiction was transferred. The archbishop meantime was sequestered, and confined to his house in Kent. Fuller asserts that his casual homicide was the alleged occasion of his disgrace;[*] but Heylyn[†] omits the charge of homicide, and relates that the archbishop was suspended because of his leaning to the puritans;—his real offence, no doubt,—the other was but a pretext. It was one of Charles's msot infatuated acts, and it recoiled upon himself.

Dec. 1628.

Within two years he was compelled to restore the archbishop, and to become a suitor for his good offices; giving him his hand to kiss, and enjoining his presence at the council twice a-week. But the interval of his suspension had been employed by the commission in promoting the interests of the Laudian party; that is, in harassing the doctrinal puritans, rigidly enforcing the ceremonies, and compelling churchwardens to place the tables altar-wise. Their ablest chronicler writes thus:[‡] "by this breathing time, short as it was, the church recovered strength again; and the disgrace put upon the man did so disanimate and deject the opposite party, that the balance began visibly to turn on the church's side." Such was the spirit in which they wrote; and such the position too at which they aimed. The Laudian party were the church. The archbishop, and all others however dignified by rank or station who

---

[*] Fuller.   [†] Heylyn's Laud, B. iii. 108, 125.
[‡] Heylyn, ut supra.

opposed them, were a mere faction—they were
puritans.

6. The archbishop was still suspended when
proceedings were taken against Williams, bishop
of Lincoln, and lord keeper of the seals. He too
was a divine of the old school, appointed to both
his dignities by the late king. It has been usual
to decry him as a weak man, and a mere bab-
bler. Had he been so, his extraordinary rise
is somewhat unaccountable. James was infirm
enough no doubt, and too ready to promote those
who flattered him. But happily he was hedged
about with wise advisers; and it exceeds belief
that they should have allowed him to place a
weak man in trusts of such importance. The
general charge against Williams was his puritanism; the proofs were distributed under two
particulars. First, he refused to discountenance
preaching; and secondly, he opposed the removal
of communion tables, so as to place them altar-
wise. We think it alike unnecessary to enter on
the accusation and the defence; though both are
ponderously written in the records of the times.
A colorable charge was added, that being a privy
councillor he had betrayed the secrets of the state.
But the single fact alleged in evidence does not
by any means sustain so grave a charge. On
being urged to punish certain puritans within his
diocese, he declined to do so; assigning as one
reason for his conduct that the king himself had
told him that for the future he meant to treat
his puritan subjects with more forbearance.

Had the lord keeper alone been made acquainted with the king's intentions, still it was no state secret, but rather a matter which, for the king's honour, ought to be repeated. But the king himself had made the promise openly, in answer to an address from the puritans of Oxford; and secret there was none. The bishop had merely repeated what was sufficiently notorious. But he was already in disgrace, and had been called upon to resign the seals. He lived for ten years in retirement at his episcopal house at Buckden, and at length in 1637, on a charge of subornation of perjury, he was fined eight thousand pounds, suspended, and imprisoned during the king's pleasure. To this sentence, Laud, now archbishop of Canterbury, consented among the rest; aggravating the crime in a speech, says his biographer, of almost an hour long. He had been, he said, five times on his knees before the king on the bishop's behalf, but at length he felt bound to consent to the heaviest punishment. In the same year a second fine of eight thousand pounds was inflicted on the bishop, upon a different charge; his servants also were fined, as sharers in the crime of subornation of perjury. If the charge were just and well proven, the punishment was slight—far too slight indeed. Two years afterwards, however, the house of commons— the long parliament—who, with all their faults, are never charged with having overlooked episcopal delinquencies—petitioned the king to release

* Fuller b. xi.

the bishop of Lincoln from his long imprisonment, CHAPTER
and to restore him in his place in the house of XIII.
peers. And, to complete the melancholy history, CHAS. I.
which needs no further comment, the king him- A. D.
self sent for him, loaded him with kindness, 1628—30.
cancelled the judgments filed against him, and
translated him to the archbishopric of York soon 1641.
afterwards. Amongst his letters, which were
seized, were some from a Mr. Osbaldeston,
master of Westminster school, reflecting upon
Laud's character. They were unbecoming and
impertinent, but scarcely even in those days
libellous; and it was not proved that the bishop
had encouraged his correspondent, or indeed that
he knew the letters were in his possession. Osbaldeston was fined five thousand pounds to the
king,* deprived of his school and living, and condemned to stand in the pillory in the Dean's yard,
and to have his ears nailed thereto, in the presence of his scholars. At this very time, it is
worthy of mention, such had been his success
in tuition, and such the esteem in which he
was held, that above four score doctors in the
university and the three learned faculties,
gratefully acknowledged their obligations to
him as their preceptor.† Osbaldeston escaped
by flight, and one of the first acts of the
long parliament was to reverse the iniquitous
decision. Each of these victims of oppression
lived to give signal proofs of loyalty; the archbishop of York, calmly maintaining his own and

* Laud, b. iv. 63.   † Fuller, b. xi. p. 403, and Heylyn, b. iv. 63.

his episcopal brethren's rights, became, ere long, almost as much the object of popular hatred as Laud himself: and Osbaldeston resigned his school,* as the parliament became more violent, and sided with his sovereign, rather than consent to hold it from a revolutionary body. The noble revenge of christian 'men was theirs: to return good for evil; and, in the instance at least of the archbishop, to do well and suffer for it, and take it patiently.

7. Davenant, the learned and exemplary bishop of Salisbury, was another victim. For a sermon, preached in the presence of the king at White-hall, he was summoned before the privy council, and charged with "at least a high contempt," for having presumed to meddle with some controverted points of doctrine. When he made his appearance, he was permitted to kneel for some time at the board, where Laud and other bishops were present; and was only requested to rise at the suggestion of a lay nobleman; and in other respects he was treated with indignity. Of his reputation in former times, let it suffice to remind the reader, that he had been one of the English representatives at the synod of Dort. In doctrine he was moderate; he was even supposed to lean towards the side of the arminians, or remonstrants: he strenuously maintained the doctrine of universal redemption. He has left on record a full account of the proceedings which took place in the presence of the king, and before the privy

* Heylyn, v. 27.

council, as well as an outline of the sermon which gave so much offence. He had asserted that eternal life was the free gift of God (from the text, Romans vi. 23) through Christ, and not procured or premerited by man; and under one of the heads of his sermon he had "considered eternal life," he says, "with respect to the eternal destination thereof, which we call election." Davenant, as his admirable writings prove, was rather a practical, than a controversial, divine. He was not, in this instance, in the least aware that he had transgressed. Charles, it is true, had repeated his father's declaration against controversial sermons and speculative doctrines; but Davenant did not admit, he said, that he had preached anything forbidden, curious, or unnecessary; or that he had gone beyond the received doctrine of the church established in the seventeenth article. However he promised obedience for the future, and the affair ended. Harsnett, who had now succeeded Abbott as archbishop of York, conducted the prosecution; and Laud was present with other bishops, walking to and fro, but making no remarks on the proceedings. Such was the treatment which one of the mildest of the doctrinal puritans received from Charles and his advisers.*

8. But the treatment of Hall, bishop successively of Exeter and Norwich, was still more unjust. He too had represented the church of England at the synod of Dort; but his views were moderate,

* Fuller iii. xi. 366.

and he had even published a treatise, which he entitled *Via media*, with a view to reconcile, if possible, the differences on both sides. Nor was his devotion to the church of England questioned: since Laud himself requested him to take up his eloquent pen in defence of episcopacy and the liturgy. He did so, and produced his well known treatise on the subject. Five of the ablest of the presbyterian divines, under a feigned title, united their learning to furnish an answer. That their answer was deemed insufficient by their own party, we gather from the fact that Milton himself came to their assistance. The greatest men, it has been said, as if to compensate for their superiority, descend, in some one instance in their lives, to the mediocrity of ordinary natures. So Milton compounded for his greatness in a pamphlet altogether unworthy of his adversary, of himself, and of his cause. Bishop Hall was then considered an elegant writer, he is still admired as a pious and eloquent one. He is at this day the oldest English prose writer who is really popular. Elder writers, Sydney, Raleigh, Bacon, and even Milton, are consulted rather than read. Their style has become obsolete, and they are perused with something of a painful effort. But bishop Hall's pious meditations are still a household volume, read by all classes, published in all forms. His graphic pictures of scripture life and manners still delight us ; his deep touches of nature still reach the heart ; his solemn tender admonitions still affect the conscience. He has had a host of

imitators, and some independent followers in the CHAPTER
same field, of whom the chief are Robinson Lei- XIII.
cester, and Henry Blunt of Chelsea ; but he is, CHAS. I.
after all, unrivalled—one of the greatest of Eng- A. D. 1630.
lish writers, one of the best of English prelates.

9. That such a man should have been disgraced
is infamy to those who dishonoured him. He had
modestly refused the see of Gloucester, but was 1627.
raised to that of Exeter soon afterwards. He was
too important a person to be overlooked, and too
sincere a protestant not to be suspected. He entered on his diocese, he tells us, amidst prejudice
and suspicion : he was averse to the Laudian
school in doctrine and in practice, and was disliked
and marked. He soon had intelligence that he
was surrounded with spies. Those who sat at the
helm of the church viewed him with great jealousy
as one who favoured the puritans ; his conduct
was watched, and his proceedings exposed to the
worst construction. Some persons of note,—if not
of reputation,—assailed him with obloquy, both in
the pulpit and directly at the court. The storm
ran high. Three several times, says the venerable
man, I was upon my knee to his majesty to
answer for these great criminations ; and his many
contests with " some great lords," the king's advisers, were too tedious to recite. At length he
appealed to the archbishop of Canterbury—a dignity which Laud had now obtained—and told him
that, rather than continue to be thus slandered and
thwarted, he would resign his sacred office and "cast
up his rochet." Meanwhile his " wary brethren,"

that large and well-compacted body who in troublous times mistake timidity for caution, and idly
think to escape danger by concealment, annoyed
him with messages of caution and letters of expostulation. Still he was highly popular, and his popularity was of that kind which comes uncourted,—the
spontaneous expression of deep respect purchased
by a blameless and consistent life. Returning home
from parliament he was met and welcomed by hundreds of the citizens of Exeter. But the storm of popular indignation now began to terrify the king; and
with a view, no doubt, of attaching to himself one
so able to assist him, bishop Hall was translated
to Norwich. But " he took the Tower," he tells
us, " in the way." The prelate who could not be obsequious to Laud, was not likely to be awed by the
frenzy of a London mob, or the madness of the
house of commons. He subscribed archbishop
Williams's protest, and with the rest of the bishops
was immediately impeached by the commons, and
committed for high treason. The Laudian party
was by this time destroyed; but the troubles of this
holy man were not ended.* Ejected from his bishopric, exposed to violence and insult, impove-
rished and in solitude, bishop Hall lived till
eighty-two, and died in peace; an object of more
veneration in his last years of poverty than in
the midst of all his honours and his usefulness.
When he could preach no longer, he became as
diligent to hear as he had once been to teach.
" How often," says the preacher of his funeral

---

* " Some especialities in his own life," &c. Hall's Hard Measure, &c.

sermon, "have we seen him walking alone, like old Jacob, with a staff to Bethel, the house of God." Five years before his death he lost her who for eight and forty years had been his dear and beloved companion through many a change. He suffered intensely from the stone, and he suffered much, no doubt, from the sad state of affairs;— the monarchy dissolved ; the church overthrown. But he had a well-spring of happiness which even these griefs could not dry. His last tract was written on the occasion of his wife's death. Its title is expressive :—" Songs in the night ; or cheerfulness in affliction."*

10. It would merely fatigue the reader to rehearse the indignities and barbarous punishments inflicted on less distinguished men. These are passages in our history which every one has read. The popular recollection of the star chamber and the court of high commission goes back, indeed, no further than the reign of Charles the first. Their names are odious to us from our childhood, chiefly because we know them in connection with Bastwick, Prynn, and Leighton, and their inhuman punishment in Palace-yard. But these are subjects rather political than pertaining to puritan history. From the treatment experienced by the leaders of the party, its inferior members could not fail to see that its extermination, and nothing less, would satisfy the court. They must bend before the storm, or resist it at their peril. The

* Hughes' Memoir of Hall, 66; Jones's Life and Times of Bishop Hall.

amount of suffering inflicted on pious members and clergymen of the church beneath Laud's tyranny was great;—greater far, we suspect, from the few incidental notices that have been handed down to us, than is generally believed. We are speaking, not of those violent acts of legal outrage which claim a place in history, but of the petty tyrannies which vex and mortify in private life ;—of the secret and malicious influence which thwarts exertion and baffles every prospect of success; which marks out its victim for the operation of the slow and secret poison under which hopes wither and reputation is destroyed. Had Laud succeeded, and the court party, the doctrinal puritans would undoubtedly have been expelled the church ; for no doctrinal puritan could have remained in it with a safe conscience to practise Laud's injunctions, and read the book of sports. And if from these he had proceeded to bind the doctrinal peculiarities of his school upon their necks, the doctrinal puritans must one and all have instantly been silent.

11. The doctrinal puritans of Charles the first are a body of men entitled to our highest reverence. Amidst formalists they were spiritual. In times of faction they were peaceable. In an age of violence they were calm and moderate. They scrupled not to wear the surplice, to kneel at the eucharist, or to sign the cross in baptism. Chanting or singing of hymns was alike welcome to them, provided the congregation "made melody in their hearts unto the Lord." They had no sus-

picions of episcopacy as a relic of antichrist, for not a few of them adorned the episcopal office: they were devout men; and prayers read from a liturgy, or uttered from the fulness of the heart in unpremeditated words, were prayers to them; for they were "the pure in heart, to whom all things are pure." They taught the doctrines of the reformation, and in their own lives they revived the spirit of the reformers. Their historical fate is that which generally befals good men whose lot is cast amongst the violent and factious. They rushed into no extremes; they set up no popular cry; they headed no party; and they followed none. When the king was under an evil influence, they remonstrated; when Laud played the tyrant, they withstood him to the face. When the house of commons in its turn entered upon its career of violence, they again protested, were insulted, imprisoned, and ruined. The church itself was overthrown, and the doctrinal puritans disappear with it. The evangelical principles of the reformation had begun to decline, under Whitgift and Bancroft, into a dry and sapless orthodoxy. Under Abbott, Hall, and Carlton, and a great number of the clergy likeminded with themselves, the true spirit of the reformation was revived; sound doctrines were taught; the christian virtues inculcated; and the religion of the bible practised, without enthusiasm and without superstition. These men were the evangelists of their age. But the storm thickened, and the rising tide beat every hour more angrily; and in the darkness and wild confusion that en-

CHAPTER XIII.

CHAS. I.

A. D. 1630—40.

sued they disappear from sight. They were the true successors of the reformation. If Laud had attended to their warnings they would have saved the church: had the parliament taken heed to the example of their moderation they would have saved the monarchy. They seem to have been raised up, like the prophets of old, to foretel impending ruin, and to leave both factions without excuse. The sin of neglecting such counsellors was great, and the retribution that followed was appalling.

CHAPTER XIV.

1. To relate the disastrous events which now begin to crowd upon each other, belongs to secular historians, and to those who write the history of the church of England. Our own less frequented path lies apart, though not far remote, from either. The puritans neither composed the nation nor the church; but they were a body of men whose varying fortunes, whose triumphs and defeats, influenced both church and state, and from time to time left upon them traces which are yet indelible. We have arrived at the period at which the history of the early puritans is drawing to a close; they melt away and disappear from sight; and henceforth the history becomes that of non-conformists, not of the puritans properly so termed.

2. Occupying an intermediate space, however, another class appears. These are the democratic puritans; strange men, whose history can be likened only to a tornado which bursts on some devoted land without a warning, covers it with ruin and desolation, and hurries away. In times of revolution it is only the violent who are

heard. The voice must be loud and shrill that swells above the roaring of the tempest. The elder puritans had long since decayed, and their numbers were insignificant. The church puritans were men of peace. Whatever their opinions might have been in the abstract as to the lawfulness of an armed resistance, they were extremely reluctant to make the appeal to the sword in this instance. They could not identify themselves with either party. They were neither cavaliers nor roundheads. For Charles it was impossible for them to fight with alacrity. They knew too well his popish tendencies; they were too keenly alive to the danger of his un-English principles. For they understood far better than their predecessors the English constitution in church and state ; and were far more competent than any who had gone before them to advance the interests of the one, and yet maintain the independence of the other. Nor, on the other hand, could they join the parliament: for then they must have arrayed themselves against the social order they revered as God's appointment; against a liturgy; against episcopacy ; against the church itself. They seem to have stood aloof, and to have shared the usual fate of those who are neutral in a civil war—plundered by each of the contending parties, protected by neither; and when the scene brightens again, and the mists disperse, they have wasted away, and their place is nowhere to be found.

3. The democratic puritans felt none of these perplexities. They were men of ungoverned pas-

sions ; intense fanaticism ; and in general, we may
add, and with a few exceptions, profoundly ignorant. They were sectaries, hating the presbyterians scarcely less than they hated the prelates.
The policy of Laud is usually blamed as having
called them into existence ; and his violent measures, it is true, contributed in no small degree to
recruit their numbers and to render them important. But they were already powerful when
Laud was an obscure person ; they threatened the
state with mischief long before he goaded them
into actual rebellion. James was still upon the
throne when the sectaries excited painful apprehensions ; and the symptoms of the terrible con-
vulsion which shook England to its centre were
already unequivocally apparent. Bishop Hall
himself—and it was not his character to be des-
ponding—in a sermon preached before James, in
1624, takes up his prophetic lamentation, and
deplores the sudden outburst of fanatical sectarianism. " Unless it can be repressed speedily,
we shall be," said he, " as when God overthrew
Sodom and Gomorrah, and it shall be with us as the
prophet speaks of proud and glorious Babylon."*
But the plague was not stayed, but rather aggravated by the impotent severities of those in power.
In a speech delivered in his place in the house of
lords, some years after, he once more called attention to the impending danger, the imminent hazard
of which, he intimates, was not perceived even then.
" Alas ! my lords, I beseech you to consider what it

CHAPTER
XIV.

CHAS. I.

A. D.
1640–42.

1641.

* Hall's Work, v. 236.

is: that there should be in London and the suburbs no fewer than fourscore congregations of several sectaries, as I have been too credibly informed, instructed by cobblers, tailors, felt-makers, and such like trash; which are all taught to spit in the face of their mother, the church of England ; and to defy and revile her government. From hence have issued that inundation of base and scurrilous pamphlets, in which papists and prelates, like oxen in a yoke, are still matched together." And, in a tone of becoming warmth, he adds ; " give me leave humbly to beseech your lordships, to be tenderly sensible of these woeful and dangerous conditions of the times. If the government of the church of England be unlawful and unfit, abandon and disclaim it. But if otherwise, uphold and maintain it. Otherwise if these lawless outrages be yet suffered to gather head, who knows where they will end ? My lords, if these men may, with impunity and freedom, thus bear down ecclesiastical authority, it is to be feared they will not rest there; but will be ready to affront the civil power too. Your lordships know that the Jack Straws, and Cades, and Wat Tylers, of former times, did not more cry down learning than nobility : and those of your lordships that have read the history of the anabaptistical tumults at Munster, will need no other item ; let it be enough to say, that many of these sectaries are of the same profession. Shortly, therefore, let me humbly move your lordships to take these dangers and miseries of this poor church deeply to heart : and upon this occasion, to give orders for the speedy redressing of these horrible insolencies; and for the stopping of that deluge of libellous invectives wherewith we are thus impetuously overflown. Which, in all due submission, I humbly present to your lordships' wise and religious consideration.* But the house of lords was now afraid to act alone; and the house of commons was more disposed to foment the evil, than to punish it. Sectarianism spread; each congregation became a focus of turbulence, if not of sedition. In general it professed neither allegiance nor affinity to any other sect or church whatever: each stood alone; the monstrous creation of unnatural times. These assemblies soon became the political clubs of later revolutions. When the presbyterians had overthrown the church, combining for once, they overthrew the presbyterians; but their impotence was then discovered; their power was merely destructive; the field was clear before them, but they could establish nothing—they had nothing to propose; and they brought religion into a state of the profoundest anarchy. It was thus in fact that the violence of the fanatics, exciting disgust and abhorrence in all reasonable minds, contributed powerfully, as if in atonement for their early excesses, to the restoration both of the church and monarchy.

4. There are times in the history of nations when the multitude suddenly break loose, and every existing institution is threatened with de-

* Bishop Hall's Works, vol. x. pp. 65, 66.

struction. Such outbursts may in general be traced to grievous oppressions; to a long period of misrule; or to criminal neglects. But sometimes it appears, in these frightful times of anarchy, as if a strange delirium was abroad, of which the causes are inexplicable. Those who have least to complain of are most clamorous; those who have been most highly favoured are loudest in their discontent. The people are wearied with repose, and jaded with prosperity. The foundations of the earth are out of course, and God's judgments are abroad. And when the wild frenzy of the democratic puritans is to be explained, at the beginning of the reign of Charles the first, it will be found that, since no other sufficient cause can be assigned, it no less becomes an historian than a humble christian—it is not less philosophical than devout —to ascribe their full weight to these solemn considerations.

5. In alliance with the democratic puritans there were undoubtedly not a few men of different principles, who united with them against popery and the common foe, and were drawn into some of their excesses. They did not see their error till it was too late. Their fault was great; but the charge, from which it is impossible to relieve the memory of the Laudian party and the king, is, that they drove them on to madness. Men of saintly minds —bishops Hall, and Carlton, and many thousands of their followers—could bear oppression and insult meekly. But the lofty standard of what a christian man will forbear and suffer, is the ex-

ception at all times ; most of all in times of revolution. The political grievances were sufficient
to have provoked resistance in any country, even
the most servile, and would undoubtedly have
done so ; and the religious hardships and wrongs
of the times, were even more intolerable. Vast
numbers of the laity forsook their pastors, and
plunged headlong into the war ; and of these, a
great proportion were hitherto members of the
church of England. Baxter, who seldom mis-
leads us with regard to facts, declares, that of the
long parliament, which drew the sword against
the king, only one member was a presbyterian ;
all the rest conformed. And lord Clarendon,
a courtly historian, confirms the general truth
of his statement. Yet their conduct afterwards,
proves that they were not church puritans. They
belonged to another class ; they were not the
pupils of bishop Hall, for they imprisoned him ;
no more than of Laud, whom they put to death.
They took other grounds, chiefly political, though
flavoured with a religious pretext and colour-
ing. Thus parties were combined afresh. Names,
long venerated, remained on each side ; but they
were no longer the symbols of the old party, or
of the old distinctions.—We proceed to relate
the grievances under which the great body of
the English people were induced at length to
array themselves against the church of their forefathers, and to regard its overthrow with indifference, if not with exultation.

6. The want of able preachers was great ; for the
policy of the court had for some time been to

CHAPTER
XIV.

CHAS. I.

A. D
1640—42.

1628.

discourage preaching as much as possible. To remedy the evil, the puritans, with great activity, established lectureships both in London and through the country. Private gentlemen retained the lecturers as chaplains in their mansions; the pious nobility had several, according to their rank, who were engaged in a kind of preaching mission upon their estates, and in the neighbouring towns. Laud regarded these proceedings with great uneasiness. The lecturers were looked down upon by the high church party with great contempt; for they were mostly puritans, and evaded strict conformity. They were neither parsons, nor vicars, nor stipendiary curates. " In fact," says Heylyn, " they were neither fish nor flesh, nor good red herring." The king, at Laud's suggestion, issued instructions to the bishops, commanding them to suppress the lecture, if preached in the afternoon ; turning it into catechizing by question and answer, and in other respects to insist upon strict conformity.* Gentlemen beneath the rank of nobility, if not qualified by law, were forbidden to retain their private chaplains. These proceedings gave great uneasiness. Some of the bishops, Hall of Exeter among the number, refused to interfere where the lecturers were men of known character and piety, and in his diocese the exceptions, he tells us, were few. The fatuity of Charles's counsels became daily apparent. A proclamation was issued, and rigidly enforced, to prevent the emigration of the puritans to lands where they might enjoy

* Heylyn's Laud, book iii. 127.

their religion undisturbed: and yet they were
sternly forbidden the exercise of their religion
at home. A company of foeffees was formed for
purchasing impropriations. They erected a kind
of corporation amongst themselves, consisting
of twelve persons,* clergymen, citizens, and lawyers, who soon collected large sums of money,
bought up advowsons, and established lectureships, especially in corporate and market towns.
Laud regarded the proceedings as dangerous both
to church and state. The attorney-general was
commanded to prosecute. The foeffees were called
into the court of exchequer, the foeffment condemned, the impropriations they had bought con-
fiscated, and the further merits of the cause deferred for a final sentence. But other troubles
arose, and the matter appears to have been carried no further. For the present, however, the
lectureships were suppressed.

7. Equally irritating, and far more criminal,
was the conduct of the court, urged forward by
the Laudian party, in the revival of the sabbatarian question. At an assize held at Exeter,
an order had been made by the judges, one of
whom was the chief baron, and the other a puisne
baron of the court of exchequer, for the suppression of Sunday revels in the western circuit. The
lord mayor exerted his authority in London to
prevent the desecration of the Lord's-day. In
such times the most insignificant occurrences are
important. A woman was prohibited by the lord

* Heylyn's Laud, book iii. 134.

CHAPTER mayor from selling apples on the Sunday in St.
XIV. Paul's church-yard. Alas! he could pretend to
CHAS. I. no jurisdiction there; and for that offence he was
A. D. questioned and reproved by Laud, then bishop of
1640—42. London.* The bitterness and scorn with which
a devout observance of the Lord's-day was treated
is perfectly incredible. The vilest heresy could
not be more unsparingly denounced; of all crimes
the greatest might have been to remember the
sabbath-day to keep it holy. In short, the book
of sports was reprinted, and issued anew, with a
declaration subjoined by the king, commanding
its publication through all parish churches; and
this was done, it declares, "out of a pious care for
Oct. 18, the service of God." The sober part of the nation
1633. was struck with horror; vast numbers of the
clergy refused to read the hateful document, and
were silenced.† Many, still more deeply to be
pitied, did violence to their consciences, and retained their livings. Some complied with the law,
and read the book of sports, and then, immediately afterwards, the fourth commandment;
calling upon the people to compare the two and
judge accordingly. An act of tyranny irritates
and inflames thousands more than it oppresses.
The book of sports was degrading and oppressive
to the clergy, who were obliged to read it; but to
the laity, who were only compelled to listen, it was
merely insulting and offensive. It proclaimed a
licence to sin, but they were not bound to make
use of it; it perverted God's word, but it could

* Heylyn's Laud, book iv. p. 8.   † Fuller, book xi. anno 1634

not make them accept the perverted interpretation. But the indignation of the English people
was not the less, upon that account; nor ought it
to have been less. The book of sports was an
outrage upon the feelings of the nation, and the
parliament expressed their opinion of it signifi-
cantly. By their command it was burnt ten years
afterwards by the common hangman in Cheapside,
and the sheriffs were ordered to demand that every
copy in private hands should be given up to them.

8. The affairs of Scotland contributed to increase
the anxiety of the puritans at home. James had
attempted to introduce episcopacy, and Charles
was now determined, at whatever hazard, to carry
the project into effect. The odium of these proceedings fell chiefly upon Laud, who succeeded to
the primacy in August 1633, upon the death of
Abbott. The indignation of the Scottish nation
was inconceivable; it contained in fact the germ
of a revolution, and of a dreadful civil war. Their
animosity was especially roused when they discovered, not only that the institutions of Knox and
of their presbyterian discipline were to be superseded on the mere fiat of the sovereign,—to whom
in spiritual things a presbyterian church assigns
but a subordinate authority; but further, that
while the liturgy to be imposed upon them varied
in several material points from that of the church
of England, every alteration betrayed a tendency
to popery. Other grievances were added. The
Scotch nobility complained of the pride and assumption of the Scotch bishops. The meanest of

CHAPTER XIV.

CHAS. I.

A. D. 1640—42.

July 23, 1637.

1638.

the people were indignant that their church, which claimed to be as free and independent as any church in christendom,—a sister, not a daughter of the English church,—should be compelled to submit to the dictation of an English bishop. When at length the new service book was introduced at Edinburgh, in the presence of the privy council, the two archbishops of Scotland, several bishops, and the city magistrates, a tumult broke out in the church, which was in effect the opening of a rebellion. At first it seemed to be a mere outrage of the mob, "the scum of the city," it was said ;* but a few days after, the whole nation took up the cause, and the enthusiastic cry was heard :—" God defend all those who will defend God's cause ; and God confound the service book and all the maintainers of it."† The bishops barely escaped by flight or by concealment. Then followed, in quick and disastrous succession, the solemn league and covenant ; the abolition of episcopacy in Scotland, with the king's extorted consent, and soon afterwards, and as the consequence of this re-action, the ruin of the English church, and the entire subversion of episcopacy.

9. The solemn league and covenant was in substance the same which had been already twice subscribed. It was now sworn to, and subscribed once more with an enthusiasm equal to the danger which threatened the church of Scotland. By the common people it was regarded as

---

* "The king's declaration concerning the tumult in Scotland," 17.
† Neal ii. 260.

a sacred oracle ; and was taken by all who wished CHAPTER
to have it thought they were not indifferent ^{XIV.}
to the protestant faith, and to the liberties of CHAS. I.
Scotland. They bound themselves by this solemn A. D.
oath, to defend the ancient doctrine and discipline 1640—42.
of the kirk, under all the penalties which might
befal transgressors in this life and in the life to
come ; and, under the same awful sanctions, they
swore, " by the great name of God," to resist all
those "errors and corruptions, (namely, the late innovations brought into the kirk), to the utmost
of their power, all the days of their lives." The oath
was illegal, since the chief magistrate forbad and
denounced it ; but indeed the whole proceeding de-
fied the ordinary forms and usages of civil government.* When, five years afterwards, the parliament, now in arms against the king, sought 1642.
assistance from the Scotch, the latter made it the
condition of their co-operation, that the solemn
league and covenant should be embraced in
England. To this dictation the parliament submitted,—but not the people of England. And
hence resulted the pertinacious though futile endeavour to establish a presbyterian church, when
our own episcopacy was overthrown.

10. There was still another cause for discontent.
The king assembled a parliament, and with it a
convocation, in April 1640. The parliament was
dissolved within a few weeks; and the convocation,
according to the practice of the English constitution, ought to have been dissolved with it. But

* Neal ii. 260.

its sittings continued after the dissolution, under a special commission from the king. The legality of this step was questioned by the great lawyers of the day. The long parliament not only reversed the proceedings of the convocation, but impeached its leading members. One of the heaviest charges in archbishop Laud's indictment when brought to trial, was the part he took in this affair. Its proceedings were rash and violent, and produced the worst consequences. It enacted new canons and constitutions for the church. One of these extended the penalties already in force against popish recusants (penalties which could only be justified, if justified at all, by the most extreme necessity) to all anabaptists, brownists, separatists, or other sects or persons whatsoever who did not rigidly conform, and receive the holy communion according to law. Other canons followed in a similar strain. The state was no doubt in extreme peril from the madness of the sectaries. But the severity of the canon was indiscriminate, and therefore powerless. It was right to denounce sedition and to punish it; but it was monstrous to punish all non-conformity with fines, imprisonment, and exile. The canons served no other purpose than to increase the universal irritation. Six articles were also passed which asserted, in unqualified terms, the divine right of kings and the doctrine of passive obedience. In seeming anticipation of a doubt which was soon to perplex so many wise and loyal hearts, the convocation declared that for subjects to bear arms against

the king, either offensive or defensive, upon any
pretence whatever, was to resist the powers ordained of God; for the order of kings, they say,
is of divine right; being the ordinance of God
himself, founded on the laws of nature and revelation.* This doctrine the clergy were commanded
to teach publicly once in each quarter of the
year; or if they maintained any contrary position
they were to be excommunicated and deprived.

11. In quiet times these propositions would
have passed unnoticed. The duty of obedience to
civil rulers is unquestionable; the exact point at
which disobedience becomes right, no casuistry
will ever determine. In general terms it may be
stated thus: it is the point at which the subject's
duty to God is plainly and unequivocally in opposition to the commands of the civil ruler. Under
all conceivable circumstances it is right to obey
God rather than man. Peremptory decisions like
those of 1640, raise more doubts than they set
at rest. In the ferment which then existed the
canon could only be mischievous. It exasperated
the one party; the other, the king's adherents,
did not require the stimulant.

12. The convocation imposed an oath which
has ever since occupied a foremost place among
puritan grievances. It is known as the et-cetera
oath; and the clause which gave so much offence
was this: "Nor will I ever give my consent to
alter the government of this church by archbishops,
bishops, deans and archdeacons, &c., as it stands
now established, and as by right it now ought to

* Canon i. convocation, published June 30, 1640.

CHAPTER XIV.

CHAS. I.

A. D. 1640—42.

stand." But how much did this et-cetera comprehend? And to what did it refer? to the question of church government by archbishops and bishops merely? or to tables placed altar-wise: and bowings to the east? How would it be construed by the star chamber and by the court of high commission? And how ought it to be construed in the bosom of every man of conscience and integrity? These were no trifling questions. They were anxiously discussed in every parish in England, and in every parsonage. For "all such as were then in any ecclesiastical dignity," all clergymen having benefice or cure of souls, were called upon to take the oath; and the penalty was, suspension for the first refusal, sequestration for the second, and deprivation for the third; a month's deliberation being granted between each refusal.* The oath was also imposed upon all the members of either university, and upon candidates for holy orders. Of the clergy many absolutely refused to take it. The London clergy, amongst whom occur the names of Goodwin and Calamy, petitioned the privy council for relief. Many denied that the convocation, or synod, was a lawful assembly, and spurned it with contempt. Bishop Hall so explained it in his diocese, as he tells us,† (and an et cetera seems to afford great latitude in the construction of an oath, whether in contracting or expanding it) as to make it sit lightly on the conscience. But many of the bishops compelled the clergy to take it on their knees; ‡ a

* Heylin's Laud, book iv. 141.   † Jones's Life of Hall, 181.
‡ Fuller xi. 171.

ceremony never required in England but in the
oaths of allegiance and supremacy. Sanderson,
afterwards bishop of Lincoln, wrote to Laud that
multitudes of the clergy utterly refused to take
the oath, or were brought to submit to it with the
utmost reluctance. And that these were not men
of the preciser sort, but such as willingly conformed; and that, in short, the peace of the church
was in the greatest danger. Laud appears to have
been, as usual, obstinate and inflexible; but happily the king was at York and he at Lambeth;
and milder counsels prevailed. A letter was
addressed in the king's name, by the secretary of
state, to the archbishop, requiring him to dispense
with the oath entirely till another convocation.
Bishop Hall declares that he never tendered the
oath to any one minister of his diocese, though
he had many expostulatory letters from the
archbishop,* and sundry cautions from his wary
brethren. He explained it for the satisfaction of
others who might be called to submit to it.

13. But the terrible crisis had at length arrived. On the 3rd of November, 1640, the long
parliament met. Three days afterwards, on the
6th of November, the proceedings of the convocation came beneath review. The indignation of the
house overflowed : and it chiefly directed itself
against the usurpation of the prelates, and " the
bottomless perjury of an et-cetera oath ;" an oath
" to be taken," said lord Digby, " in the literal
sense, whereof no two of the makers themselves,

CHAPTER XIV.

CHAS. I.

A. D.
1640—42.

Sept. 30,
1640.

---

* Fuller xi. 171.

CHAPTER XIV.

CHAS. I.

A. D. 1640—42.

that I have heard of, would ever agree in the understanding of." The debate was adjourned to the 15th of December, in order to give time for the report of a committee, who were appointed to collect such materials as might assist the house in its decision. It was resolved unanimously, that the clergy assembled in convocation, or synod, or otherwise, have no power to make any constitutions, canons, or acts whatever, to bind either the laity or clergy, without consent of parliament. That the synod or convocation of 1640, was illegal; that its canons and constitutions contained many things contrary to the king's prerogative; to the fundamental laws and statutes of this realm; to the rights of parliament; to the property and liberty of the subject : matters tending to sedition, and of dangerous consequence; and that the grants, or contributions they had levied on the clergy for the king, were illegal. On the 16th of December, the first assault was made upon the unhappy Laud, under three heads. First, he was charged with forcing episcopacy on Scotland : secondly, for obtruding upon the Scotch a book of canons; for establishing a tyrannical power in the person of their prelates over the people; and for abolishing the kirk of Scotland : and, thirdly, with having introduced the book of common prayer without warrant from the kirk. Of each of these grievances the archbishop was said to be the chief author : they were first presented to the house of lords ; and reported to the lower house at a conference. The door once opened, a furious

storm broke in. The archbishop was voted guilty
of high treason by the lower house; and on the
26th of February, the impeachment was laid upon
the bar of the house of lords in fourteen articles.
On the 1st of March, surrounded by a mob which
followed him with huzzas and insults until he
arrived within the Tower gate, he was carried to
the prison from which he only came forth, after a
long and mournful captivity, to his trial and execution. None of the charges amounted to high
treason : the punishment inflicted upon him was
not justice but revenge. His faults are great,
but they are overlooked in comparison with his
misfortunes. The spectacle of greatness suffering
is more touching, and the impression it leaves
more lasting, than the remembrance of its crimes.
Wherever the story of archbishop Laud shall be
told, it is not his follies, his bigotry, his arrogance,
but his death, that will be had in everlasting remembrance. So violence defeats itself ; and thus
the memory of the injured is righteously avenged.

14. The immediate consequence of Laud's impeachment was, that the spirit which broke out
in parliament was caught up out of doors. The
populace of London became little better than a
mob frenzied with fanaticism. Petitions poured
in demanding the abolition of episcopacy " root
and branch." The words, first used in a violent
address from the city of London, became a rally-
ing cry. Root and branch petitions, with their
thousands or tens of thousands of names, loaded
the tables of both houses. The city apprentices

prayed that prelacy might be rooted up. The city porters complained that episcopacy was a burden too heavy for their shoulders. These petitions were received by the house with evident satisfaction ; for as the storm increased, parliament was driven helplessly before it. Wren of Ely, and several other bishops, were imprisoned or censured by parliament, upon general charges of severity against the puritans, and of entertaining Laudian principles. A bill was presented, and finally carried, degrading them from the peerage, and excluding them from parliament. In the

interval before it passed, the mob were permitted, if not encouraged, to insult them as they passed along the streets on their way to the house of lords. Some, even of their friends, suggested that it would be but prudent to keep away, at least during the Christmas holidays, while the apprentices and the rabble were idle and at large. But they nobly determined to do their duty ; and, unable to pass through the streets, they went by water in their barges to Westminster ; but as they landed, the mob rushed down upon them with a volley of stones, and compelled them to retire. They met together, twelve in number—all the bishops who were in London at the time, except Laud and Wren, who were prisoners—and drew up a becoming protest, in which they declare that they had been deterred by violence from the discharge of their duty, and protest against all the proceedings of parliament during their compulsory absence " as in themselves null

and of none effect." Archbishop Williams of
York, the chief offender, with the other bishops,
was immediately voted guilty of high treason by
the house of commons ; and they were committed
to the Tower. The impeachment was never carried
out, nor were they brought to trial; the object,
indeed, was already gained.

15. Nothing less than the overthrow of the
church of England would now satisfy a vast number of those who, a few months ago, had sought
only for moderate and reasonable reforms. In
revolutions this is almost invariably the case ; for
a revolution is a fever ; the delirium of a nation's
brain ; a judgment that God has sent to punish
the pride and selfishness of rulers, the insubordination of the multitude, or the wickedness of both.
Even the puritan clergy were insulted in the streets,
and interrupted while they read the prayers. The
Laudian party or the Romish priests were not
more obnoxious. The clergy usually wore their
canonical habits abroad ; and to be seen in a gown
and bands, was to be hooted at if not assailed.
Be the cause good or bad it is painful to observe
how, when the populace break loose and take the
work of reformation into their own hands, they
resort to the same excesses. In the days of queen
Mary, an over-zealous protestant, moved with indignation at the idolatrous service of the mass in
St. Margaret's, Westminster, struck the officiating
priest, and dashed the vessel from his hands ; and
paid the forfeit of his rashness at the stake. In
the same Saint Margaret's church at Westmin-

ster, while the house of commons were assembled there, when the officiating minister began the eucharistic service at the communion table, the congregation began a psalm, and the minister was silenced. At Saint Saviour's in Southwark, the mob pulled down the rails which surrounded the communion table. In other places they contented themselves with tearing up the surplice or the prayer book. Multitudes who knew little of prayer, denounced the liturgy as a lifeless form. And those whose lives proved that they knew neither what they spake nor whereof they affirmed, were ready to declaim against all forms, because they quenched, they said, the holy Spirit.*

16. A last effort to conciliate was made by the house of lords. On the 21st of March in this eventful year, they appointed a committee for religion : it consisted of ten bishops and twenty peers ; and they were to call in the assistance of other divines. Laud heard of it in his prison in the Tower, and entered in his journal the follow. ing words : " The lay votes will be double to the clergy. This committee will meddle with doctrines as well as ceremonies, and will call some divines to them to consider of the business. Upon the whole, I believe this committee will prove the national synod of England, to the great dishonour of the church. And what else may follow on it God knows."† It does not seem to have occurred to him, that if the church of England had root in the affections of the people, the ten earls and ten

* Neal ii. 314, 315.   † Laud's Diary, p. 24.

barons on the committee had no reason for abandoning it; that if it had not, the only method of
re-instating it was, to call in those who had the
people's confidence, not necessarily to take their
advice, but to listen to their objections. The house
of lords was still warmly attached to episcopacy,
though very sensitive of late of some of its abuses;
and the divines called in to assist were the best
men of either party. On the one side—or rather,
perhaps, raised, by the greatness of his mind and
the simplicity of his character, above all party
considerations—was Usher archbishop of Armagh,
as well as the bishops of Durham and Exeter, Dr.
Samuel Ward, Saunderson, and others. Of the
presbyterian party, or those who were so inclined,
were White, Marshall, Calamy, and Hill. The
conference lasted during six days. First, they
took into consideration the recent innovations of
doctrine; and it was complained that all the tenets
of the council of Trent had, by one or other, been
preached and printed; except those regarding the
king's supremacy, which the statute had made
treasonable: That good works were made to co-
operate with faith for justification: That private
confession, enumerating particular sins, was inculcated as needful to salvation: That the oblation
of the elements in the Lord's supper was held to
be a true sacrifice: That prayers for the dead, mo-
nastic vows, and other grievous errors, were inculcated. Secondly, the committee inquired into matters of conformity, and discovered that candlesticks
were placed in parish churches "on the altars so

called :" That canopies with curtains, in imitation of the veil before the holy of holies, were drawn around it : That a *credentia,* or side table, was made use of in the Lord's supper : That a direct prayer was forbidden before the sermon; and that ministers were forbidden to expound at large the catechism to their parishioners; from which we infer that the bidding prayer only was allowed in the pulpit, and that no explanations of the catechism were permitted : They objected too, that children when baptized, were carried to the altar and there offered up to God. And thirdly, they consulted about the common prayer book : whether some legendary saints ought not to be expunged from the calendar, and the apocryphal chapters from the lessons, and whether the rubric ought not to be amended in many particulars.* But the day for conciliation had now passed. Laud and his party, in danger of losing all, would give up nothing. They distrusted the doctrinal puritans as men who intended to betray the church into the hands of her enemies, and they thwarted their efforts. The democratic party, upon the other hand, now dreaded moderate reforms as men resolved on the destruction of the church, and anxious to aggravate its faults. The committee sat till the middle of May, when, amidst the crash of revolutionary measures and the approach of civil war, it broke up, and accomplished nothing. Even then it was the opinion of moderate men

---

* Fuller, book ii. 416. "This I write," he says, " out of the private notes of one of the committee."

that the conference, had it been permitted to continue, might have produced much good; that it
might have saved the church, and rescued the
monarchy; and that the civil war would still
have been averted. It was the last effort. Political disquietudes followed each other in quick
succession, and religious affairs soon occupied
but a secondary place. Soon afterwards deans
and chapters were abolished. The bill to abolish episcopacy was introduced again into the
house of commons on the first of September: with
what deliberation so grave a measure was discussed, we may infer from the fact that it passed
the house of lords upon the tenth. In effect, the
constitution of England was suspended both in
church and state; and in August 1642 the king
set up his standard, and the civil war began.

17. There were few puritans in the army of
king Charles when the war began. They were
chiefly on the side of the parliament. It would
be a study of the deepest interest to class, if it
were possible, the various and discordant parties assembled in the popular camp; to investigate their motives, and to dissect their characters. Human nature, in our own land at least,
never presented such a study; so difficult, so
varied, and, could we succeed in comprehending
it, so instructive. There was (for this is the sub-
stratum in every revolution) a vast mass of floating

discontent. There were protestants, who dreaded the return of popery; patriots, who trembled for the liberties of England; and earnest men of real piety, worn out with insults and persecutions, who believed that they took up arms in the cause of true religion, and therefore in the cause of God. There were enthusiasts, who sighed for a perfection unattainable on earth; and fanatics, who sought for it by the most unjustifiable means. And mingled with these, no doubt, there were the selfish, who hoped to gain in the general uproar; and the purely rebellious, who fought for the parliament, simply because the parliament fought against the king. All these took the name of puritans in history. But it is only with those to whom it more properly belongs, the religious puritans, that we are now concerned. What were their motives? What were those considerations that induced religious men, and these neither few in number nor inconsiderable in rank and fortune, but in truth one half of England, to draw the sword against the king whom they still acknowledged to be their lawful sovereign? Whether posterity choose to regard them as rebels or patriots, it has the same interest in discovering, if possible, the motives by which they were impelled.

18. Their cause they knew was good; the only ground for hesitation was, whether the time had come to defend it in arms. That they sincerely believed the reformed religion to be in the greatest danger, admits of no doubt; and that their fears were too well founded, admits of

none. The queen was a papist, and the king
was almost at her disposal : in all matters of
state her influence was unbounded. A horrible massacre of the protestants in Ireland had
just taken place, and the court was charged with
connivance and encouragement. The accusation
is too horrible to be credited, except on the fullest
evidence : and none such has yet appeared. The
weakness of all the king's measures, his uncertainty of purpose and feebleness of action, had however been severely felt by his protestant subjects in
Ireland. He had rendered them no timely assistance ; and it is possible that the queen, a bigot
to her faith, may have secretly rejoiced. The
courtiers displayed none of that depth of sorrow
which even decency required. And the suspicion,
if not the firm belief, that the court was a party to
the massacre, universally prevailed on the side of
the parliament. The favourable eye with which
popery was looked upon by the court, and the tendency of the Laudian theology in the English
church, added greatly to the universal apprehension. Was it right to take up arms in defence of
the protestant faith ? If so, said the puritans, it
is right to take up arms against the king.

19. But while they fought against the king's
person, they denied that they fought against the
king's authority. They drew a distinction, by
no means frivolous or unconstitutional, between
Charles Stuart, the king of England, and the
same person at the head of the royalist army at
Nottingham. The king, they argued, was the

highest of those constituted powers to whom the subject owes submission. But England was not an absolute monarchy. The parliament was one of the powers, to whom a christian and a subject owed submission likewise. The powers that be are ordained of God : but this was true of the parliament no less than of the monarchy, or else the parliament would have been nothing more at any time than an insolent usurpation. The king, it was true, declared in frequent manifestoes, that the parliament was in rebellion, and called upon his subjects to arm in his defence. But the parliament issued similar proclamations. They declared that the king was acting without their advice, and therefore without constitutional authority ; that he was in the hands of papists and malignants. They fought in the king's name, and on his behalf, they said ; though such was his infatuation, or the restraint he suffered, that they were compelled to fight against his person. If it were treason to fight against the king, was it less treason to fight against the parliament ? The fiction they adopted, of carrying on the war in the king's name, could not fail to have its effect with an army which believed that the king was a dupe, if not a prisoner, in the hands of their and his own worst enemies. Thousands believed firmly through the war, that they were fighting, not to overthrow the monarchy, but to restore it ; not to destroy the church, but to purify it. These considerations perplexed many on both sides, and gave assurance to others. When we

attempt to estimate the piety of the puritans who
fought against the king, it is unjust to deny their
weight to these considerations.

20. Men in general will always judge rather by
the appearance of things, than by calmly sifting
the merits of the case and the comparative weight
of opposing principles; and to all appearance piety
was entirely with the puritans. It was a common
saying with the virtuous royalists, that the king
had the better cause, but the parliament had the
better men. The licentiousness of the king's
army was deplorable; his best friends spoke of it
with shame, his enemies with indecent triumph.
The king's chief officers were men of profligate
lives, who made a jest of religion. The private
soldiers, whose pay was irregular, lived chiefly on
plunder, and they chiefly plundered the puritans.
But the popular camp resounded, not with oaths
and ribaldry, but with the murmurs of devotion
or the louder strains of thanksgiving. Frequent
preaching and exhortation, the reading of the
scriptures, and religious conversation, filled up the
intervals of martial duty. Around the army, property was safe; and modesty passed by without a
blush. The times did not permit neutrality; and
pious men naturally took their side with those by
whom piety was respected. Numbers joined the parliament, and filled up the ranks of the army, merely
because they saw the appearance of fervour and
piety there, and the utter want of it in the royal
camp. In time, the clergy who had been oppressed by Laud; those who dreaded popery and

wished for a reformation of discipline; the deprived and silenced ministers, not a few in number; the lecturers and popular preachers whom Laud had in vain endeavoured to suppress ; all these, compelled to choose their side, attached themselves to the army of the parliament. After the indecisive battle of Edge Hill, Baxter tells us that he found at Coventry upwards of thirty ministers who, like himself, had fled for refuge to a parliamentary garrison, from the fury of the royalists; though they had not yet interfered in the war on either side. This was the great cause of the strength of the parliament, and of the ruin of the king. A debauched rabble, encouraged by his gentry, and seconded by the common soldiers, took all puritans for their enemies and treated them as such ; and every man was a puritan in their eyes who was heard to repeat a sermon, sing a psalm, or pray in his family. Such treatment filled the armies and garrisons of the parliament with sober and

pious men. The king deplored these outrages, and issued a proclamation to repress them ; but it had very little effect.* These again are considerations which those who would understand and do justice to the puritans of 1642 will not hastily dismiss. They were of sufficient weight to influence the minds of such men as Howe and Owen, Marshall, and Calamy, and Baxter. The latter, writing long afterwards,—when age and reflection, and the utter failure of every hope entertained when the war began, may be supposed to have

* Baxter's own Life, fol. p. 26—44.

chastened something at least of his party zeal—
still thought the war had been inevitable. He cast
a retrospective glance over the whole field of blood,
from Edge Hill and Naseby to the execution of
king Charles, and then again through the turbulent protectorate of Cromwell, and he still thought
that the war was just, and that his own course as a
chaplain to the army had been right in the sight of
God. Upon the justice of his opinion men will differ; but what must have been those times and provocations which could leave a doubt in such a mind
as Baxter's ;—a doubt upon such a question as the
alternative of submission to a lawful sovereign, or
civil war with all its horrors ?*

21. These are the justifications of the puritans ;
on the other hand, their faults were great. We
speak of them in their religious character, and
with reference to the particular points on which
their conduct was affected by their puritanism.
One fault of the party always was a strong tinge
of enthusiasm; which means, not in its perverted
sense, that they had too much devotion, but that
they were too ready to assume that their own impressions were the voice of God. Whatever may
have been the case with those who were drawn into
the conflict in the manner we have just described,
there was a vast multitude who entered upon it
with very little hesitation or reluctance ; and these
were soon sufficiently numerous and powerful to

---

* Baxter's Holy Commonwealth, pp. 470—480. This work was published in the last year of the commonwealth. On the restoration, a
burst of censure fell upon its author, which he bore for ten years, when
he suppressed the work, but without retracting the principles advanced
in it. See Orme's Life of Baxter, 710.

impress their own character on the parliamentary cause; and as moulded in their hands, it has, in fact, been handed down to the present times in history. And the accusation of history against them is, that they followed their own will, while they professed to follow the will of God. This may seem severe to those who only call to mind their frequent seasons set apart for prayer and fasting, and observed with an awful solemnity. But if we compare the events of the times with the devotions of the parliament, it is too often evident that the former were already decided on without much reference to the latter; and that in truth God's direction was not sought upon their counsels, but his approbation upon their decisions already made and taken. Something of this was apparent from the first; but a few years afterwards, a solemn fast was notoriously the signal for an outrage; the feint to divert attention, just as the assault is about to be made in earnest. Even true religion had already lost much of its sobriety; and heat and passion were substituted instead of the real life of fervent piety—a decay which, we conceive, was at once a cause and a consequence of the neglect into which the established church, with its calmness and its liturgy, had fallen. Thus the puritans were led on, and entangled first in excesses and then in crimes. The best of them felt that they had been duped, and would gladly have withdrawn. But the storm rushed onward, and they were swept before it. They had given an impulse at first, under which they themselves were to be crushed hereafter.

22. A grievous error had long infected the puritan theology. It had been first avowed in the infancy of the party, and tenaciously cherished ever
since. The examples of the old testament in all
political affairs were asserted to be those which
christian men and christian communities were
bound to follow; the old testament was in all
these respects our pattern.* The effect of such
doctrines, preached in a camp with intense fervour, by one who was both soldier and divine,
may be easily conceived. Saul's special commission to slay the Amalekites, and Samuel's judicial hewing of Agag in pieces before the Lord,
were enforced as precedents which it was a want
of faith not to receive and practise. The outrages
on the side of the parliament, though few compared with what civil war has inflicted on other
countries, are chiefly due to this fanatical perversion ; we call it so, because it assumed the inspiration of him who undertook to copy the example of Saul or Samuel, or the heroes of the jewish
church, in those particular instances in which their
conduct was justified by the special command of
God. The Author of life has a right to resume it
when or how he will; his creatures invade his
prerogative if they destroy it without his express
permission; and his permission is now given to
us, not in special instances, but in general laws.
But the greater evil was, that religious men became more careless of shedding human blood.

* See page 60 of this volume.

CHAPTER
XIV.

CHAS. I.

A. D. 1642.

The spirit that would have fainted (though not in cowardice) after a single fight, and longed for peace, was stimulated to unnatural obduracy; the cause was God's, and the method was of divine appointment. The enemies of Christ, and of his church, were to be treated like the enemies of the Jewish church of old; this was the worst error of the puritans : eventually it destroyed their piety, their reputation, and their cause.

23. To those who study the errors of mankind for the sake of wisdom, or with the nobler view of erecting new barriers against the return of sins and calamities once endured, this point in puritan theology will afford matter for profound reflection. The notion that in the events and histories of the old testament the church of Christ must search for its warrants and precedents, was utterly inconsistent with evangelical doctrine. The inconsistency had been exposed, first by Whitgift, and then by Hooker ; and it was of so gross a nature that, once refuted, obstinacy alone can account for its retention. Indeed, we have no doubt that the sudden decline of puritanism at the close of the reign of queen Elizabeth was owing, not to her unwise severities, but to the growing conviction that this great puritan stronghold was untenable. It was held only in a modified form at all times by the wiser puritans, who seem to have been satisfied by maintaining in general, that as the commands of God were, in every point and with regard to each particular, whether of church government or national rule, precise and

full, in the old testament, an equal precision; and the same kind and degree of minute and special direction, must be expected in the new. But even this was a false position, assumed in order to convict the church party of unscriptural superstition in erecting offices not expressly named in the new testament. And when such men as Cartwright forgot their church theories, and addressed themselves to the greater work of preaching Christ to sinners, they unconsciously demolished their own fortress and laid it waste. When they spoke, and few ever spoke more effectually, on the spiritual as opposed to the legal covenant, and of the liberty wherewith Christ hath made us free, as opposed to the covenant of works, they in fact conceded everything. As types and figurations, or as an exhibition of the bondage in which men were held till Christ appeared, these histories were of the highest price; but if received as precedents on some points, why not on all points ? Why not slay the daily sacrifice if we must needs slay the Amalekite ? The coarsest minds arrive with the least difficulty at remote analogies, and reason for the most part with least hesitation. The sectaries who broke out at the close of the reign of James, and were now spreading like locusts over the whole land, held and taught without any reserve that the actions recorded in the old testament were recorded for imitation. Perhaps this was not a necessary deduction from the premises of Cartwright and his school; but at least it was a natural and easy transition; or rather an extension of the

same argument. If precedents for church government were to be raked up from the archives of
the jewish temple, why should not precedents in
politics be sought for in the archives of the jewish
state? The answer that God himself was the great
theocrat in the latter case, and that each political
action was done by his command, was not conclusive, because it was just as applicable to the
former. For God directed the temple worship,
always in the same, often in a much higher, sense
than the affairs of the jewish state. The fanatic
who invoked God's curse upon kings in the words
which prophets had made use of against Moab
and the children of Edom, or chanted in triumph
the song of Moses when the English Pharaoh and
his army perished, might have very safely challenged some of the elder puritans of a former age
to show why, upon their own principles, his conduct
should be severely blamed. They might prove
him rash and rebellious, and so far wrong; but
was the principle itself unchristian? Had they
not themselves adopted it? They had singled out
certain events and principles in Jewish history,
which they maintained were binding as precedents
and authorities in civil affairs; why might he not
extend the principle a little further; why not
make a new selection of his own?

24. But from whatever fountain the poison
had distilled, it infected multitudes. The religion
of a great number of those who now bore un-
worthily the name of puritan, was a strange compound of christian doctrine, often distorted, and

engrafted upon jewish modes of thought and
principles of action. The consequence was of a
hybrid character, which has been always perfectly
inexplicable to those who have not traced its parentage;—many christian virtues flourishing in
high perfection, and a dark ferocity unworthy of
civilized men. The jewish and the christian element by turns prevailing, and the puritan, in
whom they strangely co-existed, by turns exciting
our indignation and commanding our highest reverence.

25. Perhaps it was in some measure a consequence of the same error that the doctrine of *impressions* became popular. It was the same mixture of faith and judaism. Prayer was offered devoutly through Jesus Christ, and faith professed.
But answers to prayer were expected, such as the
seers and prophets of old times had been wont to
receive. The petition was offered upon the terms
of the new testament ; the answer was expected
after the manner of the old. As enthusiasm increased, the puritans of this school became in one
respect little better than the adulterous generation
whom our Lord rebukes. They sought, if not a
sign from heaven, some conscious impulse of the
nature of a miracle. The sin was the same. Men
demanded more than God would give. They in
effect declare that his word and Spirit were not
sufficient. Their pride must be gratified, each
man's with a special revelation: something, the
reader will understand, perfectly distinct from that
sacred peace which God distributes to his people,
and with which he fills their hearts while, in prayer

and the diligent study of his word, they wait upon him for instruction. Cromwell himself was the victim of this delusion. It was after a night spent in prayer, which ended, as he believed, in one of these divine impressions, that he consented to the death of Charles. John Howe was his chaplain, a man of whom none will speak with disrespect who have read a page of his writings, and he had preached in vain before him to expose the lamentable delusion. But it was the stronghold of the puritan soldiery. They sought their examples in the old testament. They marched to the field of battle, with awe upon their souls, as the executioners of God's vengeance. They believed that they were doing his work; doing it in the very way which he himself prescribed; to shew pity was unbelief, to turn back was apostacy from God.

26. These errors prevailed extensively when at length the civil war began; and they had been silently preparing thousands of religious men to gird on the sword without regret. Neither party seemed to have felt reluctance to make the last appeal to arms. Even the reformation of the church after the severest methods, would not have prevented it; for this had now become only one of many subjects of mutual exasperation. In the month of April, 1642, the lords and commons had published a declaration of their intention to reform the government and discipline of the church, but at the same time they were resolved, they said, to proceed with moderation.* But in

* Neal, vol. ii. 441.

August the power of the house of lords was almost ended, and the commons had, in fact, usurped the functions of both houses, and their tone was changed. They were anxious to propitiate the Scotch, and to obtain their assistance in the quarrel with the king. The general assembly urged the parliament to establish an uniformity of church government in the two kingdoms; meaning, to establish the presbyterian church in England. The house replied in a manner which sufficiently shewed that no difficulties would be raised on their part. They had by this time discovered " that the hierarchy was evil, justly offensive, burdensome to the kingdom, a great impediment to reformation, very prejudicial to the civil government." "In short," they say, "we are resolved that the same shall be taken away." In the same month the war began. Whatever the church puritans, who revered episcopacy as a sacred institution, if not divine, may have thought as to the conduct of Laud and the king, it was evidently impossible for them to side, after this declaration, with the parliament. Thus, at length, the church of England fell, and for a time the triumph of the puritans seemed to be complete. The astonishing recovery of the church, and the more astonishing discomfiture of the puritans, remain to be told; they form another history, pregnant with instruction to all men, and with solemn cautions to men of violence and strife.

27. It is a question which will never now receive a complete answer, but one so natural

that it suggests itself probably to every reader, what were the feelings, not of incensed fanatics, but of the wise, pious, and thoughtful men who sided with the parliament when the church of England fell? Had they no deep misgivings? Did they really believe that the faults of the church outweighed its usefulness; outweighed it so as to demand its overthrow? Did they really regard the subversion of episcopacy with complacent approbation? The Scotch asserted, in their letter to the parliament, that the presbyterian discipline was ordained of God. There was no other scriptural form of church government. Like the pattern of the tabernacle, it had been shewn upon the mount. Could these assertions have weight with Calamy and Baxter, or with the laymen of the party? Did St. John believe them, or Hampden? Cromwell, it is known, detested the assumption of the presbyterians. And when the experiment was made, it was found impossible to persuade the people of England to accept the presbytery : except in two counties, Lancashire and a part of Middlesex, it was not even tried. Or was it that the best men on both sides looked on in silent dismay, foreseeing evils they could do nothing to prevent? Even then, the church of England was, under God, the leader and mistress of the reformation. What other church had been blessed with so many eminent ministers, or with successes so amazing? Where else had been found such an array of learning directed to the noblest ends, the glory of God, and the present and eternal welfare of thousands

upon thousands ? Even if learning was to be depreciated, and made no longer of account, could they
hope, by the rude overthrow of a church within
which were to be found so many wise and holy
men, preachers so eloquent, and divines so deep,
to prepare the ground, strewed with its ruins, for
an institution of superior worth and greater usefulness, one more honourable to God and more
effective ? It is difficult to believe this of a great
number of those (the most discerning and devout,
we mean, and therefore least affected by clamour
and the love of change) who certainly looked on
in silence, and raised no warning voice. They had
before them living witnesses, if of violence and
tyranny in some of the prelates, in others of every
christian every ministerial virtue. They must
have been forced sometimes to reflect, that an institution which numbered amongst its members
archbishop Usher, bishop Hall, and bishop Carlton,
could not lie under God's curse. Why did they
not attempt to rescue it from violence ? Why
array themselves, at least by their silence, against
an order in the ministry and a form of government which had existed if not from apostolic, yet
from primitive ages ; which had furnished many
of its ablest ministers to the church even in its
brightest periods ; and which had often saved it
from deeper superstition, and retrieved it even in
its worst ?

28. But of such memorials, if such existed, few
or none remain. Shame or fear, the accidents of
time and civil war, have led to their destruction.

One thing alone is certain ; the great body of the puritans were consenting to the church's overthrow, and in its ruins they and their principles were crushed. Like Samson of old, in more than mortal energy, and in judicial blindness, they were like him in their end : they were the instruments of inflicting upon the episcopal church an awful punishment, not altogether unmerited, but far beyond what her greatest faults deserved ; but the moment of their triumph was that in which they seemed to be smitten with paralysis and the hand of death.

FINIS.

WORKS BY THE SAME AUTHOR.

The CHURCHMANSHIP of the NEW TESTAMENT: an Inquiry, Historical and Theological, into the Origin and Progress of certain Opinions which now agitate the Church of Christ. Post 8vo. 6s. cloth lettered.

II.

DISCOURSES for the FESTIVALS of the CHURCH of ENGLAND. With Notes. 1 vol. 8vo. 12s. cloth lettered. — This volume contains a Discourse for every Festival for which a Collect and Epistle are appointed in the Prayer-book.

III.

The RULE of FASTING, as set forth in Holy Scripture, and taught by the Church of England. A Manual for Lent. Second Edition, 1s. cloth.

IV.

SERMONS. Second Edition. 12mo. 6s. cloth lettered.

V.

The COMINGS of CHRIST: Five Advent Sermons on Haggai ii. 6—9. 12mo. cloth, 2s. 6d.

VI.

TWO SERMONS on the LIFE, MINISTRY, and DEATH of the late Rev. RICHARD MARKS; Author of the Retrospect, &c. 1s. 6d.

VII.

SERMONS from the OLD TESTAMENT. 12mo. 6s. cloth lettered.

VIII.

A TREATISE on the SPECIAL PROVIDENCE of GOD: Also Two Dissertations—1. On Prophecy, 2. On Inspiration. By the late Edmund Dewdney, M.A. With a Biographical Preface by the Rev. J. B. MARSDEN. With Portrait. Price 5s. 6d.